Renaissance Dress in Italy 1400-1500

Renaissance Dress in Italy 1400-1500

Jacqueline Herald

The History of Dress Series
General Editor: Dr Aileen Ribeiro

Bell & Hyman
London

Humanities Press
New Jersey

This edition first published in Great Britain in 1981 by
BELL & HYMAN LIMITED
Denmark House
37–39 Queen Elizabeth Street
London SE1 2QB

British Library Cataloguing in Publication Data

Herald, Jacqueline
    Renaissance dress in Italy 1400–1500—
    (History of dress: 2)
    1. Costume, Italian—History
    I. Title
    391'.00945   GT964

    ISBN 0-7135-1294-6

            First published in the USA by
            Humanities Press Inc.
            Atlantic Highlands
            New Jersey 07716
            ISBN 0 391 02362 4

Designed by Harold Bartram
Text filmset and printed in Great Britain by
BAS Printers Limited, Over Wallop, Hants.
Colour plates by Creative Print & Design Limited,
North Ascot, Berks.
Bound by W.B.C. Bookbinders, Maesteg, Wales.

Contents

List of Illustrations

Colour plates

Black and white photographs

Note on Money and Measurements

Money

The monetary terms used in Italy during the Quattrocento are virtually untranslatable into present day currency. The system was complex, for different coins were used in different cities; and values were expressed either as figures in accounts, or in tangible terms of gold and silver coinage.

The largest unit was called a *lira*, *fiorino* or *ducato*; it was then divided into *soldi* and *denari*.

$$1 \; lira/fiorino/ducato = 20 \; soldi$$
$$1 \; soldo = 12 \; denari$$

This ratio had been established by Charlemagne, and remained the basis of English currency, indicating the relationship between pounds, shillings and pence, until the transfer to decimalization in 1971.

In the Middle Ages, many different systems of coinage had evolved. The year 1252 was therefore an important moment in international trade, for it marked the first production of the gold florin, the *fiorino a oro*, of Florence. It was welcomed immediately across Europe, because of its constant gold content, and soon was followed by the Venetian ducat (*ducato*) and other imitations. The florin bore the image of Saint John the Baptist, the republic's protector, on one side, and the armorial lily on the other. The ducat was distinguished on the one hand by the image of the Redeemer, and on the other, by a figure of Christ handing to the Doge a banner inscribed '*Sid tibi Christe datum quem tu regis iste ducatus*'. The *genovino* of Genoa also became synonymous with the two denominations of the *fiorino* and the *ducato*.

However, not all denominations were minted, nor was the introduction of the new gold florin fused completely with the older silver system to which people were accustomed. The use of real gold and silver always had presented problems which were difficult to resolve, for the market value of the metals continued to fluctuate, according to availability and demand. Once the comparative values of gold and silver were systematized, it was possible to link the old and the new monetary systems.

It was decided that an old silver *fiorino* should be worth 1/20 of the new gold one; that is, it should equal a *soldo a oro*. In addition to the silver *lira*, which was minted, there had been another monetary system based on the *lira di piccioli*. The latter had never been coined, but was an imaginary method of evaluation, used in accounts. Subsequently, twenty silver *soldi* already in circulation corresponded to one gold florin coin, while twenty imaginary *soldi a oro* (no gold *soldi* or *denari* were minted) represented the imaginary *lira di piccioli*. Thus there evolved some correspondence between the two systems. Nevertheless, at intervals during the years of its production, fom 1252 to 1533, the value of a *fiorino a oro* in terms of the *lira di piccioli* did rise and fall.

Monetary systems varied from one city or state to another. For example, the gold ducat of Venice was at one stage said to equal not one *lira*, but one *lira* and eight *denari*. And in Bologna in 1496, Giovanni Bentivoglio ordered the issue of new silver coins each worth 48 *quattrini*

(1 *quattrino* = 4 *denari*). In Ferrara, on the other hand, the Duke Ercole d'Este had coined the *testone*, worth a quarter of a *scudo* or 36 *quattrini*. The *testone* was so named for the head of Ercole, which it bore on one side; on the other face appeared the image of the Duke on horseback slaying a dragon.

In its day, therefore, the monetary system must have offered enormous difficulties in business transactions. No less are the problems facing the historian's interpretation of bills, inventories and other documents of the period.

Measurements

The principal unit of length was the *braccio* (plural, *braccia*), literally meaning an arm's length. In reality, as one might expect, this measurement was extremely variable. In Florence, it measured 58 cm., in Piacenza it was slightly larger, 66 cm. The average *braccio* was probably the Italian equivalent of the English 'ell' used during the period.

If a unit shorter than a *braccio* needed to be expressed, references were made in terms of the *spanna*, *palmo* or *dito* (span, palm or finger), the average size of such measurements also being debatable.

It is therefore difficult to draw accurate comparisons between the various measurements of cloth needed for certain types of garments. The situation is further complicated by the fact that the widths of textiles varied, depending on the location of production, and on the structure of the cloth. Silks, especially the figured ones, generally came in much narrower widths than woollen cloths.

Preface

During the fifteenth century in Italy, 'even the outward appearance of men and women and the habits of daily life were more perfect, more beautiful, and more polished than among other nations of Europe . . . and even serious men among it looked on a handsome and becoming costume as an element in the perfection of the individual.'

Such eulogistic tones may not be entirely applicable today, for since Jacob Burckhardt's *The Civilisation of the Renaissance in Italy* was first published in 1860, many have studied the Renaissance in general, and the fifteenth century in particular with a far more critical eye. No one, however, can deny the splendour of costume, and the important role it played, in the life of Italian society in that period.

The aim of this book is to offer some answers to what, why and how fashionable men and women dressed in the Quattrocento. Against a lively background of political intrigue, economic activity, flourishing of the arts, philosophy and acute awareness of individual status, the scene is set. The picture is composed from a variety of documentary sources: paintings, drawings, sculpture, portrait medals and a few manuscripts, as well as inventories, diaries, letters and sumptuary legislations. To date, I have neither heard of nor seen any surviving Italian costume of the fifteenth century, though a considerable number of textiles (more ecclesiastical than secular, however) remains.

To isolate the fifteenth century is to draw artificial margins through a long and intricate progression of events running through the fourteenth and sixteenth centuries as well. Certainly, that progression gathered increasing momentum in the period in question and, for many reasons, some of which I hope will become clear, this often manifested itself in, and attached a particular importance to dress. The emphasis will be on fashionable dress, and how it is distinguished from official, academic and theatrical dress, or the costume of other countries.

What is fashion? It is surely a make, a shape, a style or a manner. Some definitions suggest that fashion refers to the usages of an upper class society, and others imply that fashion is a habit or a custom—especially, but not necessarily, in dress.

Though superficially different, costume in the Renaissance played a role very similar to that of clothing today. Fashion is a style which responds to the mood of a given moment in time and place. Occasionally, an individual will invent something new, but usually fashion is the result of 'something in the air'. There need not be one exclusive strain; for often several styles run concurrently, to satisfy the need of self-advertisement amongst different social stratifications within a community, or between contrasting cultural groups.

Not all fashion is dress; however, one of the most effective means of expressing style lies in the manner of clothing. Costume may symbolize class, or wealth, an intellectual or artistic statement, or occupation. On the other hand, it may be purely theatrical and fantastically conceived. This is true of both high fashion and all other forms of dress from the Renaissance to the present—that is the period which the encyclopaedias classify as 'modern'.

'High' fashion is something which moves with the times. It keeps a step ahead, it tempts, and one strives after it. By the time one has caught up with it, it is already out of date. In the fifteenth century, dress did not change its shape as quickly as it does today— there were no fashion magazines or newspapers, for one thing. Common to both and the intervening period, however, is the fact that the most 'fashionable' are young men and women, with considerable financial resources, who inhabit towns or cities where there is successful industrial involvement and lively cultural activity.

To be fashionable means to conform to a fashion. In one sense, therefore, fashion is uniform; but styles are forever changing, and there are no written rules and regulations. Although high fashion is constantly traced, in order to capture the cultural atmosphere of the day, it is probable that the majority of the population goes about its everyday activity wearing a conventional style of clothing, or some form of occupational dress. In fifteenth-century Italy, legal, academic, official, ecclesiastical and functional dress was probably much more widely worn than fashion itself.

The wealth of material from which I have drawn is boundless. The volume and nature of documentation varies from one household to another, from town to town, from region to region, and from decade to decade. For example, the portrait—usually the best visual evidence for the most up-to-date dress—does not become a generally recognized form of artistic expression until the latter half of the fifteenth century. Sumptuary legislations can be extremely informative, but often relate to one town, sometimes exclude the upper classes from their clauses, and besides invariably are not adhered to. Varying details in dress reflect regional characteristics, particularly towards the end of the century. Nevertheless, I accept that the general shape of dress and the development of political, social and intellectual ideas alters on similar lines and at a reasonably consistent pace amongst the arbiters of fashion throughout the Quattrocento. The imbalance of documentary detail, therefore, should not invalidate this study.

The documents referred to have all been published in one form or another; there is insufficient time or space here to annotate and discuss in any useful detail documents which have not previously been worked on. There are so many permutations of language to describe a dress, a tunic, or a mantle which cannot be translated. For this reason, the original terms, when known, will appear in italics, and are fully explained in the glossary. Otherwise, the simplest descriptions are used—made up of words which do not radically alter through the test of time. Details of construction shall be remarked upon when they become essential features for defining a particular shape within a certain progression of fashionable styles.

SWITZERLAND

HAPSBURG LANDS

Trent

R. OF

Monza
Bergamo
D. OF SAVOY
Milan
Crema
Brescia
Vigevano
Verona
Padua
Turin
M. OF MANTUA
Mantua
Venice
River Po
River Po
Modena
Ferrara
M. OF
SALUZZO
Bologna
D. OF FERRARA
Genoa
R. OF GENOA
D. OF MODENA
Prato
R. OF LUCCA
Lucca
Florence
Urbino
Pisa
River
Leghorn
Arno
R. OF FLORENCE
Recanati
THE
Siena
Perugia
PAPAL
ELBA
R. OF SIENA
STATES
CORSICA
(Genoa)
River Tiber
ADRIATIC SEA
OTTOMAN
EMPIRE

SARDINIA
(Aragon)

Rome

KINGDOM
Barletta
Naples
Bari
Salerno
OF
NAPLES

TYRRHENIAN
SEA

IONIAN
SEA

Catanzaro

MEDITERRANEAN

Palermo
Catania
SICILY
(Aragon)
SEA

Boundaries after the
Peace of Lodi, 1454

M = Marquisate
D = Duchy
R = Republic

1 The Quattrocento: An Introduction

It was in the fifteenth century in Italy that men began to talk of a rebirth in the arts and literature. Today, we consider the period to belong to the Renaissance, a term first used by historians in the nineteenth century. As a cultural phenomenon, the traditional image of the Renaissance embodies the revival and reassessment of values and cultural images of antiquity, a sense of innovation and exploration, and the increasing importance of the individual. The development of these themes becomes apparent and quickens its pace during the Quattrocento.

The Renaissance was not born overnight, nor was it precisely confined to the fifteenth and early sixteenth centuries. The study of the classics did not die in the Middle Ages, but rather it was restricted by an ignorance of many major classical texts, texts which were to be sought out and discovered in considerable numbers by dedicated collectors, particularly of the Quattrocento. Fifteenth-century humanists, first in Florence and later elsewhere, owed much to their counterparts of the preceding century, the most outstanding of whom was Petrarch. Similarly, artists and art theorists could not have ignored the advances in realism and perspective made by Giotto in his frescoes. For some time, due to the papal residence in Avignon, there had been a certain alienation from the Church in its most visible and political form: Italy was now more receptive to the thoughts and activities of men.

Though flanked by mountains and sea, the Italians had little sense of a national political identity, but there was some unity in their collective belief that they were culturally superior to those barbarians across the Alps. However, the political situation within the peninsula during the fifteenth century was not peaceful. Italian men identified themselves with their immediate environment, and tended to offer allegiance to their local communities, the city states. The development of towns and cities during the two preceding centuries was far more advanced in Italy than in the rest of Europe. Many of those cities were independent states, each ruling its neighbouring countryside, the *contado*; but by the fifteenth century, most of these had merged into larger political territories, so that Italy was dominated by five

1. Map of Italy, indicating the principal states in the mid-fifteenth century.

principal states—Naples, the Papal States, Florence, Milan and Venice.

Each of these powers was organized and ruled in a very different way. Naples was exclusive in being the only Italian kingdom, ruled predominantly by the royal house of Aragon. The Papal States were also unique, in possessing a spiritual head, who was at the same time an extremely temporal one. Constitutionally, Florence was a republic but in practice was ruled by one or a group of leading families. Through the first decades of the century the Albizzi, together with the Uzzano and the Strozzi families, held chief political power. Then in 1434, Cosimo de' Medici returned from exile and effectively became ruler of the republic, to be followed by his son Piero and grandson Lorenzo, the Magnificent. Milan was a principality, first ruled by the Visconti, when constant attempts to acquire more territory were being made, particularly in the direction of Florence and Venice. From 1450, the Duchy of Milan was ruled by the Sforza family, beginning with the *condottiere* Francesco. Politically, the internal affairs of Venice, that most aristocratic of cities, were the most stable, based on a republican constitution and ruled by an oligarchy, headed by an ageing Doge. There was also Savoy (the alpine region which seemed more French to the Italians) and a handful of smaller states, which usually sought the support of one or other of the five major states. Most were governed by feudal lords—though in theory some were republics. Following the brief tutelage of the Duke of Milan, Siena formed a republic which lasted for the major part of the century, before the emergence of a native *signore*, Pandolfo Petrucci. Bologna, though technically belonging to the Papal States was conducted as a republic under the powerful leadership of the Bentivoglio family. And Lucca, after the rule of a *signore* during the first few decades, then established a somewhat insecure republican state.

In the fifteenth century, cities and states invariably fell into the hands of lords, sometimes through the activities of *condottieri*, professional military commanders, or by purchase; the ways and means of opportunity might seem unorthodox today, but were accepted, almost expected, then. The incessant political tensions in Italy erupted into wars based on personal ambition. The balance of power, though basically lying in the hands of the large states, was forever oscillating. In the 1420s, Florence and Venice (with Francesco Sforza as captain of the latter's armies) joined as allies against Milan, but by 1454 Florence had switched her support to Milan following the ascendancy of Sforza as Duke. Loyalty to another state was less important than the protection of one's own interests. In this case, Florence had recognized the threat imposed by Venice's increasing power through trade and territorial expansion; and besides, Cosimo de' Medici had struck up a strong personal friendship with Francesco Sforza.

2. Cardinal Francesco Gonzaga Returns from Rome, by Mantegna, *c.* 1471–4. In the foreground on the left the Marquis of Mantua, Ludovico Gonzaga, is informally and fashionably dressed in a sideless overtunic and wears a ducal cap. The doublets worn by all the men have laces attached to the upper arm; these were used for tying on armour and were also treated as a decorative feature of fashion.

How was it possible that, in a century of constant turmoil, Italy could flourish in agriculture, industry, commerce and the arts? The paintings, the sculptures, and a large number of the palaces, churches, canal systems and hillslopes of mulberry trees, established during the period, have impressed many foreign tourists to Italy for five centuries, and today they are readily identifiable images of Italian townscape and countryside. Italy is considered to be the first country of western Europe to have achieved some kind of renaissance. It also happens that nowhere other than in Italy were the paths of political ambition laid so wide open to *condottieri*. These men were instrumental in causing constant changes in the dynasties of lords. A family was lucky to rule a city state for more than 50 years: the d'Este of Ferrara were exceptional in lasting for four centuries. However, to entrust the fighting to professionals was to spare time for other occupations.

Italy in the Quattrocento was still rich, but it is probable that the economics of the country as a whole were less prosperous than before. Severe outbreaks of plague at the end of the fourteenth and early fifteenth centuries caused a considerable decline in population. In the 1330s, the citizens of Florence totalled about 90,000; by 1427 that number was reduced to around 37,000, a third of whom were too poor to be taxed. With fewer mouths to feed, and a general move towards rearing sheep and other stock, so fell the demand for corn, on which the economy of the southern states had greatly relied. The balance of economic power was even more heavily weighted towards the north. In Florence, production of high quality woollen cloth waned, but the developing silk industry probably compensated for any lost profits. Amongst the acquisitions of Florentine territory were Pisa (1406) standing at the mouth of the Arno, and the port of Leghorn (1421) which opened trade with the Levant. But the greatest sea power certainly of Italy, and probably of all Europe, was Venice. After a long duel with Genoa over the dominion of the seas, she finally came out the better of the two in the war of Chioggia (1378–81). Venetian vessels carried sugar and spices to England, supplied Flemish weavers with English wool, and Mediterranean towns with Flemish cloth. Geographically, Venice was favourably placed for the overland exchange of goods with India, the assembly point for items from further east. In return, India particularly demanded certain precious metals which in Europe were mostly handled by the merchants of south German towns such as Augsburg. For them, Venice was the most convenient port and as a result of the flourishing industry and trade, the Arsenal was reconstructed between 1472 and 1487, to accommodate more and larger ships. In contrast, Genoa had a hinterland, and was constantly disrupted by the turbulent relationships amongst her landed aristocracy. Her sea trade was not as prosperous as that of Venice, but nor was it inactive. The Genoese did regularly convey goods to towns in the south of

France, ran commercial depots on the route to the Crimea, and had contacts with north Africa and Spain. Many Genoese merchants centred their businesses in Palermo, and as chief buyers of the products of Sicily—silk and cane sugar—they fed the silk industry of Genoa with raw material, and redistributed the sugar throughout Europe.

Probably the most thriving economy was to be found in Lombardy. It is no coincidence that the Visconti family, through the female line, became connected with five royal houses of Europe—the Valois, Hapsburg, Tudor, Stuart and Hanover— for a Visconti bride was a highly esteemed reward of the marriage market. The foreign traveller to Italy was particularly struck by the canal system of Lombardy, expanded considerably after interest in sluice gates was shown by the architect Leon Battista Alberti, and later developed by Leonardo da Vinci. Milan was enriched by her agriculture (much encouraged in the policies of the Visconti rulers), and by her silk production and industry in arms and armaments. So Lombardy, based at the head of a great commercial route across the Alps, was in an outstanding position.

Lombard Street in the City of London reminds us that at one time the name Lombard was synonymous with banker or money-changer. The increase in importance of exchange is reflected by the title of the Florentine Bankers' guild, the *Arte del Cambio*. In the middle of the thirteenth century, the Florentine florin, with its reasonably consistent gold content, had become the international currency, as the silver coinages issued elsewhere fluctuated in value. This factor, coupled with the gradual change from Germanic to Roman law—that is, from a bartering system to one

3. The Arrival of the English Ambassadors, by Carpaccio; from the story of Saint Ursula painted in the late 1490s. The background includes part of the newly constructed arsenal of Venice.

which recognized the right to accumulate individual possessions through the use of coinage and bills of exchange—made the whole organization of banking an essential feature of international trade and commerce. The Italians were leaders in the field. A member of a Florentine family of bankers, Giovanni di Antonio da Uzzano, published in 1442 his *Pratica della Mercatura*. In it, he offered a guide to the seasonal fluctuations of the money market. During that period, traffic was concentrated on principal towns, referred to as *piazze*, which were all connected by a regular mail service. In Italy, Barletta, Bologna, Florence, Genoa, Lucca, Milan, Naples, Palermo, Pisa, Rome, Siena and Venice were *piazze*. Similar centres of commerce in Spain were Barcelona and Valencia; in France, Avignon, Montpellier and Paris (though Paris declined rapidly after 1410, in favour of the fairs of Geneva, and later of Lyons): and there was Bruges in Flanders, and the city and port of London.

Each of the most important commercial centres of Europe housed a branch of one of the major institutions of the century, the Medici bank. Founded in 1397 by Giovanni di Bicci de' Medici, in association with members of the Bardi family, the bank at first held two offices, in Florence and Rome, and then new branches were established in Naples, 1400 (but discontinued as from 1426); in Venice, 1401; and in Geneva, in 1426. But the great period of the bank was marked by the stern and skilful administration of Cosimo de' Medici, Giovanni's son. Between 1439 and 1453, branches were set up in Bruges, Pisa, London, Avignon and Milan.

Typical of the economic and political approach during the period was the way in which a situation would be assessed, and plans and administration reorganized in order to take the best advantage of any given situation. Thus the Medici bank opened a temporary office in Basle in 1433, to handle the financial business of the Church council; and so in around 1464 the Geneva branch was moved to Lyons, where the fairs recently established by Louis XI attracted far more trade. Another feature of the Medici bank, common also to many other enterprizes of the day, was the range of its involvement. In its most successful years, the whole bank incorporated the 'bank' in Florence, the branches in other Italian cities and abroad, and three *botteghe* within Florence—two for the manufacture of woollen cloth, and one for silk. Foreign branches of the bank undertook trade as well as exchange. For instance, in 1469, Tommaso Portinari was managing a staff of eight at the branch in Bruges where, during the rule of Philip the Good (1419–67), the Medici represented the most important Italian firm. Its success abroad was due in part to Cosimo's policy to allow foreign branches of the bank only to deal with princes when he granted permission. The next head of the bank, Piero, had less control over the Bruges branch manager, Portinari, whose friendship with Charles the Bold (Duke, 1467–77), caused Medici finance to become entangled in some of the Duke's ambitious pursuits. Politics and finance were inextricably linked, and nowhere was this more evident than from 1462, when new alum sources were discovered in the Papal States. The Medici, as Papal bankers, were inevitably drawn into the political web of shifting Papal policies which manipulated this abundant supply of raw material, essential to the Italian textile industries. In such ways the flow of trade and commerce in the Quattrocento spread far and wide.

There was a move towards a much more closed society at the end of the century. Those men who acted as merchants and bankers were gradually withdrawing from trade. Relatively little land was left in the hands of the Church, and small properties were swept into the expansive territories of the big landowners. The wealth of the country was becoming concentrated in the hands of fewer noble families.

Any distinctions made between the classes of fifteenth-century Italy are arbitrary, and inevitably based on the theories and political beliefs of the social and economic historians who have attempted such an exercise. However, it is necessary at this point (and at the risk of oversimplification) to offer an idea of the social structure, so as to establish who were the arbiters of taste and style. There existed five main social groups: the clergy, the nobility, the merchant and professional class, artisans and shopkeepers, and the peasants and extremely poor. For the study of fashionable dress, we will turn to members of the nobility, and of the merchant and professional class.

An Italian in the Quattrocento would classify a noble as one who lived nobly, but who was not necessarily a member of the landed aristocracy. One might be a noble by birth, or ennobled by a prince; or, in Venice, one would be considered noble if the family was included in the Golden Book, a social register which had been closed at the end of the thirteenth century. Perhaps most important to the nobility was a sense of common values. They considered themselves the only social group capable of esteem (*onore*). Inwardly, this entailed courage and loyalty; outwardly, esteem was recognized by the bearing of titles and official positions, and by generous acts displayed through gifts of alms, clothes, hospitality, and through the patronage of the arts. A certain grace of movement and upright composure, the visible signs of nobility, were not necessarily hereditary, but were harmonized by a series of highly cultivated traits. In 1469, on viewing Clarice Orsini, the future wife of her son Lorenzo, Lucrezia Tornabuoni Medici remarked the manner in which Clarice walked about with her head held 'not boldly as ours is'.[1] She went on to forgive this slightly shameful demeanour, attributing it to Clarice's shyness at meeting her prospective mother-in-law for the first time. The Orsini, a Roman family of outstandingly aristocratic lineage, had not given Clarice the

4. Lorenzo de' Medici (the Magnificent) attired as the young magus in The Journey of the Magi by Benozzo Gozzoli, 1459.

sparkling confidence and proud posture held by the noble, but thoroughly bourgeois, Medici. Even when married to Lorenzo, poor Clarice remained the doleful, timid creature she had appeared from the start, and never quite came to terms with the splendidly cultured life of Florence: a considerable contrast to unfashionable Rome.

More often in the south of Italy and the Papal States were nobles to be found engaged in their traditional pursuit—war. A business in the fifteenth century, some nobles were still engaged in fighting, on an amateur or professional basis. But all over Italy the skills of equitation and the use of weapons were mainly employed by the patriciate for the more pleasurable pursuits of hunting and jousting. The nobility primarily constituted a leisure class privileged enough to afford to pay the mercenary soldiers, the managerial merchants and bankers, the artists and humanist scholars, the political advisers and the managers of their country estates.

'Professional' was not a term used in the Quattrocento, but here refers to that class of doctors, members of the legal profession, university teachers (usually lawyers or doctors themselves), and full-time officials, such as the staff of chanceries. The merchant class, on the other hand, included those men involved in commerce and banking: some would manage businesses themselves, whilst others would employ men to do that job for them. The strength of the professional group lies less in wealth than in education—usually at university, and invariably in law. However, within such stratifications there are very subtle differences of status; for example, judges and lawyers, addressed 'messer', took precedence over the notaries, who were merely called 'ser'.

It was principally the nobles, professionals and merchants who had surnames, the acquisition of which assisted the identification of a family's standing. An individual was account-able not to a small family unit as we know it, but to the extended family or *casa*. This included not just the legitimate and illegitimate children, but all the relatives and slaves; it was a group of people with the same surname. As the relations were traced through the male line, the birth of a son was a cause for celebration; but a daughter was seen primarily as a means of linking one *casa* with another.

Girls were legally of a marriageable age when they were 12 years old, by which age the children of the social classes just discussed were often quite sophisticated. If a daughter were not married by the time she had reached 16, her parents would probably show some degree of concern: that is, if the intention to marry had ever been expressed, for convents were far cheaper than husbands! Compare the 1000 florin dowry of Paolo Niccolini's wife in 1429 with the house he bought in Via San Procolo in 1461 for 870 gold florins, and the 60 florins he had spent on their wedding feast in 1433.[2] A marriage was the result not of individual will, but of a collective decision, and canon law termed invalid any marriage which took place without the parents' consent, either during or after the mother's and father's lifetime, for there are cases of wills in which the details of marriages were laid down. Sometimes, arrangements were made soon after the birth of a child: in May 1477 at Milan, the betrothal of the infant Alfonso d'Este, heir to Ercole, Duke of Ferrara, and Anna Sforza, four-year-old daughter of the late Duke Galeazzo Maria and his Duchess Bona, was announced. Two weeks later, the nuptial contract was signed at Ferrara and the union was celebrated with great processions and thanksgivings, the baby bridegroom being solemnly carried in the arms of his chamber-lain to meet the Milanese ambassador, sent to Ferrara on Anna's behalf. Bonds between the Sforza and Este families were more

5. The Wedding Feast of Nastagio degli Onesti, by Botticelli. This is the last of a series of four panels probably painted in 1483 to commemorate the marriage of Giannozzo di Antonio Pucci with Lucrezia di Piero di Giovanni Bini. Above the capitals of the front pillars appear the arms of Pucci (left), Medici (centre), and Pucci impaling Bini (right). It is likely that the presence of the Medici arms, as well as the Medici *impresa* of the diamond ring and the laurel bush set in a bracket on each of the front columns, relate to Lorenzo the Magnificent who may have negotiated the marriage. The scene depicts the serving of sweetmeats, while Nastagio offers wine to his bride.

firmly established in 1480, when Ludovico il Moro, recently proclaimed Duke of Milan, offered his hand in marriage to Isabella d'Este who was, as it happens, already engaged to Francesco Gonzaga of Mantua. Ludovico, however, raised no objection when Isabella's younger sister Beatrice was offered to him instead. She was only five years old at the time, and he 29.

Marriage was one way of drawing together possessions of land and money, cultures and styles—not an attitude peculiar to Italy or to the fifteenth century, but one which was exploited to the full. A flavour of Spain reached both Milan and Ferrara via Naples through the marriage in 1473 of King Ferrante's daughter Leonora to Ercole d'Este, and in 1489 through the marriage of Gian Galeazzo Sforza, Duke of Milan, to Isabella of Aragon, daughter of King Alfonso of Naples. Political and economic motives for marriage were not confined to the illustrious houses just mentioned: there are many instances of merchants' daughters marrying the sons of lawyers. The facts would suggest that lawyers were socially more acceptable, and that the merchant class was intent on penetrating a higher rank by financial arrangement.

Paolo Niccolini, a successful wool merchant of Florence who

later rose to the highest office of the state, *gonfaloniere* of justice, began to write a book of records in 1429. Commencing in that year, his notes demonstrate how a marriage (in his case to a certain Cosa Guascone) consisted of a series of ceremonies, and how between each rite, months or even years might elapse.[3] A document concerning the bride's dowry was drawn up by intermediaries who were appointed to organize the legal formalities of the marriage. This was confirmed in church by the *impalmare*, or shaking of hands, at which the mediating notary and members of the two families were present; but the bride did not appear on this occasion. Subsequently the solemn betrothal took place, usually, though not always, in church. The third instalment involved the presentation of the ring in the house of the bride's father, and afterwards bride and groom would retire to a closed chamber, and a notary recorded the fact. The only truly religious part of the ceremonies, *la messa del congiunto*, was said as soon as possible after consummation. The final, and most celebrated, often lavish event of marriage procedure was the

6. The Giving of the Ring, by a Veronese artist, *c.* 1490.

nozze, the formal welcome of the bride into her new home. In the case of Cosa Guasconi, she continued to live in her father's house for a further three years following the initial marriage rites, and did not move to her new home until the dowry had been paid, in 1433. For some marriages, an additional ceremony took place: the official girding of the bride with a beautiful belt (a feature of every trousseau), in memory of the *cestus* given by Vulcan to Venus. It was believed that by this gesture, the bride would be gifted with every grace.

A daughter was not valued as highly as a son, for she did not continue the family name and direct blood-line. But this did not mean that the education of women—particularly those of the noble classes—was in any way neglected. Nor were the true qualities of women considered inferior to their masculine counterparts. Some of the most illuminating and perceptive letters handed down to us were written by women. Had Beatrice d'Este only been graced with charm, she certainly would not have been sent, aged 18, as Ludovico's ambassador to Venice in 1493. Her brilliant elder sister Isabella was involved in a lively exchange of correspondence with Ludovico il Moro's son-in-law, Galeazzo di San Severino, during the summer of 1491. Their argument was founded on the respective merits of the heroes Rinaldo and Orlando. Isabella's conscientious determination to substantiate her view caused her to request from Matteo Boiardo, a friend of hers, the concluding part of his *Orlando Innammorato* (still in manuscript form at that time); she also wrote to the faithful agent in Venice, Giorgio Brognolo, to send her a complete list compiled from the Venetian booksellers of all the works available in Italian, concerning ancient and modern heroic legends and stories of battles, particularly those in which the protagonists were paladins of France. Another of her correspondents, also a great friend and almost identical in age, was Elisabetta Gonzaga who in 1488 married Guidubaldo Montefeltro: as the exalted Duchess of Urbino, Elisabetta commands great intellectual respect, for it is round her circle of companions at court that Baldassare Castiglione's discussions about the courtier took place.[4]

Humanist scholars were sometimes employed as tutors to children, either within a household, as Lorenzo de' Medici employed Poliziano or the Gonzaga engaged Vittorino da Feltre, or by local governments or institutions. Bianca Maria Sforza, Duchess of Milan, saw to it that Ludovico and his brothers were carefully educated, allowing an even distribution of occupations throughout the day. Their studies included theology, the art of the state, Latin and Greek; and of secondary importance were dancing, ball games, vaulting, duelling, equitation and the use of arms. Tutored by the humanist Francesco Filelfo and Giorgio Valagussa (poet laureate and author of learned works on theology) amongst others, it is said that Bianca Maria used to tell

Filelfo not to forget that 'we must make princes of our children, not men of letters!'[5]

Among some members of the professional and merchant classes, it was customary for boys to be put into a monastery at about the age of eight or ten, for their early education. At a later stage, those young men whose fathers had planned a merchant career for them, would go to an 'abacus' school, to learn the arithmetic of business. This would be followed by an apprenticeship to a merchant, beginning with the humblest duties in a shop, and eventually rising to the position of a firm's representative, perhaps in some foreign branch. Luca Landucci, author of a Florentine diary, in 1450, aged about 14, went to learn book-keeping from a master called Calandra and in 1452 he entered the shop of the apothecary Francesco in the Mercato Vecchio.[6]

The universities of Italy were different from most academic institutions elsewhere in Europe, where theology and philosophy were dominant. In Italy, law was the principal subject taught, though a qualification in medicine was also offered. The law was Roman law involving the consultation of Latin texts. Also considered essential to the training of lawyers was the art of composing letters, documents and speeches.

Many early humanists were lawyers, or at least had undergone some form of legal training, and were employed as chancellors, ambassadors, historians, composers of speeches, translators and tutors. Not one of these men would in fact have decribed himself as a humanist, but rather 'orator' or occasionally 'rhetoricus'. The popular nineteenth-century view of Renaissance humanism envisages a revival of classical themes and a study of Greek and Latin texts. This is so, but in addition to the more overt references to and imitations of Greece and Rome in art, architecture and literature, the fifteenth-century humanism offered something far more profound—a reinterpretation of the values of life, no longer based on the spiritual foundations of medieval Christianity, but on a logical observation of reality through human experience. Whilst the very devout might consider the Greeks and Romans pagans—and therefore it followed that those who studied their laws, language, art and philosophies possessed pagan tendencies—the juxtaposition of and correspondence between the sacred and profane, religious and secular, is an undeniable feature of the Renaissance. The possible accusation of paganism did not deter Pope Nicholas v (1447–55) from being one of the most outstanding collectors of classical texts of his day, whose manuscripts were to form a valuable collection within the Vatican library. And attempts to end the Eastern schism hardly proved successful in terms of the popular Christian view of what they had set out to do; rather, they provided forums at which Greeks and Romans met and exchanged knowledge of their revived classical heritage. The most prominent of the Greek scholars at the Council of Ferrara in 1438, Plethon, Scholarius and Bessarion,

7. Portrait medal of Isotta da Rimini, by Matteo de' Pasti, 1446. An interest in the antique and the discovery of ancient Roman coins and cameos encouraged the revival of the medal as an art form.

acted as a strong catalyst in the spread of Renaissance humanism. And from the Council of Constance (1414–18) appeared letters from Leonardo Bruni[7] and others, which were saturated with philosophical questions about the utter pride and the entire ceremonial nature of the prelates' way of life. Their writings offer a caricature of the Council, where the luxurious robes, the horses, the numbers of servants and the kneeling devotees enveloped the leaders of the Church.

Humanistic thought and writing demonstrate a preference for a simplicity and clarity of style in an attempt to understand the world, with the aid of classical scholarship. Similarly, in the visual arts, we find influences of the classical, initially in sculpture: for example, in Donatello's prophets of the Old Testament carved in oratorical poses on the doors of the Baptistry in Florence.[8] The classical style embodies an investigation into realistic and naturalistic detail—into drapery, anatomy and perspective— points which are discussed in Alberti's *Della Pittura* of the 1430s.[9] In addition, artists from north of the Alps, such as the Flemings Jan van Eyck (*c.* 1390–1441) and Rogier van der Weyden (1399–1464), had a direct influence on Italian painters in terms of colour, texture and landscape. The mystery and stylization of the sculpture and painting of the Middle Ages gradually give way to a more worldly interpretation of subjects.

From the works of art passed to posterity, it would appear that the majority of paintings in the fifteenth century were religious in content. However, the smaller proportion of secular subjects in art did increase during the course of the century. Probably the most frequent theme for altarpieces was the Madonna with saints, but within that subject-matter, the introduction of other figures, including perhaps a donor, became increasingly evident. Gradually, those figures were drawn into a closer relationship with each other, and with the religious figures present. The numbers of lay figures also increased, no doubt a result of developments in religious drama and saints' day processions. The individuals in these religious paintings were, at first, of a smaller scale than the protagonists; but their presence became more and more noticeable as their proportions met those of the sacred figures.

The result was a secularization of the content, form and function of works of art. A Martyrdom of Saint Sebastian or a Baptism of Christ, allowing a progressive artist to show his skills in portraying the human form or a landscape background, rarely was found at the beginning of the century. An individual was only occasionally interpreted in the form of a portrait-painting, -bust, or -medal before the latter half of the Quattrocento. And whilst the most important works of art were intended for public places throughout the period, there was a noticeable rise in the number of altarpieces and other works of art commissioned for private chapels, houses and palaces. There is also strong evidence that there was a considerable output of ready-made workshop

8. Saint Lawrence Enthroned with Saints and Donors, by Filippo Lippi, *c.* 1435–40. Alessandro degli Alessandri, a rich Florentine merchant who commissioned the altarpiece, kneels with his sons. The inclusion of saints Cosmas and Damian is a payment of homage to Cosimo de' Medici, whom Alessandro supported.

goods, such as the painted or carved and gilded marriage chest (*cassone*) and the salver presented on the birth of a child (*desco da parto*). Because these were functional objects, usually made anonymously and possibly according to a set of patterns, they were not highly valued and so few have survived. Those that still exist, however, indicate the kind of secular subject matter employed: the Birth of Saint John the Baptist, Christ or the Virgin introduced details of women assisting at something approaching the actual occasion for which the salver was to be presented. The *cassoni* called for triumphs of love and virtues, illustrated in courtly and processional tones which directly reflected the ceremonial quality of the *nozze*.

Drama was not contained within the stage and auditorium arrangement familiar today, but was often to be found out-of-doors, in churches and in palaces. The correspondence between the arts was strongly felt, and this interpenetration was demonstrated in performance. The fifteenth century saw the rebirth of the madrigal—a poem set to music.[10] Religious and secular theatre associated music and painting with literature. A member of the Orthodox contingent to the Council of Florence in 1439 visited churches where he saw plays enacted, and after seeing an Annunciation, he remarked 'The angel Gabriel was a beautiful youth, dressed in a gown as white as snow, decorated with gold—exactly as one sees heavenly angels in paintings'.[11] Saints' days, such as that of Saint George and Saint John the Baptist, patron saints of the house of Este and of Florence respectively, were celebrated with dramatic tableaux and processions illustrating the life of the saint.

A direct relationship between real events and the staging of them was shown when, in 1493, Beatrice, Ludovico il Moro's duchess, visited Venice accompanied by her mother Leonora, Duchess of Ferrara. The occasion prompted the first boat race ever held between women, but more significant was the fact that the winning boat should be rowed by a mother, her two daughters and one daughter-in-law, thus paying a great compliment to Leonora, who herself had two daughters (Beatrice and Isabella) and one daughter-in-law (Anna Sforza).[12] The processions of Alfonso of Aragon and his officials, the whole court of Milan to a hunting-lodge or summer residence, and many more, all offered wonderful spectacles. The diary of Luca Landucci offers a lively picture, viewed from a lower social position, of scenes of visitors entering Florence with their entourages; battles won and lost; deaths and imprisonments of the well-known higher ranks, as well as of the anonymous guilty of theft or murder. He marvels at the expenditure of the classes of higher rank than his own, and in particular the cost of the altarpiece by Ghirlandaio for Santa Maria Novella, first shown to the public on 22 December 1490. Any artist, intent on portraying a realistic picture, with which contemporary spectators could

9. A salver, depicting the Triumph of Love, by Dello di Niccolò.

identify, would find it difficult to ignore such events.

From what standpoint did artists view their subjects? Painters, sculptors and architects, unlike the writers, scientists and humanists, tended to be the sons of artisans and shopkeepers. Artists were at the same time both designers and craftsmen, and were all generally considered artisans—whether painters, stone-masons, goldsmiths, or some other form of skilled manual worker. Being of a lower social group, and often identified by the town from which they came, rather than by a family name, may offer one explanation why many artists settled in republican states—particularly Venice and Florence, states which proclaimed the virtues of liberty. But a far more convincing reason for the thriving schools of art in those two centres is due to the number and variety of patrons to be found there. In the development of art and letters, the division of the Italian states can be seen as an advantage, for the variety of patronage allowed artists, to a certain degree, to develop individual styles. But was the flourishing of the arts dependent on patronage? It is difficult to answer such a question; but whilst the details which contribute towards an individual style are left to the artist's initiative, the general control would appear to lie in the hands of the patron. The wording of surviving contracts for commissions supports this opinion, as do certain letters. One such, of 12 November 1491, addressed from Ferrara by Isabella d'Este, Marchioness of Mantua, to the painter Luca Liombeni, concerns the decoration of her *studiolo* in the palace at Mantua.[13] Knowing how Liombeni tended to work at a sluggish pace if not pressed, and anxious that the room should be finished before her return to Mantua, Isabella wrote:

> In answer to your letter, we are glad to hear that you are doing your utmost to finish our *studiolo*, so as not to be sent to prison. We enclose a list of the devices which we wish to have painted on the frieze, and hope that you will arrange them as you think best, and make them as beautiful and elegant as possible. You can paint whatever you like inside the cupboards, as long as it is not anything ugly, because if it is, you will have to paint it all over again at your own expense, and be sent to pass the winter in the dungeon, where you can, if you like, spend a night for your pleasure now, to see if the accommodation there is to your taste! Perhaps this may make you more anxious to please us in the future. On our part, we will not let you want for money, and have told Cusatro to give you all the gold that you require.

An artist's reward for completing his work well and on time was usually a letter of apology from Isabella, explaining that any threat she might have made was done so purely in jest. Notwithstanding such belated excuses, it is clear that fifteenth-century patrons displayed a combination of ruthlessness and benevolence towards those whose work was dependent on them, so forcing that anxiety to please.

Apart from the private pleasure gained by possessing and looking at works of art, there were more public and historical reasons for patronage. The commissioning, particularly of religious works of art by official bodies, individual personalities and ruling households offered a public declaration of pious intentions. At the same time they gave prestige in the eyes of contemporaries and of posterity. Such prestige might be shown either through the portrayal of the donor and his relationship to the subject-matter, or through the size of the work and the qualities of

10. The Birth of Saint John the Baptist, by Ghirlandaio, 1485–90. Conspicuously looking out from the foreground is Lodovica Tornabuoni.

THE HISTORY OF DRESS

materials used—or both. A painting was the outcome of a financial agreement: bespoke works were calculated by the square foot, by time and materials. Details such as the use of gold, numbers of figures, the quality of ultramarine, and the types of costumes to be featured were often laid down in contracts. The use of new techniques and ideas very much depended on the taste of the patron. A letter of Matteo de' Pasti to Piero de' Medici, written in 1441, illustrates the eagerness of an artist to make advances with his own ideas: but these are checked by his employer's specifications:

> By this letter I beg to inform you that since being in Venice I have learnt something which could not be more suited to the work I am doing for you, a technique of using powdered gold like any other colour, and I have already begun to paint the Triumphs in this manner, so that you will never have seen anything like them before. The foliage is all touched up with this powdered gold, and I have embroidered it over the maidens in a thousand ways . . . and if you so please, send me your instructions to go ahead with the Triumph of Fame, because I have details of the fantasy already, except that I do not know whether you want the seated woman in a simple dress or a cloak as I would like her to be. I know all the rest of what is to go in: the four elephants drawing her chariot, though I do not know whether you want young men and maidens surrounding her or famous old men . . .[14]

Piero de' Medici was also responsible for the commissioning of a tabernacle, on which an inscription records that the marble alone cost 4000 florins, an enormous sum.[15]

Conspicuous consumption was considered a sin of usury. However, gifts of altarpieces and suchlike could expiate the danger of damnation, for they were of course acts of charity and generosity. In Italy during the fifteenth century, although guilds still played an important part in the organization of industry, it was really the leading members of those guilds and the prominent families who exercised political power. The majority of the population was therefore somewhat depressed and so those with authority and the financial means probably realized some benefit could be gained from keeping those people entertained. Thus events like the carnivals provided for by Lorenzo de' Medici were arranged.

Vespasiano da Bisticci's description of the life of Federigo, Duke of Urbino, constructs a picture of a paternal figure, generously acting in the interests of the general population of Urbino.[16] Federigo regularly went about the town on foot,

11. The Duke of Urbino, Federigo da Montefeltro, with his son Guidubaldo; attributed to Pietro Berruguete, *c.* 1476.

calling into shops and stopping to talk in the street to anybody who had some misgiving to relate. He would walk down to a large meadow with a beautiful view, beside a convent of Saint Francis which he had built, and young men and boys would go down there with him, strip down to their doublets and play games. Vespasiano's chapter on Federigo concludes with a list of the wonderful buildings all erected under the Duke's patronage. In a way, the possession of money and property was morally justifiable, for they helped participation in the life of the city or state, and served to uphold the future position and activities of the family. Such a viewpoint was expressed in 1472 by a proud Florentine merchant, Benedetto Dei, who when writing a fine letter in oratorical tones to a Venetian, upheld the attributes and noble heritage of his home city.[17] He illustrated this concept of inheritance:

> . . . though Cosimo is dead and buried, he did not take his gold florins and the rest of his money and bonds with him into the other world, nor his banks and storehouses, nor his woollen and silken cloths, nor his plate and jewellery; but he left them all to his worthy sons and grandsons, who take pains to keep them and add to them, to the everlasting vexation of the Venetians and other envious foes whose tongues are more malicious and slanderous than if they were Sienese.

There was inevitably a good amount of pure self-indulgence, vanity and rivalry. The letters of Beatrice and Isabella d'Este bear witness to this fact—their wardrobes left nothing to be desired. In 1493, Beatrice's wardrobe contained around 84 gowns which she had had made for her in the two years since her *nozze*, and what is more, she had another wardrobe of clothes in Milan.[18] And Isabella forever demanded the highest quality of goods, declaring that if a piece of cloth of a quality frequently seen worn by other women was bought to make a garment for her, it had not been worth the trouble of purchasing.[19] The two sisters were both, like their high-born contemporaries, extremely partial to games of cards like *scartino*. In 1494, when Ludovico learnt that his wife had won as much as 3000 ducats during that year through gambling, and that she had spent it all on alms, he could hardly believe the sum, and even when she owned up to having paid some of that money to embroiderers and craftsmen, he still considered it an over-indulgence.[20] Not that Ludovico himself was a paragon of virtue. His generous acts can also be seen as self-centred ways of outdoing others; they included prizes of money or of cloth to those jousters whom he admired in tournaments. One such event was organized by Ercole d'Este, in honour of Ludovico's visit to Ferrara in 1493. On one day Ludovico gave 100 ducats to a winning combatant, and on another, a single-handed contest between a

Milanese and a Mantuan man-at-arms was held in the courtyard of the castle, and won by the Mantuan, on whom Ludovico, the Marquis of Mantua and others proceeded to bestow fine gifts.[21]

The examples of extravagant expenditure are too numerous to mention, but how did they afford the enormous sums they paid out? Income came from their estates, banks and businesses, but the major part of their wealth was expressed in terms of the value of land and objects in their possession. If ready cash was not available in large quantities, by what means did they succeed in changing fashion and finding new novelties so frequently? The Gonzagas in 1491 owed Pagano, a Venetian jeweller, the sum of 8000 ducats.[22] One way out of debt was by pawning. It was Francesco's wish that Isabella should pledge many of her jewels in order to raise money to assist Sigismondo Gonzaga's rise to the position of cardinal. She did not, however, give away a golden belt, which she had recently worn in Milan and which she had just lent to one of her father's courtiers to wear at a masque. At that time, all her other jewels were in pawn in Venice, as she reminded her husband.[23] In one anxious moment Maximilian, the Emperor of the West, was forced to pawn not only many jewels, but also some linen, blouses and undergarments (*biancheria*) belonging to his wife Bianca Sforza![24]

Although such indulgence was widespread throughout Italy in the period, the degree of extravagance varied. So impressed were Galeazzo, Duke of Milan, and his consort Bona of Savoy, when Lorenzo the Magnificent visited the Duchy in 1469 to become godfather to their infant son, he presented an enormous diamond to Bona, who exclaimed delightedly 'You must be godfather to all my children!'[25] But two years later, the visit of the Duke and Duchess of Milan created a far greater public show of wealth, for their suite consisted of around 2000 people, and in Machiavelli's opinion was to be blamed for initiating a notable decline in public morals.[26]

How might such luxury be checked? Sumptuary legislations were issued throughout the century to restrict extravagance in clothes, jewellery and ceremony; the laws usually were passed by the local government in question, and were normally instigated for either moral or economic reasons, or both. However, despite the pedantic detail of some legislations, invariably these laws were quite ineffectual for they often only applied to women, and exempted from their clauses the ladies of knights or doctors. It appears that the higher classes of office were creating such laws to ensure that the lower social orders could not compete with them.

Some cases of sumptuary legislation were quite ridiculous. In Milan in 1498 there was a ruling that the use of dark-coloured clothing worn in mourning should apply only to the wife of the deceased, his brothers and sisters and descendants in the masculine line.[27] Was it to be literally interpreted that parents could not wear mourning for their children? Conversely, in

Brescia there was one group of women—the prostitutes— who were positively encouraged to wear as many forbidden items of clothing as they could. It was believed that all women of esteem (those described as *oneste*) would not wish to associate themselves with those of ill repute, and thereby ensure the enforcement of the sumptuary law.[28]

If such secular attempts were unsuccessful, then perhaps to scorn luxury on religious grounds might appeal to the moral fibre of the noble and professional classes. Denunciations of all 'vanities'—his comprehensive word for superfluity, especially in women's dress and artificial accessories to fashion—were proclaimed wherever San Bernardino preached. Born in 1380 of a noble family of Siena, the Albizzeschi, San Bernardino spoke with a curiously intimate knowledge of costume and cosmetics:

> It would seem a strange thing if a woman on the death of her husband or father should go to Mass with her head decked with flowers. But it is much more strange for a woman redeemed with Christ's blood, the daughter and spouse of the Supreme Father, to go to Mass with her head ornamented not with flowers only but with gold and precious stones, with paint and false hair; for every Mass is celebrated in memory of Christ's passion. . . . O the vanity of thee, woman, who deckest thy head with such a multitude of vanities! Remember that divine Head at which the Angels tremble . . . that Head is crowned with thorns while thine is adorned with jewels. His hair is stained with blood, but thy hair (or rather that which is not thine own) is bleached artificially. His cheeks are befouled with spitting,

12. (opposite) Madonna and Child with Saints, and with Ludovico il Moro and Beatrice d'Este; known as the Pala Sforzesca, Lombard School, *c.* 1495.

13. (above) San Bernardino Preaching; attributed to Vecchietta, *c.* 1440.

blood and bruises, but thine are coloured with rouge and varied pigments. His beauteous eyes, which the Angels of God contemplate, are darkened by most bitter death, but thine seem to sparkle with the ardour of lust and flames of wantonness.[29]

The saint's sermons resulted in public bonfires upon which were piled masses of false hair together with musical instruments and song-books, charms, masks, dice-boxes and other vanities. Such violent tones and visual parallels must have stirred the emotions of his audiences, but had little long-term effect.

In public, a sense of ceremony and theatrical spectacle, and in private the enjoyment of dreaming up and possessing something different, gave costume a vital role in the lives of men and women of the Quattrocento. Whether fashionable, legal or academic gowns were worn, whether a figure was dressed in resplendent ecclesiastical vestments, motley livery, earthy peasant clothing or sombre mourning, the language of dress was highly expressive. The growth of commerce and travel, and the unions between different royal and noble families through politics and marriage; the skill, variety and originality of the artists, and the development of new techniques in textiles; the classical revival and the assertion of personal status; the use of heraldic devices and the belief in allegory; all were instrumental in stimulating new ideas in art and fashion.

2 The Making of Renaissance Dress: 1400-1430

I n the first half of the fifteenth century, the development of Renaissance ideals in art and literature is mainly focussed on Florence. Correspondingly, a large part of the contemporary evidence for costume in pictures and documents is Florentine. Leonardo Bruni, who twice held the position of Chancellor, enthusiastically proclaimed the virtues of 'liberty', a word very much in vogue in Florence in those earlier years of the Quattrocento. A new secular approach to the freedom of an individual's status was emerging, and these recently awakened attitudes towards man's assertive role in society were bound to have repercussions in the manner of dress.

All over Italy, petty wars between feudal lords and greater victories, leading to the emergence of the five principal states, were being fought. In the opening years of the century, two key political figures emerged, each attempting to conquer vast stretches of land. The first was Gian Galeazzo Visconti, Duke of Milan, and the second, King Ladislas of Naples. Visconti possessed ambitious schemes which no doubt included dreams of commanding at least the Italian peninsula, if not a complete empire, and probably Ladislas thought likewise. Had Gian Galeazzo not suddenly died of the plague in 1402, or had Ladislas not suffered a fatal attack of syphilis in 1414, who knows what the political and cultural story of the Quattrocento might have been?

Regional warfare was never to cease. Many battles and petty intrigues were short-sighted and lacking in political ideal. However, much wider horizons were being reached through the world of commerce, in which Italian prestige was unquestioned. The variety and scale of the traffic of goods through the hands of Italian merchants brought many luxury materials, such as silk and wool, dyestuffs, spices and precious metals, from all round the Mediterranean, the Orient, and north and west of the Alps. But the consequences of a succession of sudden and hard-hitting outbreaks of plague meant a smaller manufacturing workforce and a diminished consumer market. Consistent with political developments, business gradually became concentrated in fewer hands. From both a political and a social point of view, the newly enhanced status of certain families allowed them more leisure

time and spare capital to invest. This state of affairs partly explains the abundance and brilliance of the arts in the Renaissance.

The rich, detailed International Gothic style was prominent throughout Italy in the first years of the fifteenth century. Strangely, one of the most flamboyant tributes to Gothic architecture is the Duomo at Milan, begun towards the end of the fourteenth century: such pointed arches hardly penetrated the rest of Italy, except on a smaller scale in some secular architecture. It was in the areas around Lombardy and Venice that northern European influence was felt most strongly, and so the gem-like qualities of Gothic lingered there longer than in Tuscany. To a man like Leon Battista Alberti, the Gothic style embodied a sense of something outdated, and quite undesirable.[1] He as an architect, the sculptor Donatello and the painter Masaccio were consciously breaking away from tradition, and are key figures in the story of early Renaissance art. On the other hand, the Florentine workshops devoted to the working of gold and silver (where Donatello, like many artists, had served his apprenticeship), and those shops which produced decorative and functional painted objects, such as chests and salvers, retained more of those gothic qualities of elaborate detail. Their subject-matter added more classical legends of Gods and the story of Paris and Helen to the popular medieval themes of Alexander the Great and knights in shining armour. Nevertheless, they retained a somewhat nostalgic, romantic atmosphere. A similar contrast is displayed in the dress depicted on the one hand by Donatello and Masaccio, and on the other, that represented by the majority of artists of the day. The former presented a timeless costume, based on an idea of Roman togas and mantles, moulded by weighty folds but delineated by few decorative trimmings. The latter portrayed dress as it was worn by contemporaries: that is, they displayed rich, sumptuous garments, which reflected the extravagant

qualities of a Gothic style, and some of the wealth and fickle nature of politics and society.

Costume is not an isolated phenomenon: people and their clothing are part of an environment. The colour and shape of dress and its ornamentation are inextricably linked with composition and movement in painting, three-dimensional form in sculpture, and the comparative orders and elevations of architecture. This is not to say that one medium takes precedence over any other; for all art and design forms are interrelated, as much in the fifteenth century as happens in the twentieth.

So in the early years of the Quattrocento, the form of dress and the details of its accessories correspond to the Gothic style. It is generally thought that Italian dress in this period was influenced by France, where the International Gothic style was epitomized in the *Très Riches Heures* of the Duc de Berry. A notable interchange of culture and influence in fashion had come about through the marriage in 1387 of Valentina, daughter of Gian Galeazzo Visconti, to the Duke of Orleans, brother of the French king. The fashionable silhouette is outlined by a high waist for women; and both male and female dress have long full sleeves and sweeping hemlines slightly trained at the back. Rising necklines and tall bulbous headdresses appear to elongate the neck and give the whole stature of the body extra artificial height. The impression is enforced by hairlines plucked back to make ladies' foreheads higher. And consonant with the female profile, men's hairlines were shaved (usually up the sides and back of the neck), if only to accommodate the extraordinary tall collars. Gradually, a more natural representation of the human figure is clothed by sober shapes—only to return to a variety of extreme forms again at the end of the century.

In his *Codice Urbinate*, Leonardo da Vinci includes a satirical picture of the extremes of fashion. He was not just speaking of changes in the shape of dress within his own lifetime. For he was born in 1452, and the early part of his description of fashion is particularly appropriate to the turn of the fourteenth and fifteenth centuries. The following passage serves to illuminate and satirize the much broader concept of fashion, whilst presenting in a nutshell the patterns of change in fifteenth-century Italian dress:

And I remember having seen, in my childhood, grown men and young boys going about with every single edge of their clothing dagged, from head to toe, and down right and left sides. At the time, it seemed such a wonderful invention that they even dagged the dags. In this way, they wore their hoods and shoes: and even the crowns of their heads looked like cockerel's combs. Such fashions appeared from all the tailors' shops, in a variety of

14. (opposite, above) Female costume study, by Gentile da Fabriano, *c.* 1410–20. The extremely pointed shoes are a feature of the gothic North. Leafy dags (*frappature*) decorate the shoulders of her overgown (*pellanda*) whilst the fur-lined sleeves *a gozzo* hang freely behind.

15. (opposite, below) The Adoration of the Magi, by Masaccio, 1426. The young magus wears a *gonnella* soberly trimmed with fur about the hem, and with a device on his left sleeve. The two onlookers behind appear as conventional men of office, wearing cloaks (*mantelli*) over their *gonnelle*, and on their heads a reduced form of hood (*cappuccio*), by this time referred to as a *berretta*.

16. (above) A tarot card, by Bonifacio Bembo. The plucked hairline, high waist, and long, ample hems give exaggerated height to the figure.

colours. And afterwards I saw the shoes, caps and purses, the collars of gowns, the hems of their ankle-length doublets, each tail-end of clothing and even offensive weapons: in effect, everything I saw, right to the tips of the tongues of whosoever wished to appear beautiful, was forked in sharp points. In another era, sleeves began to grow and were so huge that each one of them on its own was larger than the main body of the garment. Then of course the clothes began to creep higher and higher up the neck until they finally smothered the whole head. Then collars began to peel away so that the clothes were no longer supported by the shoulders, because there was nothing left covering them. Then dress became so elongated that men had to bundle

17. Saint John Baptizing the Multitudes, by the Salimbeni brothers, 1416. Though not visible here in their most extreme forms, the use of dagging and applied decorative cutwork is evident. The young page holding the horses wears an open-sided tunic, a *giornea*, dagged all round.

the excess textile into their arms to avoid trampling over the hems with their feet. Following this, the cut of the garments swung to the opposite extreme, and hems only reached down to the hips and the elbows: the clothes were so narrow that they suffered unbearably, and many split under the strain. And feet were so squeezed into slim-fitting shoes that the toes bunched up one over the next and developed corns.[2]

The tailoring of cloth into closely-fitted garments had, to some extent, been resolved in the fourteenth century, with the mastering of buttoned closures. However, new layers of clothing and different ways of wearing them, as well as advances in the construction of garments, were yet to be achieved in the Quattrocento.

Women's clothing comprised three principal layers: the chemise, a simple dress, and some form of overgown. The fundamental garment in the Quattrocento remained the fourteenth-century *gonnella*, *gonna* or *sottana*. By this date it was generally called a *gamurra* (*camurra/camora*) in Florence; and in the north of Italy was known by the terms *zupa*, *zipa*, or *socha*. Worn by women of all classes, the *gamurra* was a simple dress with sleeves; as some inventories list examples which are worn out (*triste*),[3] it must be considered a lasting functional garment. Earlier in the century, the sleeves were attached: but soon the use of wearing detached sleeves, held to the main body of the garment by means of *aghetti*, laces, becomes more general. Following the natural contour of the body, the *gamurra* was unlined, and invariably made of wool, sometimes with sleeves of silk: it was worn over a light chemise (*camicia*) of cotton or linen, on its own at home, and under another garment when going out or on formal occasions. When Alessandra Macinghi Strozzi wrote to her son Filippo about a girl whom she would like him to marry, she related how the girl visited her *in gamurra*; she therefore implied the informality of the occasion.[4]

There was a difference between summer and winter garments, the distinction usually being made by the weight of the cloth. In warmer weather, the form of the *gamurra* probably took on the name of *cotta*, constructed from silk rather than woollen cloth. *Cotte* were not necessarily as humble as the *gamurre*; for in 1466 the trousseau of Nannina de' Medici, the wife of Bernardo Rucellai, was to include a *cotta* of white damask brocaded in gold with flowers, and with sleeves of pearls.[5] The relative fullness of the *cotta* compared with the *gamurra* is difficult to determine: Marco Parenti, a silk merchant of Florence, recorded that 18 *braccia* were sufficient to make a *cotta* of *zetani vellutato di chermisi* for his wife.[6] The garment was to be lined with 20 *braccia* of red *gualescio*, costing seven *soldi* per *braccio*. Gold trimmings and little

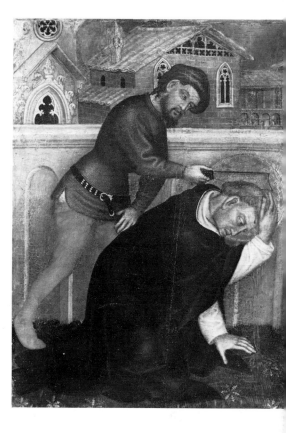

18. The Assassination of Saint Peter Martyr, by Gentile da Fabriano, *c.* 1400. The doublet (*farsetto*) worn by the saint's assassin has sleeves cut in one with the bodice. The tailoring of sleeves around the shoulder was, by the second decade, to become reasonably accomplished; but this man of lowly means wears the unsophisticated cut of an earlier period.

47

pearls for embroidering the sleeves of the same *cotta* indicate that the garment, though basically forming the same layer of clothing as the *gamurra*, was a more prestigious article of clothing, formal enough to wear alone over a chemise, especially in the summer. Sometimes, however, it was worn with an overgarment—usually a *giornea*.

The *giornea* corresponds to the fourteenth-century *guarnacca*, and in the Quattrocento was still sometimes called by that name. It was often sleeveless: but its main feature was that instead of only opening down the front, it was also left open at the sides, to reveal the textile of the *gamurra* or of the *cotta* underneath.

19. Detail of The Mystic Marriage of Saint Francis, by Sassetta, 1437–44. Each of the three young women wears a humble *gamurra*.

The most important women's overgarment was the *cioppa*. So-called in Florence and Naples, it was known by different terms elsewhere. In the north of Italy it was called a *pellanda* (*opelanda*) and must therefore be related to the *houppelande* of northern Europe. Elsewhere, it may be called a *veste* or *sacco*: but later in the century the terms *sacco* and *pellanda* became obsolete, and were replaced by *vestimento*. The *cioppa* was invariably lined, and usually opened down the centre front. It had sleeves—often of majestic shape and volume—and was often a resplendent garment, displaying borders of some fine fur. Listed in his family inventory of 1449, Bartolommeo Pucci's wife had three velvet *cioppe*, two of

20. The Queen of Sheba Adores the Holy Wood; from the Legend of the True Cross, by Piero della Francesca, *c.* 1452–66. In the central foreground, a young woman wears a white *giornea* with *frappature* down the edges over a dark red *cotta*. The figure to the left of her wears a *cioppa* with fur-lined open sleeves over a *gamurra* or *cotta*. The kneeling queen wears a *mantello* over her *cotta*.

black lined with marten (*martore*), and a fine one of *velluto chermisj paonazzo* with open sleeves (*maniche aperte*) lined with ermine (*ermellini*) and the *buosto* (*busto*) with *pancie*, skins from the underside of the animal's belly; the ermine would therefore be visible around the sleeves.[7] In other cases, the *cioppa* remained simply cut and unadorned, continuing its essentially functional origins: for example, when one impoverished young woman had to mend her *gamurra*, she was forced to wear her *cioppa* directly over a chemise, *la cioppa in sulla camicia*.[8] Considering her circumstances, she would hardly have much decoration on her *cioppa*.

Alternatively (or in addition) out-of-doors, a woman might wear some form of cloak, a *mantello*. It was a practical garment, worn habitually by older women, or occasionally by women of all ages when out riding or travelling. To wear a mantle with the hood drawn over the head would seem a custom of widows—at least in Lucca, where a law specified that women who had not been widowed were prohibited from wearing cloaks over their heads, except when it was raining.[9] There are numerous names of cloaks, each referring to a slightly different fashion or function. Among those to appear during the course of the century were the *mantechello*, the *mongile*, the *sbernia*, and the *passatempo*.

Underneath these layers of clothing, women wore *calze*, stockings usually made of woollen cloth: but how they were supported we do not know. For underneath the chemise no other garment was worn. There are no records of ladies' underpants and only the very occasional reference to other forms of hidden clothing, such as a woman's *farsettino* (related to the *farsetto*, the padded doublet worn by men) recorded in an inventory of 1411.[10] Shoes are listed sparsely through the inventories and trousseaux, although they were worn regularly.

On her head, an Italian woman might wear a *ghirlanda* (*grillanda*) or a *balzo*, both of which appear early in the century. A *ghirlanda*, literally a garland, was a head ornament, often taking the form of a padded roll placed round the crown. A *balzo* is a bulbous headdress, consisting of a wire or possibly willow understructure which was then covered by textile. Both *ghirlanda* and *balzo* were often covered with gems, usually pearls, and with velvet or often some more lavish figured textile. They served as purely ornamental headwear, and are features of high fashion, corresponding to the steeple and horned headdresses of northern Europe. In the middle of the century, Italian women also began to wear horns (*corna*), but by the end of the Quattrocento, headwear was not so large, though equally ornate. Fashionable headwear contrasts strongly with the veils and towels worn in a practical and modest way by women of lower classes and by widows and the elderly. Veils were usually made from pieces of linen; but some were made of silk, and came either from Italy, or from the East, where they were woven with colourful patterned borders.

21. (above) Drawing of a nude woman holding two torches and wearing the understructure to a *balzo*, probably made from steamed and bent willow; Tuscan School, *c.* 1430.

22. (opposite) Two young women attendants and the Virgin; detail from The Adoration of the Magi, by Gentile da Fabriano, 1423.

In The Adoration of the Magi by Gentile da Fabriano, two young women standing behind the Madonna and Child wear interesting, probably Turkish, towels wrapped turban-style about their heads. Similar textiles are often worn by the Madonna.

Throughout the century, much attention was paid to all the decorative trimmings which embellished fashionable clothing. Also essential to the resplendent image, as well as to the general silhouette, were the accessories to women's dress: jewels, embroidery, buttons and belts, veils and purses.

The vocabularly of costume is wide and complex. Names vary from region to region, and spellings alter from one line to the next in a manuscript. The idea of fashionable influences also changed, causing many variants in the names for garments, despite the fact that they do not radically alter in form and function.

23. Scene from the Story of the Holy Cross, by Michele di Matteo, c. 1440. The painter's fanciful application of gold reflects a general interest in embroidered motifs, braids and little decorative metal ornaments (tremolanti), which hang from chains.

Masculine attire usually related in silhouette to that of women's clothing. In particular, the many shapes of sleeves corresponded to both sexes—both strictly observing what seems to have been a universal rule for Italian women to cover the arms. Over a shirt (*camicia*), a man wore a doublet. The doublet was known by many different terms—*giubbetto, zuparello, corpetto, farsetto, zupone*. A close-fitting garment with a low-standing collar, and usually with sleeves, the doublet reached to a little below the waist. Its function was to give warmth and protection, but its most effective feature was the delineation of the torso. It was padded and quilted, the shape varying from decade to decade, depending on the fashionable silhouette. Doublets were sometimes made of extremely rich fabric, and in other cases of a simple linen or cotton stuff. To remain *in zuppone* was an expression equivalent to today's 'to be in shirt sleeves'.[11] It has been suggested that some forms of doublet were meant to show, whilst others were intended as hidden undergarments. Levi Pisetzky suggests that the *giubbetto, zuparello* or *corpetto* is often confused with the *farsetto* or *zupone*, the latter two forms being concealed layers of clothing. This may be so, but the confusion is understandable, since *farsetti* are sometimes recorded as being made of fine velvet, and elsewhere of linen or cotton. However, the fact that doublets were made by *farsettai* suggests that *farsetto* was a generic term for a range of garments all similarly constructed.[12]

Attached to the doublet by means of laces were the hose (*calze*) into which the ends of the *camicia* were tucked. However the immodestly short doublets did require a pair of underpants, *mutande* (confused with *brache* at the beginning of the fifteenth century); these would have been made, together with the rest of the *biancheria* (shirts, handkerchiefs, coifs, collars), at home. Invariably, hose were worn with no shoes or boots over them, but to protect the sole of the foot a piece of leather would probably be attached to the underside of the *calze*, when hose were worn alone.

Over the doublet a man wore some kind of tunic—a *gonnella* or a *cioppa*—with sleeves. Younger men generally went about dressed in shorter tunics (*gonnellini* or *vestini*); whereas older men, particularly those holding official positions, wore long robes.

Another masculine item of clothing, which corresponded precisely to the women's garment of the same name, is the *giornea*. Worn long or short, with or without a *gonnella* between it and the doublet, the *giornea* is a sideless tunic. According to San Bernardino, it rendered indecent anyone who stripped it off: on the other hand, when worn, it looked quite pretentious:

Have you ever considered how the *giornea* is made?
It is made like a horse-cloth, with the fringes down
the sides and round the bottom: in which case you

24. A study for David, by Ghirlandaio. The *camicia* hangs out from beneath the *farsetto* which, left unbuttoned at the wrists for freedom of movement, is tied to the *calze* by means of laces.

53

wear your clothing as a beast does. It therefore
follows, from all appearances, that you are a beast.
May one conclude from seeing you dressed thus,
that your inner being is also bestial?[13]

The saint from Siena also had strong words to say about the
fashion for the long hood, *cappuccio*, which had survived from the
Trecento. Though still long, it was not worn hanging down in
the way that it had been in the previous century. Rather, it was
draped round the crown of the head, to resemble a turban. For the
major part of the Quattrocento, however, the *cappuccio* was
obsolete as fashion although vestiges of it did remain and became
an element of official and academic dress—less to be worn than to
be carried over the shoulder. More frequently, men in the
fifteenth century wore some form of cap, the *berretta*, especially a
brimless conical form, though straw-brimmed hats, coifs and
other forms of headwear were often to be seen.

A form of cloak, *mantello*, would also feature in a man's
wardrobe. However, cloaks, like their feminine counterparts,
were forever changing names and the ways of being worn.
Alternatively, they were to be seen in a purely ceremonial
context: for example, the *manto* of the Doge of Venice. A
fashionable set of clothes was not complete without the usual
belts, brooches, buttons, laces and neckchains. Men in the
Quattrocento were as anxious about their appearance as were

25. (opposite) The Whim of the Young Saint
Francis to Become a Soldier, by Sassetta,
1437–44. The saint, here represented as a young
knight, donates his *vestito* and is left with a
gonnella. The knights' clothes are slit from knee to
hem, back and front, to facilitate riding on
horseback.

26. (left) Scene of a Miracle; School of Pisanello,
c. 1435–40. The young man in the left foreground
wears the type of *giornea* so scorned by San
Bernardino.

27. The tomb of Ilaria del Carretto, by Jacopo della Quercia, 1406.

Colour plate 1 (opposite) A hero and heroine, from The Fountain of Youth, by Jaquerio, 1418–30. The young man wears the leafy dags (*frappature*) and a garland headdress (*ghirlanda*) appropriate for a festive occasion. The heroine's sleeves are of a length and width prohibited in some sumptuary legislations. There is a northern gothic feel about the painting which is reflected by the dress – particularly the lady's *sella* (saddle-shaped) headdress.

Colour plate 2 (overleaf, left) Detail of The Adoration of The Magi, by Gentile da Fabriano, 1423. The feathered headdress worn by the middle magus here corresponds to that worn by the same character in Benozzo Gozzoli's Journey of the Magi of 1459 (see colour plate opposite page 97). The rich textile of his tunic shows an early use of pomegranates in Italian brocaded velvet. The skirt of the young king's tunic is composed of fringed and embroidered tabs.

women and the extremes of fashion, in shape and in the use of decorative trimmings, applied equally to both sexes.

The dress of Ilaria del Carretto shows the long drapes of fashion evident at the beginning of the Quattrocento. Her *cioppa* is undecorated, except for the trim of buttons fastening the high collar, a simplicity more appropriate for a tomb sculpture than would be dagged edges, fringes, and bejewelled ornaments. The long trailing sleeves, open from the shoulder, might be described in contemporary documents as *aperti* (open) or *ad ali* (like wings).[14] In profile, the sweep of the long drapes would follow in her path, collecting dust in summer and mud in winter—or so San Bernardino would have reminded her, had she lived to hear his sermons.[15] The bird-like profile was emphasized by the extra weight of cloth hanging from the back of the shoulders, causing the torso to thrust forward. This accounts for the greater bulk of cloth below the woman's high waistline in front—a feature which is evident in the tomb of Ilaria, and also later in Jan van Eyck's portrait of the Arnolfini couple.[16] The bird imagery is followed through to the sleeves *a gozzo* of the *gamurra* that Ilaria wears which were likened to a bird's crop, on account of their bulbous shape. In addition, the tightly buttoned cuffs of the *gamurra*, which then bell out and are turned back over the wrists, are an interesting feature. It is difficult to say whether they are part of fashion, or whether they hold a significance, for such details are not often seen. They may be the reason for references in some sumptuary legislations which forbid sleeves to cover the hands.[17]

Hemlines and the widths of sleeves expanded to vast proportions. The exaggerations that Leonardo spoke of were not isolated incidents, but part of a general trend.[18] The clothes of late Gothic and early Renaissance are not simply moulded around the human anatomy but rather, they become sculptural forms in their own right, transforming men and women into larger-than-life creatures. Here and there, they conceal, reveal and distort the natural figure, in the way that fashion has done ever since.

The qualities of cloth at hand and the increasingly magnificent figured silk textiles must, for those who could afford them, have been inspirational in selecting or devising fashionable shapes and details. The behaviour of cloth was particularly important as there was little artificial understructure to support a complete transformation in the shape of dress. It is true that men's doublets were filled and quilted and could alter the profile of the torso. But in women's clothing, the lack of boning and of corsets or hooped petticoats made the drape of the cloth, aided by some linings and facings, an essential feature of dress. The tightness of fit was, however, adjustable, for the *gamurra* had either a laced front opening or laced side openings, or both. The impoverished young women in Gentile's story of St Nicholas of Bari show how the *gamurre*, though following the natural line from shoulders to wrists and to hips, swing out in the lower part of the skirt. The

Je fuy dus de loraine apres mes ancesfoies
esteen de boucelon le palais victoires
emplari de romania iey aquis les mersours
hauy em baron crine asoire e asfours
ierusalen aquise antesours
emori ki c ous agres nosse seignore

＋godefroit de buisson＋

emplase a beques sa suer
oraise qui sb de grant euer
aliede de sur desumes
sut acenix delsebes auis prises
car tout la cite pillirent
z les cineuns fuerest
les vures auf tous abolirent
et de pois la cite ardirent

fullness about the hem of the *gamurra* must assist in the shaping of the silhouette of the *cioppa* worn on top.

Moreover, fashionable *cioppe* and other garments were growing so rich and voluminous that measures had to be taken to check their proportions. A sumptuary legislation of 1405, issued in Recanati in the Marches,[19] asserted that sleeves should be no more than four *palmi* wide, and that they should not be so long as to cover the hands. Not more than two colours or two types of cloth should be employed in one outfit of clothing; and restrictions were also imposed on the amount of gold and silver fringing worn. Traditionally extremely reactionary characters, the people of the Marches were considered somewhat avaricious by Florentines and other more showy, fashion-conscious Italians. This aspect of their contrasting natures had been put into caricature by Boccaccio.[20] Nevertheless, throughout Italy, local governments were obliged to draw official attention to the excess of fashion, and attempted to curb such extravagances.

In Pistoia, a statute of 1420 prohibited sleeves which were more than five *braccia* round the bottom; while the total width of the hem of the dress should not exceed 12 *braccia*.[21] And a decree published in Siena in 1412 advocated that clothes only of woollen cloth (*panni lani*) were to be permitted:[22] and no more than 16 *braccia* per garment should be used. Sleeves should be modestly lined with nothing but *panno lino*, *gualescio*, *bocchaccino* or *taffeta*: no embroidery or pearls were permitted, except for a

Colour plate 3 (previous page, right) The Rape of Helen, by a follower of Fra Angelico. Helen is made to stand out from the crowd by her rather exotic form of headdress and the extremely long flowing composite sleeves. This is an example of a painting in which it is difficult to relate the pigment colours to the shades of dyed cloth that were actually worn.

Colour plate 4 (opposite) Detail of a dapper young Sienese man from Pope Celestinus III Grants Privilege of Independence to the Spedale, by Domenico di Bartolo, 1443. The coloured *calze*, the fur *balze* and the sleeve turned back toga-style (*togata*) are all features of contemporary fashion. The Sienese were noted for their particularly ostentatious manner of dress.

28. Saint Nicholas Throws the Golden Balls to Three Poor Young Women; by Gentile da Fabriano, 1425. Behind the bed, one young woman takes off her *gamurra* to reveal the *camicia* underneath. The old man wears a coif (*cuffia*) and cap (*berretta*) on his head, a gown (*veste*) – probably second-hand – and low wooden shoes to protect the feet of his hose (*calze*) from wet and muddy streets.

garland (*grillanda*) on the head, up to the value of 25 gold florins: no jewels, fringes, or paternosters could be worn round the neck and no more than 18 *oncie* of silver should be applied to each dress in the form of buttons or other gemless ornaments. A belt was permitted, but was not to exceed the value of 12 florins, and no decoration with pearls was allowed. Should any clause of the law be defied, a fine of 25 gold florins was to be paid to the commune.

Any tailor found guilty of using a greater amount, or a richer type of fabric than was permitted was also in danger of such a forfeit. Such precautions had little effect, for this law only applied to women, and exempted the ladies of knights or doctors. In 1427 the Sienese friar, San Bernardino, was to make reference to the monstrous size of sleeves: they were, according to him, so vast as to take up more material than all the rest of the costume.[23]

The same Sienese sumptuary law of 1412 included a restriction in the expenditure on marriage rites. It imposed a limit on the number of gifts presented in public or private: at the *giure* (the declaration of marriage), the two families concerned should not invite more than 25 guests each, excluding very close blood relations and lawyers or others involved in drawing up the marriage contract; and at the *nozze*, no more than 20 platters should be offered, allowing for two people per platter. A limit of two main courses was laid down—the first to have no more than two types of meat in addition to the vegetables and salad, and the second (roast) course no more than three. On each platter one capon and a pair of other birds—no more—should be served; and to finish, only the smallest of *confettini* (little sweetmeats) were permitted.

That such sumptuary legislations were thoroughly discriminating and hypocritical is proved by the action of Gian Galeazzo Visconti. He had published a series of laws in 1396, the '*rubricae generalis de infrixaturis et diversis vanitatibus*',[24] which began with a condemnation of all excesses of vanity. It warned of the consequences of luxury, insisting principally on the difficulty imposed on marital relationships: married women should not prove too great a temptation for other men. The clauses of the law prescribed fines to the women who decorated their clothes with pearls; except that the wives of soldiers were exempted. Notwithstanding, six *pellande* appeared in 1420 in the trousseau of the Milanese Jacobina Resti, wife of Michele Trivulzio: mainly of woollen cloth of dark colours, the hems of some were decorated with pearls.[25] Besides pearls, they prohibited silver and silver-gilt chain ornaments worn on the head or on gowns, and banned the use of dagged work and fringes (*affrappatori*). However, the utter pomp and ceremony involved in 1402 at the funeral of Gian Galeazzo himself are surely proof that the style and excesses of life at the Milanese court were a far cry from that moral guidance issued by the Duke to his citizens. Forty-seven days passed after the Duke's death before the preparations for the funeral

29. A young woman holding a helmet; School of Pisanello. The hem-lines and widths of sleeves grew to excessive proportions, complemented by the bulbous *balzo*. Here, the headdress is covered with layers of false hair.

ceremony were ready. A sea of thousands, comprising relatives and officials of the Duchy of Milan, foreign ambassadors, soldiers and ecclesiastics, punctuated by men carrying the various devices of the Duke, accompanied the Duke's coffin from the Castello di Porto Giovo (now called the Castello Sforzesco) to the Church of S. Maria Maggiore. The coffin was surmounted by a canopy of cloth of gold lined with ermine—even though it was empty.[26]

Ceremony and the order of precedence were essential considerations in the placement of figures within a painted composition. So also was the identification of the protagonists' clothes an active feature of narrative. The recognition of subtle differences between the different shades of garments and manner of wearing them is, for the most part, completely lost on us today. The contemporary ability to discern status through men's official clothing is comparable with our judgement of men's suits today. Pin-stripes, and brown, linen or denim suits are traditionally associated with different occupations and life-styles. Of paramount importance to the most discerning eye is the cut and the quality of cloth. So it was with Roman togas—and so it was also with men's costume in the Renaissance.

Masaccio's frescoes in the Brancacci Chapel at Florence draw a parallel between the religious story of Saint Peter, officially the founder of the Papacy, and contemporary political events. Felice Brancacci, by whom the frescoes were commissioned, was a member of the newly-formed Board of Maritime Consuls. Following the capture of the port of Pisa by Florence, he had been sent in 1422 to Cairo to meet the Sultan and secure Florentine trade with Egypt. In all probability, Brancacci wished Masaccio to illustrate that the wealth of the Florentine state was to be found in the ocean. One wonders whether Brancacci liked what he saw. Instead of promoting this theme, in the Tribùte Money Masaccio relegated to the background the only miraculous incident in the whole story—the finding of the money in a fish's belly. A tax collector demands payment and Christ instructs Saint Peter to hand over the money. The totally unemotional interpretation of the religious content makes for an objective study of contemporary secular activities within the Florentine republic. The incident is related to proposals of 1425 to introduce a new tax, the *castasto*. Figures are draped classically in high grade woollen cloth in the colours that everyday official gowns would have been made up in. In strong contrast to the protagonists of the religious story, two young men, painted by Masolino, walk by in the Resurrection of Tabitha scene, apparently ignorant of the collection of taxes and other incidents. The men are dressed in the height of fashion, the one on the left wearing a gown of voided velvet (*raso vellutato*) with sleeves *a gozzo*, and the other a cloth gown.

The shape of their gowns is no different from the shapes worn by men in official garb. Indeed, certain elements of clothing, when they are no longer fashionable, will linger on as features of

official or ceremonial dress. The sleeves *a gozzo* and the *cappuccio* are cases in point. Here one *cappuccio*, that on the left, is worn in turban fashion, with the hanging end wound round the crown; the other is a smaller, but slightly bulbous hood which demonstrates the transition between the long *cappuccio* of the Trecento and the *berretta* of the Quattrocento. When worn in an academic or official capacity, the old *cappuccio* is draped over one or both shoulders, and is left to hang down over the back of the gown.

Both men's and women's dress follow similar proportions despite differences in class or the functional value of garments. For example, while the fashionable young ladies of the earlier part of the century go about in *ghirlande* and *balzi*, the non-fashionable women (the elderly and lower-class) often have their heads covered with some form of veil.

The binding of the hair and winding of the plait round the crown of the head is to the headwear as the *gamurra* is to the *cioppa*. Ilaria del Carretto dealt with her hair in exactly the same way as did the three poor girls in the story of St Nicholas of Bari, or the Madonna in an Adoration of the Kings. By nature, fashionable dress is often impractical in its restrictions imposed either by excess volume, or by very tight clothing; nevertheless, the basic sense of proportion remains constant and by winding the plait round the head, the faces are framed similarly in every case.

Sometimes, garments are cut with continuous pieces forming sleeve and body. In other cases, sleeves are squarely set in at the shoulder. The illustration of a game of *civettino* (the aim of which was to knock off the opponent's hat) indicates the clean cut of the young men's doublets, and the various pieces from which they have been constructed. On the other hand, the doublet worn by the executor of Saint Peter (plate 18) was probably made not with separate sleeves set into the shoulders, but with sleeve and body cut in one. New ways of cutting garments were to develop during the Quattrocento; the differing shapes of garments earlier in the century reflect the general lack of sophistication of tailoring at that time but emphasize the quality and cost of the cloth.

Compared with the value of textiles and jewels, the amounts paid to tailors were minute. A statute issued in Florence in 1415 fixed the maximum charges allowable for the making-up of garments by tailors.[27] For women's dresses, not more than four or five *lire* should be paid. And tailors were allowed only one florin for each item made from a very precious textile, whilst the price fixed for the tailoring of masculine dress was even less. The tailors did not have their own guild, but were associated with people of other professions. Not all tailors were men, as a late fourteenth-century document suggests. For the most part in Florence, tailors were linked to the *rigattieri* (second-hand clothes dealers) and with the *lanaioli* in the woollen cloth trade.

A list compiled in 1427 of the occupations of the citizens of Florence indicates the different ways in which individuals were

30. Two fashionable young men in The Resurrection of Tabitha by Masolino, *c.* 1425–8. The left-hand figure's tunic is made of a silk satin with the pattern picked out in velvet (*raso vellutato*). The two men wear alternative forms of fashionable headdress, each being a version of the scaled-down hood (*cappuccio*) of the fourteenth century.

61

31. (above) A *desco da parto*, illustrated with
boys playing a game of *civettino*, Tuscan School,
c. 1430. The young men strip down to their shirts,
doublets and hose for ease of movement.

32. (opposite) A market-place selling second-
hand and ready-made clothes; from the statues of
the Society of Drapers in Bologna, 1411.

involved in the clothing and textile industries.[28] There were 101 tailors (*sarti*) compared with 52 *farsettai* and 153 men who fell into the category of *rigattiere*, *linaiuolo* and *cenciaolo* (second-hand clothes dealers, merchants of cloth and rag-pickers). The market for second-hand clothes was very large. Either they would be worn as purchased, or they might be recut and remade. The clothes displayed in the market-place depicted in the statutes of the Society of Drapers of Bologna may include some ready-made garments, but probably most are second-hand goods.

The quality of textiles was so good that clothes tended to last for a very long time. In many cases, garments were passed down from mother to daughter, or from one woman to another. This must have been practised on such a vast scale that at one stage in Siena, each transaction was subject to a tax.[29]

There must therefore have been an extremely slow rate of change in fashionable shapes. Besides, if the tailors generally earned such low wages and were not highly regarded, they must have had little incentive to develop new ideas in the form of garments, and in some cases had been positively restricted. A statute issued in Florence in 1388 had specified that tailors and seamstresses were forbidden to make new, recut existing clothes, or keep in stock any garments for women which were not of a style already established.[30] Alberti, in his book on the family, talks of the necessity for only three sets of clothing. In Gianozzo's words, Alberti offers a reply to the question regarding the most suitable way to dress:

33. Clothing the Poor, by a follower of Ghirlandaio.

. . . good clothing for civic life must be clean, appropriate and well made. Cheerful colours are right to wear, in whichever shades suit the wearer best; and they must be made from good cloth [*buoni panni*]. These fringes [*frastagli*] and embroideries [*ricami*] that some people wear have never seemed attractive to me, except if they are worn by buffoons and trumpeters. On public holidays, dress in the newest suit of clothes [*vesta nuova*] and on other days, an outfit that has been worn; but very old clothing should be reserved only for wearing inside the house. Well Lionardo, your dress gives you respect, is it not true? Therefore you should have some regard for your clothes. . . . Maybe to men who spend liberally this next remark may not be a matter of concern; however, it must be said that belting your gown [*vesta*] is harmful on two counts. Firstly, it makes your dress seem less full and rather undignified; and secondly, the belt [*cinto*] makes the cloth shiny, and very soon you will have rubbed the nap of it away, so that your gown will look completely new, except for where the belt has been tied round. Beautiful clothes should not be belted. . . .[31]

Such sound advice and logical thought was hardly likely to be followed by the fashion-conscious. After all, a good quality cloth can be given a new lease of life when spruced up with new trimmings; ornamentation in the form of linings and facings, dags and fringes, gold and silver chains and other jewellery, was essential in adding striking interest to a garment. It would seem that many ideas about dress came from the wearers themselves. Tailors had their craft, but little influence. Even they were subject to penalties, should they comply with their clients' wishes and make a garment shorter, tighter or more voluminous than was morally permissible in the eyes of the local government.

3 Cloth of Gold

'Now we have invested in our silk industry a capital of ten million ducats and we make two millions annually in export trade; sixteen thousand weavers live in our city.'[1]

Muttering from his deathbed in 1423, the 80-year-old doge Tommaso Mocenico recalled some of Venice's achievements during his term of office. By the fourteenth and until the early seventeenth century, Italy was the most outstanding producer of silk fabrics in Europe. Her textile industries manufactured some resplendent cloths of wool, and silk, and cloth of gold, the production of which contributed considerably to the successful phases of the Italian economy. The markets of Bruges and Geneva, and later Lyons and Basle, were teeming with traders from all over Europe. At the fairs, the Italian merchants would distribute cloth for bills of exchange and foreign goods, including furs from the north, fustians and linens. Although both silk and wool products remained important, the fifteenth century witnessed a tendency towards the production of more luxury goods for a rich and exclusive market.

34. (right and opposite) Florentine merchants barter textile goods, a) wool for silk and cloth, and b) grain (dye) for woollen cloth.

The highest grade of woollen cloth was produced in Florence, the prime centre for the cloth trade in Italy. Made from English wool, some cloth was woven up in Flanders, and then sent to Florence to be dyed and finished. In other cases, the entire process of manufacture—spinning, weaving and finishing—took place in the city. The import of English wool to Tuscany was dealt with principally by those Tuscan firms who had offices in London. They would send their buyers on horseback round the English countryside to collect wool from individual farmers and monasteries, or to buy it from local woolmen. The papers of Francesco di Marco Datini, the merchant of Prato, record that the wool he was ordering between 1382 and 1410 came mainly from the Cotswolds (written as 'Chondisgualdo')—especially from Northleach and Burford, and also from the land around Cirencester and Winchester.[2]

The woollen industry was quite widespread thoughout northern Italy but each centre tended to specialize in particular types or qualities of cloth. Genoa had its own industry, engaged in the weaving of some cheap low-grade wool from north Africa. The area around Milan was occupied with the production of some quite fine cloths, whilst Venice developed a highly lucrative trade in inexpensive rather coarse woollen cloth made principally for its home market.

To speak of 'industry' in the modern sense is somewhat misleading, for there were no factories as such, but a series of small workshops (*botteghe*) and a considerable amount of home-based manufacture—a situation that was to remain in Europe until the late eighteenth century.

In fifteenth-century Florence, two of the largest and most powerful guilds, the *Calimala* and the *Lana*, indicated the division of labour and organization within the woollen cloth industry.

The former was involved with the processes of cloth finishing, whilst the members of the *Lana* were the weavers. Only a few processes were performed in the *bottega* itself, usually the beating, carding, and combing of the wool. All other operations—spinning, weaving, dyeing and finishing—took place elsewhere. Presumably, the *botteghe* were attached to warehouses, which controlled the traffic of both raw materials and the finished products.

A contemporary description of Florence in the later years of the Quattrocento indicates the number of workshops in the city.[3] By far the largest proportion was devoted to the working of wool; that is 270, compared with 83 for silk, or 74 goldsmiths' shops. However, by that date the silk industry was offering much greater financial rewards, and Italy merely sought to protect its cloth industry by introducing import tariffs and concentrating on its home market. The supremacy of the Florentine workers in the cloth trade was also, ironically, a contributing factor to the decline of her industry in the fifteenth century. Their technical skills were gradually transferred to and developed by their Flemish counterparts, for not infrequently Florentine artisans were invited to work in other cloth centres of Europe and boost their industry.

35. Spinning, winding the warp, and weaving in a workshop of the Umiliate, a religious group who specialized in clothmaking; a miniature by Fra Giovanni da Brera.

Despite the occasional uprising involving textile operatives, the fate of the textile industry lay almost entirely in the hands of newly rich merchants and bankers, many of whom had an invested interest in other enterprises as well, and at some stage in their careers would have held some official position in the government of the state. The same men were also influential in the organization of the major guilds, amongst which in Florence was the *Arte della Seta*, that of the silk weavers. It was based in the area by the Ponte Vecchio, around the Church of Por Santa Maria.

A greater demand for Italian silks was the consequence of several changes in society and commerce. An accumulation of wealth amongst the noble and professional classes, and the assertion of individual status, both encouraged the effective use of dress and textiles. The manufacture of cloth in the north of Europe had greatly developed, where consequently competition from the Italian wool trade was discouraged. Supplies of fur from the East were strictly limited, once the Turks had control over the Black Sea after the fall of Constantinople in 1453: some fur trimmings therefore, were replaced by the use of figurative silks. And besides, the skills of the Italian silk weavers were directed towards the development of new techniques, creating sumptuous fabrics which any lover of dress could not resist.

Had the efforts of foreigners to entice Genoese weavers away from Italy been successful the story of silk production would have been very different. King Louis XI invited weavers of silk to help set up a French industry in Lyons in 1466, and in Tours from 1470. Louis, and later Charles VII, gave great privileges to Genoese weavers who settled in France, but French silks did not begin to compete seriously with Italian ones until the seventeenth century.

By the late tenth century, silk weaving had been established in Sicily. The occupation of the island by Byzantines and then Arabs contributed to the cosmopolitan Near Eastern style of the textile motifs, inherited by the Normans and later dynasties, making the particular origins of the silks of that early period almost indistinguishable to the eye. But by the fourteenth century, a silk industry on the Italian mainland, based principally in Lucca and Venice, had developed from the early style some distinctive characteristics.

The production of silk in Lucca was under way in the twelfth and thirteenth centuries. Records of commercial agreements indicate the routes that grey silk took to reach Lucca: treaties of 1153 and 1156 with Genoa concern goods transported by sea, and in 1182 with Modena refer to overland trade routes. Later, in 1314, in the confusion of Guelf and Ghibelline warfare, the tyrant Uguccione della Fagginola proclaimed himself master of the republic; terrified, a good 300 families, mainly artisans and including weavers, fled from the city. Nevertheless, the silk industry, its production and commerce, remained the basis of the

Lucchese economy throughout the Trecento. However, according to the chronicle of Sercambi[4] the situation in Lucca had become precarious in 1419, and from then on the silk industry steadily diminished, despite subsequent attempts to revitalize it.

In Venice, decrees proclaimed in the thirteenth century make specific references to weavers and dyers, and the influx of Lucchese weavers after 1314 encouraged a steady growth in the production of silk textiles. A Vatican inventory of 1295 listed a fabric as '*venetico sive lucano*'[5] and it is presumed, therefore, that a close stylistic correspondence had already grown between the two centres.

Other Lucchese weavers settled in Florence, where they boosted the silk weaving in the Trecento. Then in the mid-fifteenth century, Filippo Maria Visconti, anxious to develop such an asset to the Milanese economy, invited a Florentine master, Piero di Bartolo, and a Genoese, Giovanni Borlasca, to set up an industry there. First assisted by weavers from Florence and Genoa, and managed by three men from Perugia, the project thrived under Francesco Sforza and his descendants. Further immigrant weavers from Cremona, Bergamo and Venice, received special privileges in 1459; but during the following year, the Duke forbade more to enter. In 1467 a protest to the Duchess Bianca Maria was signed by 300 or more weavers; but when the production of silk velvets and brocades was at its height in Milan in 1474, entries in the city's records indicate that there were 15,000 people involved in the silk industry, out of a population of less than 100,000. At that stage production was limited only to Milan itself, but plans were under way to extend it to Pavia.

The statute of 1432 relating to the silk guild of Genoa attests to the advanced state of the industry there. Second only to the construction of ships, silk weaving constituted one of the most commercial activities. The mid-fifteenth century witnessed a considerable expansion in the industry, and the increasing importance of the *Arte della Seta* in the economics and politics of Genoa. The aggrandizement of the guild coincided with the involvement of some of the great noble Genoese families—the Spinola, Doria, Grimaldi, Di Negro, and Fieschi—traditionally in banking and shipbuilding, but now also in silk. One aspect of the Genoese silk industry, much feared by the guild, was the emigration of weavers from the city, beginning in the later fifteenth century and continuing with increased momentum in the sixteenth, due to the economic, political and social climate. Genoese weavers instigated and monopolized the silk industry both abroad and in several towns elsewhere in Italy; for example in Tours (1470), and Lyons (1466 and 1536), Milan (1442), Mantua (1501) and Ferrara (1462), and later in the 1520s in Piedmont and Reggio Emilia.

Despite opposition from the principal centres of silk weaving (Florence, Genoa, Milan and Venice), smaller towns began to

36. (above) An early fifteenth-century Lucchese silk. Floral forms begin to dominate the paired animals.

37. (opposite) An Allegory of the Month of March; The Triumph of Minerva, detail, by Francesco del Cossa, *c.* 1470. Fashionable young women like this might pass their time embroidering; but weaving and other processes involved in clothmaking were usually carried out on a professional basis.

develop their own silk industries in the fifteenth century. Siena and Ferrara encouraged the settlement of weavers from Genoa and under the protection of Borso d'Este and Ercole Gonzaga they assumed a certain importance, but perhaps more in the manufacture of plain satins and velvets than in figured textiles. In 1462, led by a certain Urbano Trincherio, four Genoese master-weavers approached Borso d'Este (Duke of Ferrara, 1451–71).[6] They offered to produce silk textiles of all kinds and various colours, and emphasized the need not only to set up their own looms, but to establish a dyehouse for such textiles. Their suggestion to introduce their art of weaving in Ferrara was accompanied by the demand for certain concessions to be made, and guaranteed for a decade. It listed provision for all four men, a place to practise their art, accommodation for their families, and the exemption of excise duties on the necessary silk, silver and gold materials imported to their workshops from outside the city. They also wished to be excused the payment of personal taxes, and called for the prohibition in the city of non-Ferrarese produced textiles of a type similar to their own. This clause should be made effective for as long as their silk-weaving business managed to supply sufficient quantities for the consumption of the city itself and the surrounding areas under Ferrara's control. The Genoese masters proposed to work 20 looms, with which they would give four months' supply of materials to the 50 people who were to help them set up the project. Therefore they demanded from Duke Borso an advance loan of 300 gold florins, to buy and to transport to Ferrara tools and other necessary items. The Duke did grant their wishes, but recommended that the privileges be allowed only for five years, during which period Trincherio's monopoly of the silk industry was protected, for attempts by other weavers to start workshops were halted by the commune's refusal to grant planning permission.

Similarly, Modena and Piedmont expanded their silk industries in the Quattrocento, and flourished in smaller scale enterprizes. Beginning in 1445, Alfonso of Aragon decreed a series of privileges to weavers and dyers in Catanzaro, Calabria. Further concessions were later granted to men working in the silk industry by Alfonso's son and successor, Ferrante. In Naples, from 1450, the silk industry got off to a flying start under the direction of a Venetian, Marino Cataponte, called to the city by King Ferrante. Weaving was carried out by already skilled Genoese, Venetians and Florentines who had settled there.[7]

Concurrent with the development of its production into textiles, silk was being cultivated in Italy. The silkworm feeds on mulberry trees, and hillslopes all over Italy bear witness to the intensity of sericulture in the fifteenth century. The well-established medieval silk industry of Lucca had, by 1400, covered its surrounding countryside with numerous mulberry trees. Elsewhere, special measures were beginning to be taken to ensure the consistent rearing of silkworms: a legislation drawn up under the rule of Galeazzo Maria Sforza, and issued in 1470, demanded that every 15 acres of suitable land in the undulating region to the south of Milan should be planted with at least five trees. The country around Mantua, the plains of Crema, Brescia and Bergamo, and much of the Tuscan landscape beyond Lucca was also characterized by similar vegetation.

Though the climate of the Italian peninsula permitted sericulture, the scale of the silk weaving industry was such that the supply of raw material had to be supplemented by imported fibre. The geography of Italy was additionally fortunate in being extremely well placed for the reception of silk cultivated in Sicily, Spain, the Levant and the Far East. Following the advancement of the Turks around the Black Sea, towards the end of the century, Italian merchants purchased large quantities of silk from the markets at Bursa in Turkey, and Aleppo and Damascus in Syria, whence it was shipped from Mediterranean ports such as Beirut.

In the fifteenth century, the range of textile techniques broadened immensely. The earlier silk fabrics of Lucca and Venice generally fell into the category of diaspers (*diaspri*), a form of lampas.[8] The dullness of the ground of the fabric, usually a tabby or twill weave, contrasted with extra light-reflecting brocaded wefts in the pattern. However, the interplay of texture and the absorption and reflection of light was never so dramatic as in the Quattrocento, when damasks, shot silks and brocaded velvets took on new dimensions.

A true damask (*damaschino*) is a monochrome figured textile with a ground of warp-faced satin, and a pattern in weft-faced satin (sateen). The origins of the technique are unknown, but it is tempting to suppose that such textiles were first imported from Damascus. Viewed from a distance, and in certain lights, single-colour damask displays subtle differences in tone between the figurative design and the background. However, such appearances are deceptive, for the warps and wefts are of exactly the same colour. There were also damasks with strongly contrasted colours in warp and weft, a deep red and rich yellow being one of the most common combinations. In such cases, the use of chequered fills-in and other small details of draughtsmanship create a much bolder effect than is to be found in the more discreetly patterned single-colour damasks.

Another intriguing fabric which appears in the fifteenth century, though it was known before, is shot silk. Again, like damask, its effect is the result of changing lights reflected from warp and weft: but, unlike damask, the pattern is neither figured nor dependent on a special woven structure. A shot silk is a taffeta with the warp of one colour, and the weft of another, favoured combinations being red and green, and red and yellow. The paler or clearer colour usually predominates under

38. The Coronation of the Virgin; School of
Gentile da Fabriano, c. 1425. The velvet textile
worn by the Virgin illustrates bold lobal forms
which gradually develop into the more complex
'pomegranate' motifs of the latter half of the
century. This textile is an early example of a
foliated stem meandering about a vertical axis.

light, while the darker one is evident in shadow. The behaviour of this kind of textile is brilliantly depicted in the dresses of the Madonna and Saint Mary Magdalen in an altarpiece by Mantegna in the National Gallery, London. The contemporary term for such silks, 'changing' is fully justifiable.

Certainly the most dramatic of all textile effects to appear in the fifteenth century was created through the production of richly figured polychrome and brocaded velvets. We know that plain coloured velvets had been woven in Italy for some time, but the exact origins of velvet weaving have never been determined. In Venice, the first guild of velvet weavers was founded in 1247. The wardrobe accounts of Edward III of England (1312–77) record purchases of velvets. Archives of Florence indicate that there were large warehouses and a considerable number of workshops being erected in the Via dei Velluti. Nevertheless, such facts still leave entirely open the question of the technical origin.

In order to weave the complicated velvet structures of the Quattrocento, weavers must already have been highly skilled in both the art of controlling the regularity of an intricate pattern repeat by some mechanical means and have mastered also fine warp-pile fabric. The textiles of the thirteenth and fourteenth centuries, especially those diaspers of Lucca and Venice already mentioned, are amazingly fine and require numerous and complex sequences of sheds to form pattern. Today, such designs would have to be woven with the aid of a jacquard mechanism (first used early in the nineteenth century) or, thanks to the microchip, by computerized methods.

Prior to Joseph Marie Jacquard's invention, figured textiles were woven on drawlooms. In the gradual development of the drawloom there must concurrently have existed several variations on the basic technical theme. The essential feature of such looms is the harness system which, by means of leashes, allows the warp threads to be raised and lowered independently of the shafts. The drawloom harness controls the pattern whilst the shafts regulate the ground or binding structure. The task of drawing the correct combination of threads for each shed of the pattern repeat was given to one or more 'drawboys'. Before the mechanization of the drawloom, those drawboys would sit up at the top of the loom and pull up the leashes one by one, according to the weaver's instructions. It remains a common belief among many that the drawloom originated in China. However, Agnes Geijer implies that the technically superb production of silks excavated at Antinoë in Egypt are the earliest extant examples of textiles patterned on a drawloom.[9] Probably they were manufactured in the area now called Iran, under the Sassanian dynasty (224–651).

Changes in the structures of silk textiles are probably indicative of the development of looms. Italian silks of the fourteenth and first half of the fifteenth centuries measured

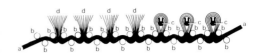

115–20 centimetres across from selvedge to selvedge. Around 1450, however, the selvedges abandoned their thick cords in favour of plain weave edges, often striped in different colours. At the same time, the width of the cloth was reduced to 60–70 centimetres and no doubt the reduction in width allowed for much greater control of the tension in increasingly more complex designs of velvet and brocade. But also, the type of loom was probably altering. An Italian from Calabria, recorded as a certain Jean le Calabrais, is accredited with the introduction of a new type of loom, a 'button drawloom', installed in Tours in 1470, under the orders of the French king.[10] Though attention is drawn to this incident, there must have been a thousand ways in which the Italian weavers devised new techniques and effects, as a general feature of their working process.

The architectonic quality of the velvets is achieved through various permutations of different pile weaves. A velvet depends on the use of two warps; one is structural, and lies on the ground of the fabric, the other forms the pile of the textile. Following every two, three or four rows of weft, depending on the density of the weave, a velvet wire (*ferro da velluto*) is inserted, over which the warp pile passes. The type and gauge of the wire determines the nature of the pile. For uncut loops, a round or rectangular wire is used, and is drawn out of the textile structure as soon as the loops have been secured by a further two, three or four rows of weft. Cut velvet pile is formed by the use of an oval or oblong shaped wire, which has running along the entire length of its upper edge a groove. The wire is placed between the ground and pile warps and secured in the same way as the wires for uncut velvet. Before the wire is removed, a sword is passed along the groove, thus slicing its way through the pile and freeing itself.

The figured velvets (*velluti operati*) are created by the combinations either of cut and uncut velvet, or of velvet with satin or brocade. Voided velvets (*velluti rasi* and *velluti inferriati* or *a inferriata*) consist of a single-height cut pile which contrasts with the 'voided' pattern, that is the area where the ground structure (invariably a satin) shows through. Two-pile velvet (*velluto alto-basso*, *rilevato*, or *controtagliato*) is that which has two heights of cut pile; the higher of the two absorbs more light and appears the darker shade. Ciselé velvet (*velluto cesellato*) is a textile incorporating cut (*tagliato*) and uncut (*riccio*) piles, the cut being higher than the uncut. Analogous to the ciselé velvet, is *velluto ricamo*, in which the uncut pile is deeper than the cut.[11] The associations formed between masters of weaving who specialized in different areas of silk production must have aided the development of such compound weaves. Two such partnerships set up in Milan demonstrate the interest taken in drawing together technical skills under one roof. In 1457 Marco Rota of Bergamo, master of cloth of gold and cloth of silver, and Mentino Prata, master of velvets, joined in partnership. And a certain Matteo Rancati and

39. (opposite) A brocaded damask, possibly Florentine, of the mid-fifteenth century.

40. (top) Diagram to show the cutting of velvet pile:
a = velvet pile warp
b = weft
c = velvet wire with groove along upper edge
d = cut velvet pile

41. (above) A voided velvet (*velluto raso* or *velluto a inferriata*) of the mid-fifteenth century.

Antonio da Caslino, velvet masters, joined Bernardino Ghili and the Capelli brothers, producers of satins (*zetanini* and *rasi*) in 1480.[12] Such arrangements must have held financial and legal advantages too.

In addition to these combinations of velvet weaves, many fifteenth-century textiles which remain evident today are highlighted by gold, silver or silver-gilt threads. The weavers did not use pure gold or silver membrane but a thread composed of a core, sometimes of linen but more often silk, around which is spirally wrapped the fine metal wire. So constructed, the thread is much more flexible for the weaver to use than would be a plain strip of metal. Always fed across the fabric, as a supplementary weft, the metal threads sometimes give a silver or gold sheen to

42. A velvet of the latter half of the century, which might have been described as *panno d'oro vellutato e allucciolato*. The gold threads illuminating the plain weave ground of the textile have mostly disappeared. The pattern is defined by a single height cut velvet pile which, like some of the smaller pomegranate motifs, is highlighted by raised loops of gold.

the flat ground of the fabric, in which case the velvet pile stands out in relief between the metallic areas. In other velvets, the metal weft is raised higher than the silk pile to form little loops which catch the light and their sparkling effect accounts for the name given to such fabrics which incorporate this technique, *velluti allucciolati*. Here and there, are found the same metal loops grouped together, to form a heavy-looking patch of gold or silver, rising above the height of the velvet (*velluto riccio sopra riccio*). Unfortunately, today much of the silver and gold used in textiles has either tarnished, or been worn down to the yellow silk core. Rarely does one catch a glimpse of what such velvets must have looked like when brand new and of the latest design.

An amusing tale recorded by Vespasiano da Bisticci in his life of Alfonso of Aragon, King of Naples,[13] demonstrates the vulnerability of such textiles:

From time to time His Majesty the King delighted in some harmless pleasure or pastime. There was in Naples a Sienese ambassador, extremely haughty in the way that Sienese can be. His Majesty the King usually dressed in black, with the occasional hat-brooch or with a gold chain around his neck: he was rarely to be seen going about in brocades and silks. This ambassador, however, would dress himself in really rich gold brocade, and always when he visited the king he wore this cloth of brocade. On many an occasion the king and his courtiers had a good laugh amongst themselves about this manner of wearing brocade. One day, the king turned to one of his men, smiled and said 'I think we should have a go at making that brocade change colour!' So he arranged that one morning he should give audience to the ambassador, in a mean little place; and he asked for all the ambassadors to be summoned. He also gave instructions to some of his courtiers that in the throng they should each jostle up against the Sienese ambassador, and rub his brocade. And that morning, the brocade was so rubbed and jostled not just by the other ambassadors but also by the king himself, that when the Sienese took his leave from the court, there was not one man who could refrain from laughing, on seeing that brocade. For it was crimson velvet sparkled with gold [*chermisi, col pelo allucignolato*] and all the gold had fallen from it, leaving nothing but the yellow silk, which appeared the most ugly sight in all the world. His Majesty went out of the little audience chamber, and he could not stop laughing either, to see this brocade

43. (next page) The Madonna and Child, and Saint Augustine; two panels of a triptych by Leonardo Boldini, illustrating different forms of pattern into which the so-called 'pomegranate' motif was integrated.

Colour plate 5 (overleaf, right) An altarpiece of the Virgin and Child with the Magdalen and Saint John the Baptist, by Andrea Mantegna. The clothes worn by the Virgin and the Magdalen on the right show that shot silk was available in the fifteenth century (see page 75).

tangled up and completely ruined. And for several days afterwards, they continued to have a good old laugh over this story of the Sienese ambassador; whilst he never realized the trick that had been played at his own expense.

The majority of Italian textiles of the Quattrocento fall into the category of 'pomegranate' patterns—a collective term first applied in the nineteenth century. Such designs occur most frequently in the period *c.* 1420–1550. They appear to dominate the textile production to such a degree that any other designs which may have been produced tend to be considered of secondary importance. There are many variants on the theme of the pomegranate, both in terms of the kind of pattern repeat, and in the manner of drawing the pomegranate itself. In fact, in many cases the so-called pomegranate resembles more closely a pinecone, a thistle, a lotus flower or a pineapple.

The most expensive fabrics of the century, those with intricate pile weaves and a lavish gold or silver content, invariably featured the pomegranate. They were used principally for important occasions, in church or at court. The ceremonial nature of such pomegranate textiles probably accounts for its persistence as the principal textile motif. It is comparable with the lotus flower in China, or the Indian *buta* (translated into later Western decorative art as the 'paisley'). The pomegranate itself was considered a symbol of immortality and fertility in Eastern religions. Historians often stress the significance of this fruit, and the possibility that it was incorporated into Christian iconography with a similar meaning. It is far more likely, however, that the decorative qualities in the outline shape and organic details of the pomegranate were recognized primarily as a wonderful pattern source.

The influence from the East, especially China, came over very strongly in the fourteenth century. Particularly noticeable was the asymmetrical arrangement found in Venetian fabrics with their diagonal emphasis in the repeat. Monstrous dragon-like creatures and the Chinese 'tschi' symbol of a cloud formation with sun-rays mingled with the griffins, eagles and stags of gothic Europe. The Vatican inventory of 1295 includes an entry for '*pannus tartaricus arcium ad aurum*', which Otto von Falke interprets as the sun's rays motif, woven into the stuff in gold.[14] Venice for some time had been the most important centre in Europe for trading in Near and Far Eastern textiles, which found their way into paintings; for example, the altarpiece of Saint Alexander at Brescia, attributed to Jacopo Bellini, depicts fine Chinese textiles.

The correspondence between the fine and decorative arts was very strong. Several fifteenth-century painters (some of them apprenticed in goldsmiths' shops) are believed to have designed textiles of one form or another. Botticelli and Pollaiuolo both

Colour plate 6 (opposite) Portrait of a Lady in Red, Florentine School. The bodice of her dress is made of voided velvet (*velluto raso*) while the detachable sleeves are made from more lavish brocaded velvet with *allucciolati*, little gold loops. Her coif (*cuffia*) is generously embroidered with pearls and gold thread, and hides the hair growing from an artificially high forehead, achieved by the plucking back of the natural hairline.

44. A late fourteenth- or early fifteenth-century Venetian diasper. The asymmetrical emphasis and the 'tschi' motif betray a Chinese influence; so too does the flowering lotus – often confused with the palmette. The simple pomegranates, on the other hand, play a minor role here.

45. The Annunciation, attributed to Jacopo
Bellini. Both the archangel's and the Virgin's
vestments are made of Chinese textiles.

designed panels of embroidery, whilst the Louvre sketchbook
attributed to Jacopo Bellini, and a folio of drawings attributed to
Pisanello (also in the Louvre) include drawings of woven textiles.
But are these working drawings showing designs devised by
artist-designers, or are they studies made out of curiosity and
perhaps for inclusion in a painting? Perhaps at this point it is best
not to attribute, but just to offer a date for each of the two sheets
of drawings. The textiles on the sheet from the Bellini sketchbook
all appear to be the type produced in Venice. The two on the left
of the sheet, in which the motifs are still somewhat limited by the

46. A page from the Bellini sketchbook in the
Louvre, illustrating three studies of textile designs.

47. Study of a textile, attributed to Pisanello.

roundel shape, must date to the very early years of the fifteenth century. The right-hand sketch, however, demonstrates how the roundels have broken out into a waving stem out of which sprout exotic leaves and lotus flowers or palmettes: the floral growth is beginning to take precedence over the birds and beasts, and therefore suggests a slightly later date. The drawing ascribed to Pisanello shows how the right-hand textile illustrated in the Bellini book had developed into the branching stem with flourishing pomegranates, a design of the mid-fifteenth century. The Bellini textiles would have been woven with one surface plain, similarly constructed to the diaspers of the Trecento. The Pisanello design, on the other hand, indicates areas of silk velvet pile and looped gold threads (*allucciolati*), features of the advanced technical skills of the later part of the century.

In 1421 in Venice, the guilds make a distinction between the weavers of *uniti* and *operati*; that is, between plain smooth cloths, like taffeta and damask, and those more complex patterned textiles which invariably depend on a combination of textures as well as colour and motif. The earlier part of the century witnessed experiments in the use of velvet weave. Initially, the type of detailed, almost narrative pattern of the Trecento is directly translated into velvet. But soon the weavers were to realize that to use the techniques of velvet and brocading most effectively, they really needed to introduce much bolder designs and treat them as low reliefs rather than illuminated manuscripts. Some tomb sculptures in Florence demonstrate the wonderful three-dimensional qualities of early figured velvets. The boldness of these Renaissance textiles develops at a pace comparable with the advances made in the rendering of light and perspective in painting and in sculpture.

In the course of the first two decades of the century animal motifs decline in importance, and flowers begin to monopolize the textile form and content. The repeats of the pomegranate designs fall into three principal categories. The diagonal emphasis found in the fourteenth-century Venetian textiles is retained in the earlier fifteenth-century velvets. After the middle of the century, however, the two other principal types of repeat are most evident: one is worked about a vertical axis, the other horizontal. In the first, the branching stem from which emerge pomegranates of increasing size may turn to right and to left, but the length of repeat (sometimes more than a metre) is greater than the width from selvedge to selvedge (approximately 60–70 centimetres). The pattern which emerges, despite its sporadic bursts into flower, is strictly controlled by the vertical emphasis; and by around 1500 the organic qualities of the pomegranates, palmettes and pine-cones are frozen into a much more cool, classical arrangement which continues with little inspired change until the mid-sixteenth century. The horizontally orientated repeat appears, from the outset, to be much more static. On the one hand, there are designs built up from a rhythmic sequence of ogees; on the other, there are those floral rosettes considered so typical of Florence.

Whatever the exact origins of the motifs may be, the Italians certainly built up a distinctive style of their own in the pomegranate velvets and gold brocades. One detail, the pomegranate split open and revealing its fertile seeds within, appears to be a particularly Italian feature.

The correspondence between Italy and the Orient was and remained very strong and it can be difficult, and often impossible, to distinguish between Turkish and Italian brocaded velvets during the century 1450–1550. This has led to much speculation about which country influenced the other, and how. The Italians appear to be the earlier masters of figured velvet weaving. Naturally, the Turks would prize such awesome feats in the production of pomegranate textiles. The Topkapi Sarayi Museum in Istanbul houses the Sultan's imperial wardrobe—consisting of nearly 2500 kaftans and shalvars, among which are robes made of or lined with Italian velvets brocaded with silver or gold.[15] Although most of them belong to the later sixteenth, seventeenth and eighteenth centuries, from which periods there exists a good deal of evidence of Turks buying velvets in Venice, no doubt such practice had gone on before.

Surviving Turkish velvets of the sixteenth century show that by then the Turks had mastered the skills of velvet weaving, and gradually added more and more of their own features—notably the tulip and the carnation—to the pomegranate patterns. The exchange of motifs is complex, for some of the Turkish features were influenced by Persian art, and in turn flowers such as the tulip and the carnation were incorporated into the gardens and decorative arts of western Europe. But how might one distinguish between one country's production and that of another during the transition period around 1500?

The results recorded by Nancy Edwards Reath following a detailed study of velvets in the Pennsylvania Museum reveal some interesting answers.[16] Her stylistic distinctions between Turkey and Italy can be disproved. However, a technical analysis of the velvets established two facts. Firstly, that the metal thread in Renaissance velvets known to be European is different from that found in Turkish textiles. Secondly, that in the Turkish velvets the metal thread is held in position by the foundation warp alone, and is never intersected by the pile warp. In Italy and elsewhere in western Europe the metal thread is bound by both ground and pile warps throughout the velvet and brocaded areas of the textile. The European metal consists of silver with a largely copper alloy: it is frequently gilded, but never pure gold. The Turkish metal is also silver, but the copper is barely traceable, and is therefore much softer than the European metal. As a result, when a Turkish velvet is worn, the soft metal is rubbed away,

48. A late fifteenth-century velvet, showing the strong vertical emphasis of the branching stem.

leaving behind nothing in place but the yellow silk core around which it had been wrapped. In the Italian brocaded textiles, on the other hand, the harder, more resistant alloyed metal causes the entire thread to break away from its warp binding. For this reason, the resplendent gown of the Sienese ambassador to the court of Naples (mentioned above) was reduced to a very sorry state, with threads hanging loose from it. It remains for further technical and chemical analysis to assist the development of this thesis.

Geographically, Venice's position commanded the strongest links between Italy and the Orient. The Near and Far Eastern decorative elements in fifteenth-century Italian silks are largely to be found in those textiles produced in Venice. As has been mentioned before, Venetian weavers must have been so well advanced by 1420 in their mastership of figured velvets that they demanded that specialist weavers be represented by different organizations. Other Italian silk weaving centres had their own special traits. Perugia was famous for its woven towels of linen, with figurative end borders. In Raccognini near Turin, a ribbon industry is recorded in 1460.[17] In Florence, a large number of textiles with figures such as those used for orphreys (decorative bands applied to ecclesiastical vestments), and some with heraldic significance were woven, in addition to the pomegranate type of design. Stylistically Florentine silks tended to include smaller scale stylized floral patterns, such as some of those featured in Benozzo Gozzoli's Journey of the Magi in the Medici Riccardi Palace.

Such differences did occur, but there are also many fabrics which cannot be attributed to any particular Italian town on stylistic grounds. The competitive spirit within the silk industry naturally instigated both innovations and imitations. The production of textiles was in reality the monopoly of merchants and financiers, who controlled the *maestri* (the masters, who worked in the *botteghe*) and the *cottimisti* (the domestically based workers). Designs for textiles were often assigned to the *disegnatores drapporum* or the *operarum*, invariably painters. There existed rigid protection clauses relating to these designs, for in the statutes of the silk guilds are listed very serious fines for whoever lifted a design out of the city walls and used it elsewhere. However, it made sense financially for one silk centre to produce stuffs in the style of another, if that was what fashion demanded. Concerned that Venice's exports to France should continue, Marino Cavalli, a Venetian ambassador, asked whether it would be possible in Venice, or in the Venetian provinces, to produce textiles like the Genoese and Tuscan ones. He asserted that their (the Genoese and Tuscan) work was just what the French required. That is, they were producing textiles which cost little, and which endured the minimal wear and tear, for the French would get bored if they had to clothe themselves with fabric for

49. A brocaded damask, demonstrating how the metal threads through wear and tear can become worn away from the ground structure, in some cases leaving only the yellow silk core. The pattern is arranged in a sequence of ogees (oval shapes with pointed ends).

too long.[18] In general, techniques too were closely guarded secrets; however, a slip of the tongue had its rewards. In 1476 the Florentine, Carlo Strozzi, awarded a prize to Giovan Petro di Padova for having introduced to Florence the Bolognese art of making silk veils.

There is no doubt that, whether adhered to or not, the legislations imposed on the conduct of silk manufacture and trade upheld the importance and success of this Italian industry. There was no totally Italian, national policy, but a number of statutes drawn up by individual towns and states, all of which had one common feature, the protection of the local industry. The following examples indicate a variety of ways in which this policy was implemented.

Some pressure was asserted on the weavers; for example, a decree of 11 July 1440 forbade the movement of looms or any weaving tools from Genoa. The clauses were detailed, and should have avoided any dodging of issues,[19] for they specifically stated that implements used by weavers should not be transported, sold or exchanged for other goods. However, later in the same decade, some of the Genoese weavers were found to have set themselves up in Milan, and later still others at Ferrara. Yet more Italian weavers made their way abroad, amongst them Venetians, and this happened despite the fact that in 1452 the Doge Pietro Campofregoso had prohibited the emigration of silk workers, declaring rebels those who disobeyed the order. However, the Signoria of Venice did permit weavers to move to Lucca or Florence, if they were out of work.

But Florentines too were anxious to protect as far as possible the skilled craftsmen among their own population. In 1463 a petition was drawn up and presented on 20 March to the Consiglio del Popolo:

> On behalf of the consuls of the *Arte di Porta
> S. Maria* of the city of Florence we hereby declare that
> in working unanimously in the interests of conser-
> vation and growth of the art of silk weaving, as is the
> duty of the consuls, they have known that for the
> past two years in the aforementioned *Arte* there has
> been a large stock of wires for the weaving of
> velvet—voided, two-pile and brocaded velvets—the
> majority being good quality ones. And two years
> ago there came to your city master Luigi Bianco,
> son of Jacopo, a Venetian citizen; and they are
> occupied in the making of the said wires. They
> have produced a vast quantity, and to such a
> standard that everyone who makes silk cloths
> knows that the wires made by master Luigi are of a
> better quality and more perfect than those of any
> other master living or dead.

50. Detail of a Perugian towel used as a table cloth in The Last Supper by Ghirlandaio, 1480.

And they asked for the guarantee of his safety for ten years, so that he might go about freely without being molested by his creditors to whom he owed several debts.[20]

In many instances the future of a local industry was dependent on the decisions of the government and of merchants and entrepreneurs. In Siena in 1438 a certain Nello di Francesco proposed to introduce the production of silk cloth and velvet weaving to Siena. With the aid of some acquaintances, he managed to build up sufficient capital to set up the whole business. The Commune was eager to bring work to the city and agreed to subsidize the industry by an annual grant of 100 gold florins for the following eight years. The financial assistance from public funds was given only on condition that they keep at least four looms in action, a number sufficient to produce the 30 pieces of stuff necessary to satisfy local consumption. Such a move would avoid the need to import textiles from outside Siena, but it did result in swift retaliatory action from Florence, whose weavers threatened to set fire to Sienese looms by night, or to steal their stocks of cloth. The Florentines then made a bid to buy up the entire Sienese silk business, but Siena declined the proposal. Finally, a group of Florentines managed to bribe the dyer of kermes reds and the principal dresser of cloths, who both suddenly fled from Siena, leaving the weavers in a terrible plight. The Commune immediately answered back by imposing tariffs on textiles imported into Siena at the rate of four *soldi* per *braccio*, for as long as there were at least 12 looms working in the town.[21]

Legislations were designed not just to protect the levels of employment in the silk industry, but also to control the quality of goods. The law that had been passed by the commune of Siena in 1438 to subsidize Nello's enterprize was repealed five years later; future financial aid was to be based on the quality of cloth. It ranged from four lire for each piece of 40 *braccia* for damasks, to 32 lire for pieces of cloth of gold.[22] This boosted Siena's interest in silk weaving tremendously.

Records in Venice clearly indicate how specific some legislations could be.[23] In July 1410 a decree forbade the adulteration of raw materials, and the introduction into Venice of silk stuffs which had not been made there. Five looms only were allowed for each weaver (15 January 1418), and the right to be engaged in the production of silk was to be carried out personally, not under contract (25 August 1422). Other specifications concerned the construction of textiles—for instance, the number of threads per inch—or the quality of dyes used. A later statute, issued in Milan in 1504, gives specifications of lengths and widths of damasks and brocades, and details of the prices to be paid to weavers for different types of stuff. It also mentions the quality of gold to be used, and the severe penalties, should some form of low grade or imitation silver or gold be employed.[24]

The contemporary eye was probably extremely discerning

about the quality of cloth—its finish, and the depth and tone of its colour. Today, the historian is faced with the near impossible task of matching the colours of cloths depicted in paintings with the names of colours listed in contemporary inventories, treatises, and other written documents. Certainly the artist, in building up his colour through the use of primers and subsequent layers of pigments, was extremely conscious of the nature of the textile he was trying to depict.[25] In fact, his role can be closely compared with that of the dyer. In the way that a painter prepares the ground of a panel or tints a sheet of paper, before commencing his composition, the dyer must carefully consider the colour or tone of the fibre before it is immersed in the dyebath. From the *vagello*, a dyevat containing a solution of reduction dyes (woad and indigo, both of which produce blue), a range of blues, violets and greens could be achieved, depending on the *impiumo* or *piede* (ground colour) used for the background colour.

A fifteenth-century treatise on the production of silk includes details about the choice of yarn for different structures of woven cloth.[26] Certain textiles need much whiter weft yarns than others

51. A late fifteenth-century velvet, red pile on a cream satin ground.

to ensure a much clearer tone of colour and greater translucence. The whitest silk should be used for taffetas, for it needs the sharpest of tones: second on the list comes damask, 'which had to be a little less clear [*netto*], and also rather more subtle in tone, for the damasks they make today are lighter than previous ones'. For velvets, the same yarn is used, but it does not need to be quite as clear as that used in damasks. The graded list continues with satins (*zetani rasi*), followed by voided velvets (*zetani vellutati*) and finally *baldacchini*.

The vital role of the dyers is apparent in any document of the period which relates to the making of textiles and the organization of the textile industry. By the fifteenth century most dyers throughout Italy belonged to their own guilds, except in Florence where they worked under the auspices of the major textile guilds. In this way, dyers were generally able to exert pressures on the weavers of cloth, the quality of which must be upheld if the dyers too were to maintain a good reputation for their work. The specialist nature of dyeing led to the formation of separate workshops, especially for indigo and kermes, and in some cases those men skilled in the art of using one dye created their own guild. In Genoa, for example, there was a special guild of indigo dyers.

The colour of a textile depends on the type and quality of dyes used, the mordants,[27] the level of concentration of the solution in the dyebath and the length of time the fibres are boiled or steeped there. Alum was one of the principal mordants, used in conjunction with kermes and madder dyes, both of which yield shades of red. Alum and tartar were normally combined when dyeing with brazilwood. As well as tartar there were other mordants and other agents, including gall-nut, and ashes of pinewood and lime. None, however, was as important as alum. In the first half of the Quattrocento, Fokia in Turkey was the principal source of alum, the trading of which was controlled by Genoa. But the fall of Constantinople in 1453 was followed, three years later, by the fall of Fokia. From her base in Chios, Genoa succeeded in sustaining some of her alum trade for a while, but she was being forced to draw from her reserve supplies, and between 1453 and 1458 alum prices rose by nearly 500 per cent. In the meantime Venice, who had always supplied her textile trade with alum independently of Genoa, was bargaining with the Sultan for rights of trade. And a Venetian, Bartolomeo Zorzi, did then take over the Turkish alum business for some years, until the outbreak of the war between Turkey and Venice (1463–79). The political threat had forced a reconsideration of the alum situation. The Genoese reopened old deposits of alum around Italy, but the greatest discovery in 1462 was that of a new source of high quality alum, at Tolfa in the Papal States.

From elsewhere in Europe and also from the East, dyestuffs came to Italy overland or in shiploads, together with wool, silk and spices. The many colours of red achieved on woollen cloth and on silk varied in price and in their tonal qualities. Red and blue—notably madder and kermes or cochineal on the one hand, and indigo and woad on the other—are fundamental textile dyes all the world over. The three principal dyestuffs used for red in the fifteenth-century Italian textile industry were kermes, madder and brazil-wood. Kermes (*chermisi*) was the best in quality and the most expensive. A brilliant red dye, it was obtained from the dried bodies of pregnant females of the kermes shield-louse, *Coccus illicis*. The source of this precious and sought-after insect was in the East, whence it was transported, usually via Constantinople. This shield-louse was also found around the Mediterranean, living on the leaves of an evergreen referred to as the kermes oak (*Quercus coccifera*). As the insects closely resembled scarlet berries on the green shrub, the kermes was thought of as an insect inside a berry, and was referred to in Europe as 'grain' (*grana*). Imported from places like Majorca, Provence and the Greek Islands, the *grana* was the less expensive dye to use and inferior in quality to the Eastern *chermisi*. Much prized, *chermisi* was decreed by Pope Paul II in 1464 to be the cardinals' purple (*purpura cardinalizia*), even though it was red (for there was a considerable decline in the use of purple murex, especially after the fall of Constantinople, the last bastion of medieval purple dyeing). However, following the discovery of the New World at the end of the century, cochineal—basically obtained from the same little red insect, but found in South America—took precedence over kermes.

Madder (sometimes called *garanza* in Italy), a dyestuff obtained from the roots of the madder plant, *Rubia tinctorum*, was cultivated for some time in Europe. Quite a large source was grown in Germany, and some in Lombardy, but the majority had to be imported from the Orient.

The third important source of red was brazil-wood (*verzino*) or redwood, obtained from trees of the *Caesalpinia* species. It was first introduced to the West by the Venetians through their trading with the East. Later, the country of Brazil was so named for the vast forests of this type of tree found there. As with other dyes, there must have existed many grades produced by the various *Caesalpinia* woods; however, dyers do not specify the different types. Lacquer (*lacca*), a resinous lymph born from the branches of some trees in the *Euphorbia* family through the activity of certain parasites, was imported from India and Indochina and was also used for dyeing red, but was considered rather precious and rarely utilized.

Most complex are the combinations of dyes and mordants. *Morello*, a mulberry-like colour, is equated in treatises on dyeing and on painting with *pavonazzo* (peacock-colour). The dyeing of this deep purplish colour could be done with kermes, grain, madder or brazilwood. In each case, the dyer would probably achieve a subtle difference of hue. *Alessandrino* was a vivid violet made from *oricello*, a form of lichen. Saffron was used for yellows, indigo and woad for blues, oak-galls for blacks. *Berettino* or *bigio* were shades of grey, whilst other colours and dyes are too numerous to list here.

Included in chapter 49 of the treatise published by Gargiolli[28] is a list of prices charged for dyeing cloth with various colours:

Herewith we record the prices of the dyeing of silk in all colours, which should be given to the dyer by the pound, otherwise they will not do the job:

For dyeing kermes twice (by the pound)	*soldi*	40
kermes once		20
in grain (*di grana*)		12
greenish brown (*verde bruno*)		40
alessandrino		40
kermes *pagonazzo*		35
grain *pagonazzo*		35
brazilwood *pagonazzo*		35
greens		20
vermilions (*vermigli*)		25
deep blues (*azzurri*)		24
greys		12
ochre (*tanè*)		12
sumac yellow (*giallo di scòtano*)		12
zaffiorato (somewhere between red and yellow)		25
inciannomati (light blue)		12
black		15
sbiaditi (pale colours)		12
saffron yellow (*giallo di zafferano*)		13
for using sulphur		1
for boiling		1

The cost of textiles was therefore partly dependent on the cost of materials used—dyes, fibres, and silver and gold threads. Prices also varied according to the intricacy of design and therefore the amount of work involved in threading up the loom and weaving the textile. Most expensive were the gold and silver brocaded velvets.

Whilst probably the best textiles were kept for the home market, Italian silks were much sought after elsewhere in Europe. North of the Alps, Bruges was the principal silk market. There, one member of staff in the Medici bank spoke fluent French and was responsible for the sale of Italian silks. It is likely that from Flanders the Italian silks found their way to Spain and so influenced Spanish textiles.

Lucchese merchants were also based in Bruges, and others in Paris. The accounts of the Dukes of Burgundy record a payment of 726 francs to Bethin Dathis and Bauduche Trent, merchants of Lucca established in Paris, and another entry of 820 francs 'for two and a half pieces of black velvet, figured with large leaf forms,

52. Piero de' Medici, by Mino da Fiesole, 1452–3, demonstrating the architectonic quality of rich silk velvet.

the said leaves being coloured in green and red velvet, and interspersed with little white florettes, brocaded with gold'.[29] Judging by the description, the design might well be Florentine. Genoa's silk textiles too were highly prized abroad, and England in particular was an interested customer. A statute issued in London in 1454 prohibited the import of all silk goods for the following five years, but it specifically excluded fabrics from Genoa because, the document claimed, the like could not be found elsewhere.[30]

Within Italy, whilst descriptions of urban scenes include details of shops displaying their wares, the richest Italians often demanded the services of an agent to search for textiles on their behalf. A certain Bartolommeo Seragli searched Rome for antique marble statues for a member of the Medici family, dealt in illuminated manuscripts, terracotta madonnas, chess sets and mirrors, as well as ordering cloths in Florence for Alfonso of Aragon.

The lengths of pieces varied, usually according to the type of textile. In 1489 Jacopo Trotti, who was employed to order brocades for the court of Ferrara, indicated in one of his letters that lengths of 40 *braccia* of one cloth could be found.[31] However, four years previously on 14 June 1485 Trotti had written to the Duke of Ferrara:

> Through a friend of mine, I have done a thorough search of all the shops and warehouses in Milan, where complete pieces of cloth of silk or gold measure no more than *14 braccia*; for whoever wants more must order it there. But I have found some good stuff which is still on the loom, and I hope that within eight days at the most Your Excellency will receive this beautiful cloth. If you had not been in such a hurry, I could have put in an order for cloth of silver and gold with your device, which would be finished in a month. As it is, I have placed the order with Messer Gotardo Panigarola who within the week shall be supplied with the length they are frantically weaving for you.[32]

Commission to the agent, and a payment of 25 ducats per *braccio* were to be made.

In 1492, Ludovico il Moro accompanied his sister-in-law Isabella d'Este to a merchant in Milan, from whom she was to choose a precious length of cloth. She decided on a *rizo soprarizo* of gold with some silver, figured with one of her devices, the two towers of the port of Genoa, with a motto which read: '*Tal trabajo m'es placer por tal thesauro no perder*'. (This cloth cost 40 ducats per *braccio*.)[33]

53. SS. Peter and Dorothy, by the Master of Saint Bartholomew, *c.* 1490. The painters of northern Europe effectively included Italian textiles for backdrops and clothing. Here, the brocaded velvet behind the saints resembles that used for altar frontals and princely canopies. However, despite the fineness of quality of the Flemish cloth from which Saint Dorothy's fashionable dress has been cut, it was a rare luxury to use Italian silk velvets for lining or underdresses.

Such lavish textiles ordered for the leading arbiters of fashion of the day were the exception to the rule. Even they would not have worn brocades woven with devices and containing a high gold and silver content every day. The best textiles played important roles on special occasions. A length of superb cloth, the *palio*, was often awarded as a prize for the winner of some jousting contest or race, and the importance and preciousness of gold brocades is proved by the gifts of pieces given to ambassadors to take back to their rulers. For instance, one piece of brocade worth 200 ducats was given to the ambassador of Caramania on his visit to Venice in 1463. And the following year, 20 *braccia* of very fine cloth of gold (*seta d'oro*) was given to the ambassador of Ussun Cassano to pass on as a gift to his master.[34]

Whilst the fine quality of silk was always recognized and appreciated, it would seem that the wearing of silk fabrics was more commonplace in Italy than elsewhere north of the Alps. This can be partly explained by the climatic differences, but the chief reason was that of economic policy. The Alps acted as a kind of defensive barrier lying between two areas of Europe, each of which wished, by means of tariffs and sometimes a complete prohibition of imported stuffs, to protect the home industry. In northern painting, examples of brocaded silks are certainly not often seen. Such luxury textiles as are depicted in works of art are worn by royalty, high-standing ecclesiastics, and by foreigners and saints. The 'orientals' and saints, sometimes wearing a textile woven with his or her particular symbol, feature as much more exotic characters. By contrast, in Italy the humble simplicity of saints in either poor or plain, classically draped timeless garments, are differentiated from the expensively dressed portraits.

The majority of surviving textiles has been preserved because they were used for ecclesiastical vestments or for church furnishings and their designs and woven structures correspond to the types worn in secular fashions of fifteenth-century Italy. Too strong a contrast between lay and clerical vestments should not be drawn here, for the volume of cloth and the restrictions imposed by the weight of metallic threads forced deliberated gestures and a ceremonial pace. Such textiles are therefore ingredients of a noble lifestyle amongst the rich.

Colour plate 7 (opposite) The Court of Autari and Teodolinda, by the Zavattari brothers, 1444. The *strascichi* of the ladies' dresses are so long that the young men cannot avoid treading on them. Standing behind, one lady's veil is suspended like wings by a fine structure; it is more northern than the rounded *balzo* which is typical of Italian fashion.

4 Dress as Narrative: 1430-1450

A transfer of power in the first half of the fifteenth century was accompanied by a shift in patronage. Guilds and confraternities no longer held their former strength, for their corporate decisions were, like those of the state, controlled by the activities of leading merchants and bankers. During the period 1430 to 1450 orders for paintings, monuments and buildings were placed more frequently and forcefully by the leading families in the republics, and by the growing cultural centres of princely courts.

The Medici were to prove generous and discerning patrons of art. So did Federigo da Montefeltro (1410–82), whose patronage as Duke brought the backwater of Urbino in the Marches to a brilliant level of scholarship and art. The encouragement of arts and learning was also to thrive under the Gonzaga, d'Este and Sforza families respectively at Mantua, Ferrara and Milan. For a while, Naples too was full of cultural activity, in spite of its unsettled condition due to bouts of civil war; there, Alfonso V of Aragon and Naples, known as the Magnanimous, brought together a succession of poets, painters and architects.

The interest in the classics and the hunt for long-lost texts was well under way. Italians voyaged to the East in search of them, while travellers from the Levant brought gifts of ancient texts on their visits. The visit of a convoy of 500 Greeks, including the Emperor of the East, John Paleologus, and Patriarch of Constantinople, to the Council of Ferrara in 1438 did little to improve the schism between the Pope and the Greeks, but contributed very positively to the advancement of humanist learning. The Emperor and his entourage must have offered a wonderful procession of Eastern costume, beards and head-dresses, which served as archetypal models of artists for quite some years afterwards.

The growing secularization of art at this point in the Quattrocento and the close correspondence between festive drama, prestigious processions and daily life affected the type of dress portrayed in paintings. In a conscious effort to recreate reality, artists usually chose to represent actual contemporary dress, whether it be extracted from everyday scenes in the home

Colour plate 8 (opposite) The middle magus in *The Journey of the Magi*, by Benozzo Gozzoli, 1459. This magus is modelled on John VIII Paleologus, the Emperor of the East, who visited Italy for the Council of Ferrara in 1438. Short, fur-trimmed sleeves like those featured on his tunic often denote oriental figures within the narrative of painting. The tunic is made of green velvet woven in two heights of pile, brocaded in gold and highlighted by *allucciolati* (indicated by the little dashes of gold paint). The sleeves of his *farsetto* are of red and gold damask.

54. Portrait medal of the Emperor John VIII Paleologus, by Pisanello, 1438–9. The Emperor, after his visit to the Council of Ferrara, was used as an identifiable model for oriental characters in Italian paintings. He is most closely associated with the role of the middle-aged magus.

55. Saint Peter preaching, from the predella to the Linaiuoli altarpiece by Fra Angelico, 1433. The secularization of subject matter and the more natural grouping of figures allowed for backviews in paintings, which offer more detail about the construction of clothing.

or at work, or from something more processional or theatrical. The dateless, simplified garments of friars, saints and the Madonna, gave way to more images of contemporary fashion. Natural groupings of figures, including back-views and variably angled profiles, allow a better insight into what costume really looked like and how it was made.

Not only did the form and the content of paintings and other works of art become more mundane, but the methods of creating reality were being carefully contrived. Paolo Uccello, for one, was making powerful experiments in foreshortening and perspective. There was a general tendency for individuals to explore their own special interests in a most systematic way, much aided by the notable increase in the number of manuals and treatises. In addition to those by Alberti on the arts, there were treatises on trade, on dance and movement, and on astrology—pastimes which the leisured rich took great pride and pleasure in.

Towards the middle of the fifteenth century were painted a number of murals which depict a colourful impression of courtly life. This is evident in Pisanello's tournament scenes in the Ducal

Palace of the Gonzaga at Mantua, in scenes of activities at court and card-games in the Palazzo Borromeo in Milan, and of hunting scenes on the walls of the Borromeo lodge at Oreno. All these, as well as the knights and princesses of chapel frescoes and smaller panel paintings, and the processions on salvers and *cassoni*, bring out the richest forms of costume. So much so, that some people consider them to be quite fantastical. The subject-matter of the Italian murals of the period is comparable with the large woven tapestries of northern Europe. They are equally decorative, and in the same way offer the court indoors the vicarious enjoyment of their outdoor pastimes. However, they are based on actual events, and on costumes which really existed. Any enquiry therefore should be directed at the type of occasions on which the clothes were worn, and by whom.

The ideal courtier of the day displayed a graceful ease of movement in his dress which complemented his whole being. Treatises, such as Leon Battista Alberti's on painting,[1] and that by

56. The Game of Palms, Lombard School, *c.* 1450; a detail from the Palazzo Borromeo frescoes. The dagged sleeves here are a theatrical feature of court dress.

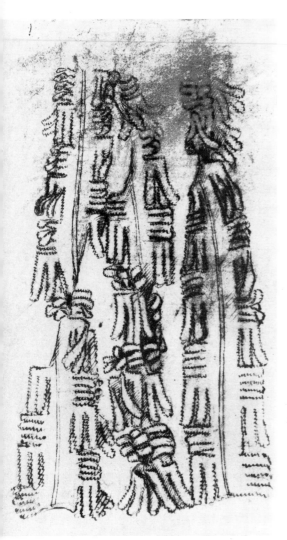

Guglielmo Ebreo on dancing,[2] show a strong interest in the way that outward physical movements echo the mental patterns and intellectual quality of an individual. The description of Leonello d'Este, Marquis of Ferrara, by Angelo Camillo Decembrio confirms this point:

> His style of dress—and one's dress can be a source of respect and good will among gentlemen—was noteworthy for its tastefulness. He was not concerned with opulence and ostentation, as some other princes are. But—now you will find this remarkable—he thought out his wardrobe in such a way as to choose the colour of his garments according to the day of the month, and the position of the stars and planets. What shall I say of his great commitment to the worship of God? Simply that he was like a saintly monk who daily offered prayers to the Lord. And though he lived among men, he was not less than the very angels of heaven who, it sometimes seemed, took counsel from him.[3]

Leonello was not ostentatious, his dress was more modified than many fashionable clothes of the period. Yet it did contain a strong element of fantasy, influenced by the increasing interest in astrology.

In general, costume was beginning to turn away from the elongated gothic forms of the early years of the century, and the silhouette was filling out. Deeply cut dags were perhaps a little outdated; nevertheless, the decorative use of fringing and gold and silver ornaments was still a desirable feature of fashion. An Este inventory of 1448 describes a *zornea de zetanino aveludado alexandrino* (a *giornea* of voided velvet) with fringes of silver and of silk, 'like those in fashion at the present time'.[4] Amongst the sketches attributed to Pisanello in the Louvre is one of a decoratively cut textile. This order of cutting strips of cloth, twisting them, and then applying them to the main body of a garment is suggested in Domenico Veneziano's tondo depicting The Adoration of the Magi. The young man whose back-view is seen in the central foreground of the picture is wearing a tunic of a type very similar to those which appear in Pisanello's studies; and the flecked lines of gold painted around the hem of his tunic are arranged in such a way as to exactly relate to the lines by which strips of cloth have been decoratively cut in the Pisanello drawing. The same idea, that of applying strips of cloth cut into patterns, is seen on the sleeves of Giovanni Arnolfini's wife, in the painting by Jan van Eyck in the National Gallery, London.

Yet, to accomplish a graceful bearing, moderation was called for in all aspects of dress. Alfonso of Aragon, habitually dressed in austere black with little ornamentation, contrasts strongly with

57. (above) Sketch of a decoratively cut textile, possibly by Pisanello. Strips of cloth are pinked into vertical and horizontal tabs, and then twisted down the central axis before being applied to the hemline of a garment.

58. (opposite) Leonello d'Este, by Giovanni da Oriolo, c. 1447.

100

LEONELLVS ✠ MARCHIO ✠ ESTESIS ✠

OPV: IOHANI

ORIOLI ✠

59. (opposite) Backview of a young man in The Adoration of the Magi by Domenico Veneziano, *c.* 1440. The flecked brushstrokes of gold around the hem of his tunic exactly correspond to the procedure of cutting the textile in plate 57.

60. (left) A very dapper Saint George; detail from The Virgin and Child with SS. George and Anthony Abbot, by Pisanello. The wide-brimmed straw hat was worn by men particularly when out hunting. His sideless tunic (*giornea*) is decorated with metal fringing; it resembles the garment which San Bernardino so despised and likened to a horsecloth.

the ostentatious Sienese ambassadors in the stories related by Vespasiano da Bisticci. The following demonstrates the ludicrously impractical qualities of fashion taken to extremes, and suggests that eccentric dagging was becoming a thing of the past.

> Another Sienese ambassador had come to Naples, and had an overgown [*covertina*] with long dags [*frastagli*], as they were accustomed to wear in the old days. . . . The King [Alfonso] on seeing this, could not help laughing. So one day, when he wanted to go out hunting, he decided to go past the house of the ambassador, and shout loudly and impatiently for him to come down. The ambassador immediately saddled the horses, and mounted, wearing his usual hose, with a long *veste* and that overgown with dagging. The King did not avoid one single hedge that morning, with the result that the ribbons and most of the gown of the Sienese ambassador were scattered about, with bits deposited in one hedge after another. It rained all day—and on returning to Naples that evening, the ambassador was soaked through from head to toe, having no cloak. So this amusing tale was passed round the court over the next few days, providing much amusement.[5]

The *strascico*, the train of a dress, often referred to as the *coda di veste*, was still long, and it was deemed necessary to check its growth. In 1430 Amadeo of Savoy asserted by law that dukes and their entourages should wear honest clothes.[6] Whether or not they had a *strascico*, they should not be allowed to become too short, and they should avoid any superficial details. This restraint should also be observed in the wearing of jewels. Duchesses were allowed the modest *strascico* of a *palmo*, but they were not allowed facings wider than three *dita*. The lengths of hemlines, rather than diminishing, must have been on the increase, for by 1460 in Padua an appeal was made against the maximum length of women's dresses (*code dei vestiti*) laid down by a law instituted by the Church. A perplexed legislator of the town addressed himself to the local bishop in this way:

> Since women are wearing the trains of their gowns much longer than is permitted, according to a papal constitution, for which the priests do not wish to absolve the said ladies in their confessions; and since the declaration of or specifications within the constitution has nothing to do with us laymen, I beseech you, Most Reverend Bishop, to declare how long the trains of women's dresses may be.[7]

It is not know exactly what papal legislation this refers to, nor is any precise length of hemline mentioned but perhaps it relates to an incident in Venice in 1437, when fashionable Venetian women were threatened with excommunication for wearing gowns with long trains; however, by appealing directly to the Pope, they won their case, and were allowed to disregard the law for three years, on payment of a tax.[8]

It is difficult to establish exactly how the *strascico* was measured, for it may have become confused with the depth of the borders around the hem. Often, overgarments—particularly the *cioppa*—were not lined throughout with fur, but just trimmed round the very edges (*filetti*), or with borders. In 1448, the 1000 florin dowry paid by Marco Parenti, a silk merchant of Florence, on his marriage with Caterina, daughter of Alessandra Macinghi Strozzi, included a trousseau.[9] His diary for 12 January of that year records a *cioppa* of white *calisea*, with embroidered sleeves *a gozzi* and edged with marten (*orlata di martore*). On the other hand, a *giornea* ordered by Marco later in the year, made of crimson velvet (*zetani vellutato di chermisi*), and lined with *valescio* and *guarnello*, must have been lined throughout with the 188 *lattizi* brought for 12 florins and 15 gold *soldi* from Francesco the furrier. The skins were intended for trimming hemlines (*fodera d'intagli e orli e filetti*). At the same time, to make a *cotta* of the same velvet cloth, Marco bought 26 *lattizi* to go into the *filetto da piè*; that is, to decorate the edge of the hem of the skirt, which was also to be trimmed with green and gold fringing.

Amadeo of Savoy also forbade women to wear tall hairstyles in horns, or rounded into some deformative shape.[10] The headwear which transformed even the profile of the face and gave height and grace to the long sweep of the early Quattrocento silhouette was the *balzo*. It is a form of headdress worn by fashionable women in the 1430s and 1440s. As the whole shape of both male and female costume added more width to its height, so the padded roll of the *ghirlanda* grew into the bulbous *balzo*. One of crimson, covered in pearls, was given by Francesco de' Medici in 1432 to his betrothed, Costanza, and is probably one of the earliest references to the fashion.[11] However, there are more documentary references to *ghirlande* than to *balzi*; although an earlier form of headdress, the garland did not go out of fashion.

The *balzo* consisted of an understructure possibly made of pliant strips of branches or reeds bent under steam and this basic shape was then covered with silk textile, and sometimes additionally decorated with ribbons, braids or strips of the textile from which the gown was made. The *balzo* was an essentially Italian fashion. The horned headdresses *a corna*, on the other hand, were features of north European dress.

A letter from the exiled Lorenzo Strozzi to his mother Alessandra, written in Valencia in 1446, describes the fashions worn in Spain. As they resemble the costume featured in

tapestries, the Spaniards are obviously dressed in the Flemish style, with pointed shoes and what are probably horned headdresses:

> Just imagine how they wear their clothes, exactly like those you see depicted in tapestries. But they do not wear that *mazzocchio*: no matter how old a woman might be, she goes about with a net of silk on her head, and over that a single veil. They do not wear their veil in the way you wear a towel [*sciugatoio*]; they wear it suspended. It looks as if they have wings on their heads, which is a charming thing. And they do not wear *cioppe* of silk: instead, all the *cioppe* are of woollen cloth, with sleeves like trumpets [*co' gozzi a trombe*], and a train five *braccia* or more long, which they have to pick up and carry. I have never seen such angelic women, never: and for as long as I shall live, I will never see any more beautiful. Believe me, when I say this. And imagine that I, like them, am wearing shoes with little laces at the sides, with points [*scarpette colle cordelline dalla latera*] three *dita* long, and I go about without leather soles [*peduli*] on my hose: it suits me very well. Praise be to God.[12]

Lorenzo's reactions, and the quaintness with which he tried to convey exactly what he was observing in Spain, suggest that never had he seen such a fashion before that date—and certainly not in Italy. Horned headdresses, being a northern fashion, were probably accepted by the women of the north of Italy before they reached Florence; and then they were only worn by young women—widows and older women covered their heads, and necks too, in veils. Among the ladies accompanying Teodolinda in the Zavattari frescoes in Monza are a number of horned headdresses, surmounted by veils suspended to look like wings. The inventory of the family of Puccio Pucci, dated 1449, includes an entry for a horned headdress (*un paio di chorna*), costing eight florins.[13]

As Lorenzo Strozzi mentioned, large trumpeting sleeves, as well as accentuated headwear, gave great stature to the fashionable impression. The variety of names for sleeves, in both men's and women's dress, evokes the imaginative forms they resembled. The *maniche a gozzo* were commonly found in both fashionable and official clothing. Likened to bells, trumpets, birds' wings and crops, or simply left open to reveal the underlying colour and texture, sleeves played an essential role in capturing the mood of dress. During this period of the century, sleeves were particularly imposing, their volume coinciding with the puffed-out hairstyles of young men, and the *balzi*, garlands

61. The head of a princess; detail from the fresco of Saint George and the Princess in S. Anastasia, Verona, by Pisanello, *c.* 1438. The *balzo* worn here consists of layers of false hair wrapped around an understructure (see plate 21), and finally decorated with braids.

107

and horned and veiled structures worn by ladies. A sumptuary law published in Pistoia on 21 February 1439, in restricting the width of sleeves to eight *braccia*, revises the proportions laid down in the same town in a statute of 1420, when sleeves only five *braccia* wide were permitted.[14] These dimensions applied only to the overgarments—*veste*, *giornee* and *cotte*, which should not be made of silk: in 1439 silk sleeves (presumably to be attached to the *gamurra*) should not exceed two *braccia* round the hem.

Some of the latest fashions to be seen were worn by young men and women parading and dancing in the streets on some festive occasion. Bartolommeo di Michele del Corazza records how, on 12 November 1435, a *brigata* (a young people's club, of which there were several in the city), numbering 16 in all, had a dance in the Piazza de' Signori in Florence.[15] They were dressed in crimson satin (*zetani in cremusi*), fur-lined, with the hem turned back on the outside (*con l'orlo di fuori*) to a depth of a third of a *braccio*. They had motley hose (*calze a divisa*) in several colours, embroidered with pearls. As it began to rain, the lady and gentleman spectators retreated to the loggia, and the dancers were not awarded any prizes that day. No doubt the honours would have consisted of one girl's and one boy's prize, as had been handed out after a similar *brigata* dance performed in 1420. On that occasion, the two prizes were a garland made from large plumes (*grillanda di penne grande*) and a *berretta* of green damask.[16]

Although one would expect young men to look totally up-to-date, it is common to find page-boys dressed in an old or past fashion, which assumes a kind of uniform or livery. The page who holds a horse in the foreground of Gentile's Adoration of the Magi wears a sleeveless, sideless tunic decorated with a serrated pattern—a form of costume left over from the second decade, which now lies dormant in current styles of dress.

As a part of livery, as well as of totally fashionable dress, the use of different coloured shoes or hose for each leg is a regular feature throughout the Quattrocento. Reputed to have been extremely neglectful about his appearance in old age, Filippo Maria Visconti may not have shaved the stubble from his chin regularly, but on festive occasions he wore a *veste togata* with a *cappuccio* over the shoulder, a light *berretta* on his head, and shoes of two colours—the right of white, and the left of an amethyst colour.[17] And at his marriage to Bianca Maria Visconti, Francesco Sforza wore a *veste* of green velvet, with a red *zuppone*: he had a red stocking on his right leg, and a blue and white one on the left.[18] Whilst these two examples relate to the Milanese court, the same use of motley was to be found elsewhere in Italy.

Much solidity of the figure must depend considerably on the style of the painter, but it is nevertheless possible to detect a general enlargement of dress into a more rounded profile. A particularly bulbous look was achieved in the clothing illustrated in a Hebrew codex, written in 1435, which contains an

62. A boy attending a horse; detail from The Adoration of the Magi by Gentile da Fabriano, 1423.

illumination of a Jewish wedding. The rolled turban hood had to develop into a proper hat, otherwise it would have become utterly uncontrollable. It is still constructed from the same component parts—a rolled base worn round the crown, from which the hood stems. But once dress had reached an extreme of bulkiness, the one way by which it can change is in a more sober, controlled direction. Sheets of studies attributed to Pisanello demonstrate the incredible volume of men's tunics, and likewise the headgear has reached outsize proportions in its various different forms—the huge straw hat, for instance. Vecchietta's painting, The Virgin Receives the Souls of the Foundlings, dated 1441, does present two extremely fashionable-looking young men in the foreground, standing within the central archway. Belts are worn round the hips—a fashionable alternative to wearing them round the waist. This does not necessarily reflect a marked chronological change in style, but is primarily a matter of personal taste. The Sienese figures here, and the outstanding young man of self-confident pose in a scene by Domenico di Bartolo, show that showiness that made King Alfonso and his courtiers laugh so much.[19] Yet the indulgent fullness of the clothes shows a contrived, carefully regulated grouping of folds. The moulding of fashionable shapes by means of precisely gored and tied pleats, as opposed to incidental drapes, is to become a prominent feature in the tailoring of dress in the latter half of the Quattrocento.

Comparable with the large hat worn by the male figure on the right of the wedding scene in the Jewish manuscript, is the headdress worn by Niccolò da Tolentino in the Battle of San Romano by Paolo Uccello. The battle was fought in 1432, and Niccolò da Tolentino died in 1435: the hat is certainly consistent with the fashions of the 1430s, although the series of panels was probably executed in the 1450s.[20] Michael Baxandall indicates

63. (above) A Jewish Wedding. Miniature from *I Quattro Ordini*, a manuscript executed in Mantua in 1435. To the trailing sleeves and hems of the elongated silhouette predominant during the first quarter of the century has been added a greater bulk of textile. The rounded shape of the groom's hairstyle echoes the general proportions of the clothing. Parti-coloured hose (*calze a divisa*) were frequently worn by men as part of fashionable dress, whilst sometimes playing a heraldic role if worn in the colours of a particular household.

64. (opposite) The Virgin Receives the Souls of the Foundlings, detail, by Vecchietta, 1441.

65. Niccolò da Tolentino in *The Battle of San Romano* by Uccello. Though executed during the 1450s, the panel commemorates an event of 1432. The exaggerated bulk of his hat adds dimension to and is a focal point within the total composition of the painting. At the same time, it is a true representation of the fashionable silhouette in the mid-1430s.

several ways of seeing the hat:

One is as a round hat with a flouncy crown; another is as a compound of cylinder and plump polygonal disc disguised as a hat. These are not mutually exclusive: Lorenzo de' Medici, who had this picture in his bedroom, would have seen both and accepted it as a sort of serial geometrical joke. It demands attention initially by its exaggerated size and splendour; then in the second stage by the paradox of the pattern on this most three-dimensional of hats behaving as if it were two-dimensional, spreading itself flatly on the picture plane without regard for the object's shape; then, in the third stage, by a dawning anxiety about the polygon of the crown. It is polygonal, certainly; but is it heptagonal, or hexagonal? It is a problem hat. . . .[21]

But was it really such a joke? The fact is that Niccolò da Tolentino's hat would have looked like that: the problems set in the interpretation of the narrative are surely those invented by modern historians. The situation is complicated because we are not faced with a simple history of dress and a straightforward method of dating a work of art. For our vision is, in certain instances, not just second-hand, but even third- or fourth-hand. We are confronted with a double past because we are looking back to what an artist thought of as being historical, theatrical or foreign. Nor are these different categories of dress in the double past always well defined. The artist often confuses clothing, his vision being drawn from a visual experience of contemporary dress, theatrical costume, figures in works of art, and his own imagination.

An interesting amalgamation of sources is built into the figure of the Emperor of the East in the Zavattari frescoes at Monza. The legend of Teodolinda dates back to the early seventh century; so here the figure ought to look both historic and foreign to the eye of the artist and the contemporary witness of his work. However, once removed from its own period, the inconsistencies in a painting are easily spotted. The head of the Zavattari Emperor is of a type extremely close to the heads of Caesars found in manuscripts of the period.[22] The wreath around his head does suggest something extracted from the past; the corkscrew curls into which his hair is arranged are a kind of password to the East—they are a distinctive feature of many orientals in painting. On the other hand, the armour worn by the Emperor and the overgown that is worn with it are totally contemporary and closely resemble that worn by Pisanello's Saint George in London; the pauldrons (shoulder-pieces) are of the same square shape. Thus a precision of detail in determining time and place is confused and lost. Moreover, the trumpeters behind herald something of a fifteenth-century pageant, but they are disguised slightly by the towels wrapped round their heads, and knotted on one side—another feature which generally signifies an oriental (but not of high station, and therefore never a magus), or a beggar. The wreath worn by the 'Caesar' is obviously an actual object—a theatrical prop—which is tied in a bow at the back of the head.

Not only do paintings include theatrical objects, but also costume. Often this is made up from, or gives the impression of, clothing belonging to the current fashion. Domenico Veneziano's tondo depicting The Adoration of the Magi looks

66. (page 114) The Emperor of the East rides on; detail from The Story of Queen Teodolinda by the Zavattari brothers, 1444. The corkscrew haircurls are a password to the East, and the laurel wreath is indentifiable with the Emperors of antique Rome, whilst the style of armour is contemporary.

67. (page 115) The Adoration of the Magi, detail; by Domenico Veneziano, c. 1440. The clothing worn by the group of young men is generally fashionable – a rounded outline with very controlled channels of folds – but with some extra theatrical props. The young page holding the crown of the old magus is made to look oriental. Over a dark coloured farsetto he wears another garment, similarly waisted and fitted narrowly about the hips; its short sleeves trimmed at the elbows with fur indicate something Eastern in both Italian and north European art; and the garment is made of a Turkish velvet featuring bold carnation motifs; the hip belt from which hang tails of fur is purely theatrical.

113

manifestly like a scene acted out for real, perhaps by members of a *brigata*. The standing young and middle magi (the latter does not look middle-aged) wear totally fashionable tunics for about the year 1445. A particularly interesting possibility is the clothing worn by the page standing directly behind the old wise man's head; it is not a garment that has been misunderstood by the painter. On the other hand, it is not a fashionable tunic, because it fits too tightly from the waist to the hips, and then suddenly billows out in a decoration of pieces of fur. The garment in fact follows the shape of a doublet, and the belt worn round his hips could be a theatrical device from which hangs strips of fur, or animals' tails; these would conveniently hide the bottom edge of the *farsetto*.

In order to divert the fifteenth-century onlooker's attention away from the present, actual contemporary items of clothing were used as studio props. The interpretation of the narrative, in a story removed from the present in time and space, depends on the understanding of current and local attitudes towards dress. Cloaks are particularly useful guises. It need not be pouring with rain for the young Madonna to wear a cloak over her head. Yet the fact that the custom of wearing hooded cloaks belongs to the role of married and elderly women and widows adds to the sobriety of the life of the Virgin. In other instances, a mantle can be usefully draped in order to assume the impression of a Roman toga, or of some Old Testament prophet. Again, this theatrical guise is not without relevance to contemporary ways of dress: for the Renaissance interest in the classical themes of ancient Greece

68. (below) The Madonna della Misericordia (detail), by Piero della Francesca, 1445–62. The kneeling women on the right wear *bende*, fine strips of linen or silk veil, in their hair. These, and the sleeve which has been turned back toga-style of the young man in the left foreground are direct references to classical Greece and Rome.

69. (opposite) Saint Eustace, by Pisanello, portrayed as a fashionable young man of the mid-1430s; a detail from The Vision of Saint Eustace.

and Rome not only stimulated a serious study of language and thought, but rubbed off in more decorative, superficial ways. In this way came the fashion for Grecian bands in women's hair, and the affected details of knotting cloaks on one shoulder or turning back big sleeves, in imitation of the drapes of a Roman toga.

Of less contemporary significance, the *gamurra* is often worn to avoid particularizing time or social class. As a practical garment, it is worn by the female friends of the expectant mother at a birth scene. As fundamental items of clothing, which hardly ever change shape, and which are barely ornamented, the *gamurra* and *camicia* or the *guarnello* are donned by many female saints and angels. The fact that the *gamurra* belongs to the woman's wardrobe and that angels are supposed to be male appears irrelevant. After all, both young men and women in enchanting costumes with golden hair look angelic to the eye of the poet.

In other cases of narrative, the painter effectively places saintly or historical figures into contemporary guise. Pisanello's Saint Eustace is a totally fashionable young man, out hunting as members of his social standing were accustomed to do. His clothes point to a date around the mid-1430s.

Whatever the subject-matter, the narrative content of a work of art is dependent on tangible examples drawn from the artist's environment. Yet the iconography in the arts and literature remains much deeper, and definitely more consistent, than in everyday life. Leonello d'Este was attuned to his own system of dress, according to the position of the stars and the planets, and the day of the month.[23] He was not alone. No quantity of sumptuary legislations could guarantee a uniformity of dress. Most colourful and ornamental details of costume were personally devised.

It is extremely tempting to ascribe a specific meaning to each colour worn. Obvious examples are those of the three theological virtues—white for Faith, green for Hope and red for Charity. Levi Pisetzky correctly points out that white was traditionally worn by the peasantry, as seen in miniatures of the fourteenth and fifteenth centuries, and that the poorest people of all wore *grigio* (meaning 'grey', but here referring to grey, i.e. untreated cloth).[24] They were wearing the least expensive cloth, unbleached and undyed linen and wool, for basic economic reasons. Their clothes are put together in the simplest way: old breeches or strips of cloth bound round the legs are used instead of tailored hose. For practical reasons, the coarse shirts and tunics never reach below the knee, and are often bunched up into the belt at the waist to allow freedom of movement. Two little figures illustrated in the Statutes of the Society of Drapers of Bologna (plate 32) appear dressed in this way. There is therefore no symbolism attached to the peasants' dress: but they are immediately recognizable within a day-to-day iconography.

With regard to colour, it is necessary to differentiate between

70. (opposite) An Allegory of the Month of April, 1407. Peasants would wear the most simply cut clothing, often left in the natural colour of the fibre used.

71. (above) A young spinster; detail from *Commentarii in Sphaera Mundi* dated 1463. A practical tuck in the skirt of the young woman's dress is a temporary readjustment of a second-hand item of clothing.

everyday clothing, and that worn on a festive occasion—between the informal set of clothes worn at home, and the more formal appearance suitable for going about one's official business. The importance attached to the identification of an individual's status was dependent on colour. However, we can be certain of intentional colour symbolism only in literature, theatrical performance (including public processions and court entertainments), and within some official settings. In fashion, vanity must be allowed to overrule some observances, for example it is claimed that Isabella d'Este often wore *berettino* (a shade of grey) because it best set off her complexion.[25] In other circumstances, *berettino* could have significance, for it was prescribed as a colour of mourning.

Some colours took precedence over others. The more precious, of better quality, were designated to higher ranking officials. Those cloths dyed with kermes were considered the most important; thus in a Florentine embassy to the Pope, the eight ambassadors were dressed in *cremisi*, whilst their 72 companions wore *rosato*.[26] Both were shades of red, *rosato* sometimes being made from *grana*. As is the case with many colours, *rosato* must have become so closely associated with a particular cloth that it often appears unqualified in inventories, and must therefore denote the type of the cloth as well as the colour. Francesco Filelfo sent from Milan a request to Lorenzo the Magnificent for two *vestiti* and for a *mantello* of *rosato di grana* lined with *zendalo di grana*.[27] This would suggest that *rosato* applies to a structure or finish of woollen cloth. Though various shades of red through to mulberry and black were indicative of specific official ranks, they were not solely reserved for the official and academic wear of men. A *cioppa rosata* embroidered with pearls, belonging to the wife of Piero Pucci, estimated at 80 florins, is listed in the Pucci inventory of 1449.[28] In other cases, certain types of cloth had become so commonly associated with particular garments that they entered the vocabulary of dress. *Saia* probably originally meant a type of woollen cloth, but it can also refer to a silk textile, and it often denotes a woman's garment, with sleeves, similar to the *cotta* and the *gamurra*, as an inventory of 1464 would suggest.[29] Amongst the Pucci possessions is listed a *saia doppia*[30] and as this entry had specified sleeves of silk, the *saia* in this case is presumably made of wool, and self-lined.

Mourning is denoted by the wearing of dark colours, some of which were part of everyday dress anyway. Dull, dark shades of mulberry, blue, green and brown, as well as black, were donned by the bereaved. However, in 1438, following a terrible attack of plague, it was forbidden in the city of Venice to wear the three *colori corozosi*, mourning colours of black, green and blue,[31] for had such a law not been passed the whole dispirited population would have been wearing those shades, for the number of dead was high. Even the wearing of mourning did not conform to one

72. Portrait of a Man, by Andrea del Castagno, *c.* 1450. The young man wears a conventional suit of clothes in red, a cloak over a tunic or gown (*veste*) and doublet. His right hand holds onto the long end of a hood worn over the shoulder in an official or academic manner.

120

set of rules; leading figures of the century sometimes specified their own mourning dress. Beatrice d'Este chose how she was to dress on the death of her mother; Ludovico did likewise when Beatrice died. And Francesco Sforza, on announcing the death of his grandmother, Agnese del Majno, said:

> We will arrange the funeral honourably, as she deserves. . . By our honour and duty we are clothed in dark green; and we will wear this colour until Christmas, when we will change to *morello*; and I intend that we should go about in that for a few months. Your brothers just dress in *morello*.[32]

Besides being a colour of mourning, green was worn at the court of Milan on several important occasions. Another shade worn in mourning was *monachino*, a brown with a reddish tint. It is the colour of an item of widow's clothing in an inventory of 1465;[33] but it also appears in non-mourning dress, though usually for a functional *mantello* or *cioppa* not of great value.

When the head of a family laid down the specifications concerning mourning, they sometimes got out of hand. To have a whole family, including the distant relatives and everybody attached to the household, in mourning, was a sign of aggrandizement. Some cases of sumptuary legislation therefore restricted the number of people eligible to wear mourning.

Excluding ecclesiastical vestments, probably the most precise regulations were applied to academic dress, worn only for public

73. The Resurrection of Tabitha, detail, by Masolino. Enveloping veils and draped hoods are indicative of mourning, as well as being the guise of older women.

ceremony. Chronicles of Bologna record how, when peace was established between the Church and the Bolognese in 1431, after the election of Pope Eugenius IV:

> At a fixed time, all the scholars appeared with the rectors and public readers dressed in their sumptuous *toghe*; *pavonazze* for the canonists, *porporine* for the lawyers, and black for those in the faculty of art. After the magistrates came the leading doctors of the nation with their staffs of office, the chancellors of both universities and the papal ambassadors, dressed in red and white stripes. Bringing up the rear of the procession all the scholars from this side and beyond the Alps were in fashionable dress, which was a most lovely and rather charming sight.[34]

Nevertheless, as the Bolognese records indicate, the variants on fashion contrasted strongly with uniform. That occasion in 1431 was a carefully staged display of the reunion of scholars and officials of the Church. For the most part, however, dress conformed to the limits of financial resources and to individual whims.

5 Extravagance at Court

The identification of the innovators of fashions in the Quattrocento poses many interesting questions. No references in contemporary accounts confirm who thought out new styles, although tailors and embroiderers are occasionally mentioned. However, with regard to the frequent processions and entertainments provided by and for the people at court, it is reasonable to expect that court artists were required to design costumes, in addition to the theatrical sets, banners, mural decorations and triumphal arches we know them to have devised.

The costume studies attributed to Pisanello demonstrate the artist's thorough understanding of three-dimensional form in dress. The extremely imaginative use of textile and embroidery suggests that some of the studies illustrate an artist's (or artists') original designs—as opposed to copies of real or painted costumes.

The name of Pisanello (*c.* 1395–*c.* 1455) immediately draws attention to the birthplace of the artist—Pisa, but it is with northern Italy that he is mainly associated. The details of Pisanello's life and activity are confusing; he appears to have begun his career in Verona, and then to have closely followed the footsteps of Gentile da Fabriano, first by painting a series of frescoes in the Doge's Palace in Venice, and then in Rome, at the Lateran Basilica (both are now completely destroyed). His interest in representing courtly life and much narrative detail are shown in two examples of his work in Verona: the Annunciation, in S. Fermo, and the later fresco (*c.* 1438) of Saint George and the Princess in S. Anastasia.

Pisanello is representative of the court artist working not solely in one medium, but as painter, draughtsman, portrait medallist, and possibly also as an illuminator of manuscripts. His career involved working for and within some of the most influential court circles of the day—notably the Gonzaga in Mantua, the Este in Ferrara, and King Alfonso of Naples. To be working in such a capacity, he must have appealed to current fashions and tastes.

With the references to Pisanello's art in the lines by Guarino and Angelo Galli, amongst others, his skills of representing or interpreting nature are highly praised, especially his draughts-manship.[1]

A sonnet written to the painter Pisanello by Angelo Galli at Urbino in 1442, reveals some of his qualities:

Art, *misura*, *aere* and draughtsmanship,
Maniera, perspective and a natural quality—
Heaven miraculously gave him these gifts.[2]

This links with Domenico da Piacenza's treatise on dancing, written in the 1440s, which states that, like the art of rhetoric, dancing had five parts—*aere*, *maniera*, *misura*, *misura di terreno*, and *memoria*.[3] This, and other treatises, show some preoccupation with the idea of the outward expression of inner reflection. Such traits were enormously admired in the personality of Leonello d'Este,[4] who in 1441 arranged a competition for the painting of a portrait of himself. It was won by Jacopo Bellini, although Leonello did very much admire the work of Pisanello, whose portrait of the Este prince may relate to the event of 1441. The portrait—though in poor condition[5]—reflects the interest in nature and diversity in all things enjoyed by the humanist poets. They looked not only for the dexterity of the painter, but also for pleasurable visual detail, such as the rendering of the different colours with which the cloth had been dyed. The attitude reflects a leaning towards romanticism which would suggest that in the

74. The Court of Solomon, miniature from the Bible of Borso d'Este, *c.* 1455–61.

renewed classicism of the fifteenth century there was not just a revival of the antique but also a feeling of nostalgia connected with it. The present-day attitude towards Pisanello is definitely a romantic one and is based, to a considerable extent, on the costume studies.

Of all the dress portrayed in Quattrocento drawing and painting, Pisanello's is generally considered to be the most fantastic. It is often thought that his clothes could not possibly have been worn, yet contemporary descriptions of his work have expressed how Pisanello's rendering of nature is not produced purely out of a keen imaginative power. Rather, the literature implies an accuracy of direct observation of all forms. With reference to costume, this is particularly true—no matter how unlikely or dramatic Pisanello's studies may look. In any case, the fashions of the day, as we have seen, were extremely fanciful in design.

75. Leonello d'Este, by Pisanello, c. 1441. The prince wears a sideless *giornea* over a doublet of rich brocaded textile; but the details are confusing.

76. Costume studies by Pisanello; Oxford, Ashmolean Museum, c. 1438–40. These fantastic, though structurally credible, men's costumes beautifully evoke the bird-like profile alluded to in the contemporary terminology for dress.

The Ashmolean costume studies may look unlikely, but structurally they are extremely sound. The man's tunic on the right would appear to follow the fashionable line of a date around the late 1430s, while the large device on the sleeve, representing a flax-hackle and a climbing tree with grafting slips (as yet, not identified with a specific prince or potentate), suggests that the garment was worn for a particular ceremonial occasion. As part of the fashion for this date, the hemline of the tunic is slightly shorter in front than behind; and this, together with the way the outline of the sleeve rhythmically grows longer and wider from the front of the shoulder at the top to its lowest point behind, accentuates the backward sweep of the whole garment, giving the outline impression of a bird's wing.

The references to birds, common in general fashion, but made much more dramatic in the designs attributed to Pisanello, reappear in the Bayonne and Chantilly sheets of studies.

The imaginative gowns in the Bayonne drawings are extensions of fashion in their use of surface decoration and extra-long trains. The edges of the sleeves look 'plumed', for the textile has been cut deeply in from the borders. Though only sketchily drawn here, the large scale and lack of repeat in the decoration on the textile show that if a garment were to be made up from the design, it would have to be embroidered rather than woven. The wavily cut edge of a sleeve, worn by the nearer of the two male figures, would then be embroidered further into the fabric, in order to give the impression of inward-growing rambling branches. The female figure's gown, on the other hand, would be decorated by an elaborate selection of applied detail. The borders of her sleeves are made to look feathered—not unlike those worn by the male figure in full-length dress in the Ashmolean studies. This decorative effect could be built up by the application of rows of single strips of cut cloth, sewn to the main body of the sleeve, most probably by the top edge of each strip, which would then hang loose. According to the type and weight of material chosen for these strips, they would flutter or sway about during any motion of the body, or movement of air. The loose, streaming lines down the central part of the sleeve framed by this border may indicate either a rambling embroidered pattern, or else a series of applied or embroidered flowers, each one issuing forth a short trail of three lengths of ribbon, which would react prettily to the slightest breeze.

The dress worn by the female figure in the Chantilly drawing is elaborated to an even greater degree, for its wing-like profile is made particularly apparent by the way she wears a double-sleeve effect—one, shorter, worn over the other, which sweeps to the ground. The upper sleeve looks as though it is designed to be ridged with pearls, to accentuate the line, while it is possible that the longer is constructed from different hanging pieces, each one representing a single 'plume'. When motionless, the total

77. Costume studies attributed to Pisanello;
Bayonne, Musée Bonnat.

78. The Feast of Herod, by Filippo Lippi, 1452–64. When kneeling still, Salome's sleeve appears to be constructed of one neatly folded piece of fabric; in the dance, however, it is proved that her sleeve is composed of separate strips of cloth.

would look as if it were made from one folded piece, but once the figure walked forward, these pieces would separate and then individually swing gracefully along. Such is the type of sleeve worn by Filippo Lippi's Salome in the Feast of Herod who, when standing still, looks as though she is wearing a hanging sleeve falling into heavy folds, but when dancing, it is apparent that her sleeve is constructed from strips. Effects of this kind must have existed, if not always in fashion, certainly in theatre or court masque.

The British Museum fashion studies are also totally possible, but it is difficult to say in what form and exactly when they existed. A date in the 1440s would seem very likely, for the main body of the tunic shown here reveals an interest in the stylistic precision of folds, while the sleeves still swing back as they do in some instances on the Ambrosiana sheet of studies. For the clothes in Pisanello's British Museum drawing to work, it would be necessary to insert narrow triangular pieces from the waist to the hem, to make the lower half of the garment stand out. This type of fluted effect, which is extremely clearly shown in the Louvre drawing, does become a fashionable construction more widely used at a later date. It is particularly evident in a sketchbook by Marco Zoppo, which includes one drawing of three male figures—a Burgundian (right), a German (behind) and an Italian (left). The presence of these three nationalities grouped together at one time may connect the drawing with a date in, or soon after, 1452, when Frederick III visited Italy for his coronation and marriage in Rome: his suite included representatives from each of those nations.

The autograph status of Pisanello's drawings and their costume content may be disputed endlessly. That such dress was worn is certain, particularly at court. However, the matter of who set the prototypes of these fashions lies open to speculation; and the possibility that the red and green colouring of some of the

79. Three fashionable young men, by Pisanello, early 1440s. British Museum.

Pisanello costume studies relates to the heraldic colours of a particular family may never be proved.[6]

Whenever a new or different style of clothing was worth mentioning, the chroniclers and diarists were eager to describe it at length. Amongst these fashion reports were included descriptions of foreign dress. Elements of this creep into everyday styles from time to time, but costumes of other countries were often used in a dramatic context, presenting the most fanciful forms of dress. For then, as today, the novelty of something different from abroad held great appeal.

A letter from Alfonso d'Este to his sister Isabella included a description of a tournament at Bologna[7] on San Petronio's Day, 1490, in which his brother-in-law, Annibale Bentivoglio, represented Fortune and Niccolò Rangoni, Lord of Spilamberto, appeared as the champion of Wisdom. The contest was the result of a discussion between Annibale and Niccolò about whether wisdom or fortune held the greater influence over affairs of men.

80. A Burgundian (right), a German (behind) and an Italian (left), from a sketchbook by Marco Zoppo. The identification of the young men is made partly on the grounds of their hairstyles, but also because of their association with figures in contemporary or slightly earlier paintings.

81. The Triumph of the Duke of Urbino, by Piero della Francesca (reverse of colour plate 11). The contemporary fondness for allegory, particularly during festivities at court, is here illustrated by Federigo da Montefeltro riding on a triumphal car of fame.

133

The event began in the Piazza, with the entry of a triumphal car in which the goddess Sapienza sat enthroned amidst representatives of ancient wisdom. Behind the car rode Sapienza's fighters, headed by Niccolò Rangoni wearing a blue gown richly embroidered with pearls. They circuited the Piazza to the sound of pipes and drums, and then stood aside for the car of the goddess Fortuna to advance, attended by Annibale Bentivoglio and his men all dressed in green. Once the procession had finished, the two goddesses recited verses in turn, pleading their case with a man robed as a Doctor of the University. He favoured neither one side nor the other, and so called on the judges of the tournament, who signalled for the fighting to begin. Fortune emerged victorious, and was awarded the *palio*.

In the following year, 1491, the marriage of Ludovico il Moro and Beatrice d'Este was celebrated in lavish style. Calco, an observer, commented in great detail on the clothes worn.[8] A tournament featuring the best knights was arranged. Amongst them was the Marquis of Mantua, followed by knights dressed in green velvet; Annibale Bentivoglio was there too, with 12 swordsmen each clothed in a *zuparello* of green satin, with pikemen also dressed in green with a motto which read '*Piu che mai*' ('More than ever'). Three jousters with overgowns of silver and of gold appeared in the procession, while the Duke Gian Galeazzo followed with 12 grooms (*staffieri*) dressed as wild men. Also, in honour of Ludovico, there was a group of men dyed with mulberry (*tincti in mori*).[9] The importance of such lavish occasions was considered a vital element of life at court: the carnival had to go on, even if it meant applying for special dispensations from Rome to eat meat at a feast held during Lent.[10]

Probably the most splendid court of the Quattrocento was that of the Sforza Dukes of Milan. Even by Renaissance standards, it was conspicuous in its luxury. In January 1489 Isabella of Aragon arrived in Milan, as bride to the young Duke, Gian Galeazzo Sforza. They had been betrothed in 1480, when he was eight, and she nine years old, but they did not meet until the year of their marriage. Ermes Sforza, brother of the Duke, had travelled to Naples accompanied by around 400 people, 'clad like so many kings', whence he escorted Isabella by sea to Genoa. The meeting of the young couple happened at Tortona, and was immediately celebrated with a grand banquet. Each course was served by mythological characters dressed in the antique style. Jason entered bearing the Golden Fleece; plates of fish were served by naïads; Hebe offered wines as sweet and precious as nectar and ambrosia; and Orpheus delivered birds which, he announced in elegant verse, had flown to hear him sing the praises of Isabella of Aragon.[11]

The wedding of Isabella and Gian Galeazzo was to take place in the Duomo at Milan: but the sad death in February 1489 of Ippolita Sforza, mother of the bride, meant that the celebrations

had to be postponed to some more suitable date. When they finally happened, on 13 January 1490, new pageants and festivities were highlighted by a wonderful performance of a masque called *Il Paradiso*, specially written for the occasion by the poet Bernardo Bellincioni to accompany an ingenious spectacle devised by Leonardo da Vinci.[12]

The spirit and splendour of court is captivated in those wedding festivities of January 1490. In a document consisting principally of the letters of Giacomo Trotti, faithful agent to the Duke of Ferrara at the court of Milan, the dramatic entertainment is described in detail.[13] Doubtless the Este family were eagerly awaiting news of the event. Beatrice had a personal interest, for she was soon to be married to Ludovico il Moro. The festivities took place in the Castello di Porta Giova, now called the Castello Sforzesco, in the great room at the top of the stairway, which was approached on horseback. The occasion provided a series of compliments to the bride; for her husband's uncle, Ludovico, and his attendants appeared in Spanish dress—a respectful tribute to the Aragonese origins of Isabella.

Invitations had been sent out to 100 of the most resplendent and beautiful young ladies to be found in the city of Milan. Other guests included all the orators, ambassadors, councillors,

82. A courtly banquet; detail from The Legend of the Argonauts attributed to Ercole de' Roberti.

magistrates and gentlemen; and of course the Duchess Bona, and Anna and Bianca Sforza. The festivities began at eight o'clock that evening.

In the large hall, decorated with the arms and devices of the house of Sforza and of King Ferrante of Aragon and Naples, father of the bride, the couple took their places on a dais specially constructed for the occasion. The sound of pipes and trumpets introduced the ceremonies, followed by a selection of Neapolitan dances played on tambourines. Then, to open her triumphant festivities, the Duchess Isabella, accompanied by the royal orator, made her way down from the dais. She was dressed in the Spanish manner, with a *mantello* of white silk over the *zuba* (*zuppa*), which was brocaded in gold on a white ground, patterned with other colours (in the Spanish style), and highlighted by a large number of jewels and pearls. She was so radiant and beautiful, like a sun; and she made her way into the middle of the hall, in front of the dais, where three of her ladies-in-waiting joined her, and performed two dances. Then she returned to her seat, and the tambourines finished playing. In a little while, eight masqueraders—four pairs of men and women—arrived on the scene, dressed in Spanish costume. They were wearing capes quartered half in gold brocade and half in green velvet; and the Spanish ladies were all dressed in silk, with their *mantelli* of various colours, edged with many jewels. They presented themselves in front of the Duchess Isabella and spoke a few words of good wishes on behalf of the 'King and Queen of Spain'.[14] Beginning with the Spaniards, each group of dancers, who were clothed in luxurious versions of their national costume, performed to the accompaniment of their own musicians a traditional dance from their country. The Spanish troupe was followed by the Poles, by the Hungarians, and then the Turks, who approached the dais on horseback. Their ambassador explained that the Sultan was unaccustomed to sending representatives to such grand occasions, and they did not know quite what to do; he was invited to take a seat in his customary way, and cushions were placed on the floor. At this point of the entertainment, Ludovico left the chamber to change into a *turcha de horo tirata*, in honour of the Turkish contingent. A knight and nobles then appeared with dancers, sent by the Emperor of the West, and the last national dance was provided by representatives of the King and Queen of France. A final performance from all the masqueraders dancing together was followed at eleven o'clock by the arrival of another eight, who only wore shirts and doublets over their satin capes. They began to dance energetically, making many quick movements with the feet and leaps into the air, which for a while was an amusing sight. Further Spanish and Neapolitan dances continued until half past midnight, when the masque began. Revealed from behind a curtain at the far end of the roon by the altar,[15] Leonardo's *pièce de résistance*, the

83. Portrait of Ludovico il Moro, attributed to Boltraffio.

136

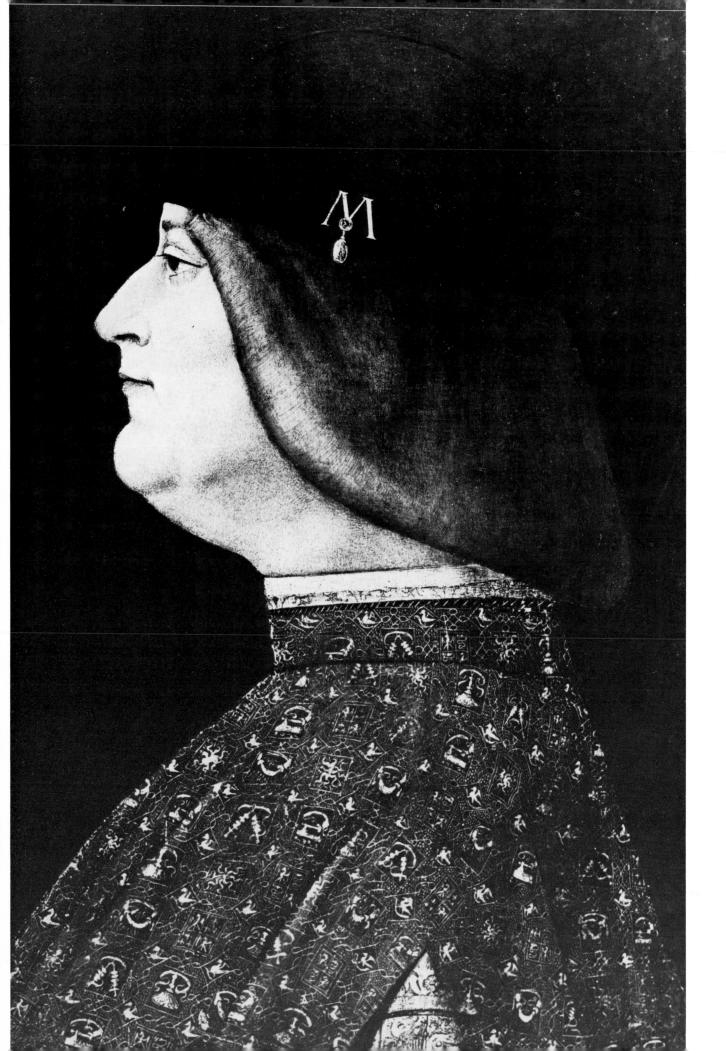

paradise, was made like half an egg, which was lined with gold, with a vast number of starlights inside, and openings revealing the seven planets. Each planet was represented by a man, and each one in turn recited Bellincione's verses in praise of Isabella, after which she was presented with a souvenir copy of the incantations. And all who had seen this wonderous masque gave profuse thanks to Ludovico, who had made the whole occasion possible.

Such festivities show the highly self-conscious use of costume within performance. In court the significance of decorative symbols and styles of dress (such as historic or foreign clothing) is used with great effect, as in painted and other works of art. Isabella of Aragon probably much resented the figure of her uncle by marriage, for when she arrived in Milan he was at the height of his power. She and Gian Galeazzo spent much of their time leading a comparatively quiet life in the castle at Pavia, from which in 1490 she wrote despairingly: 'In these jousts, they were forever shouting "Moro, Moro"—meaning Signor Ludovico—never did they shout "Duke, Duke".'[16] Tradition has passed down a story which ascribes to Ludovico the plot to murder Gian Galeazzo. It is unlikely: but the meaning behind the emblems of three *vesti* once ordered by Ludovico induce suspicion.[17] The gowns were to be made for Ludovico himself, for his nephew Gian Galeazzo, and for Galeazzo Sanseverino. The device chosen for each was rather daring behind its apparently innocuous appearance; it constituted the image of a clock with bells which rang on those clothes worn by Gian Galeazzo and Sanseverino, but there was a slight variation on Ludovico's gown which, according to the accompanying motto, made the other clocks toll. He was evidently indicating that the power was in his hands and perhaps foresaw his own usurpation of the title of Duke following the death of Gian Galeazzo in 1494.

There are many cases in which an individual's interests are symbolized by the devices chosen to decorate their clothes. Both Beatrice and Isabella d'Este were extremely fond of music, and had been taught to dance by Ambrogio da Urbino; they also sang, and were accomplished musicians, playing the viola and the lute. Beatrice enjoyed travelling with a musical accompaniment and Isabella reflected her keen interest by the frequent use of notes and other musical allusions in the embroidery decorating her gowns.

Beatrice and Isabella, through the evidence in their correspondence, enter the history books as two of the most innovative ladies of fashion. Beatrice was described by Muralto as '*novarum vestium inventrix*',[18] and the Queen of Poland also ascribed all the beautiful Italian fashions to the inventive young Duchess.[19] In contrast, Giovio looked upon her with a much sterner eye, accusing her of being thoroughly ostentatious and a lady of great pride.[20] She worked extremely hard at creating what appeared—even to some of her contemporaries—over-dramatic effects. Ludovico recalled how his consort once worked all night long, just like an industrious old woman, to get some *vesti alla turchesca* made, which she had designed herself. One afternoon in Pavia, Ludovico went out to meet the two duchesses (of Bari and of Milan), only to find them and all their ladies dressed in those Turkish costumes devised by Beatrice.[21] Both amused and delighted with the accomplishments of his spirited wife, Ludovico once had to admit: 'My wife is so good at hawking, that she surpasses me entirely.'[22] When necessary, she proved the perfect diplomat but her life at Milan was coloured by some carefree pranks.[23] Her strength of character must have won the respect of the Duke, who soon after his marriage turned his attentions away from his mistress Cecilia Gallerani, partly due to Beatrice's determination to refuse gifts which bore any resemblance to those given by Ludovico to Cecilia.[24]

Ludovico's economic policies had caused Milan to prosper, so that the annual revenue was considerable. There were apparently endless resources available for extravagant spending on the richest clothes, jewels, festivities and other displays of material wealth. Within two years of her marriage to Ludovico, Beatrice possessed no less than 84 new dresses in her wardrobe at Vigevano. Leonora, Beatrice's mother, took the opportunity of viewing the collection, and was conducted to the costly garments by the jester Mariolo. In a long letter to Isabella, Prosperi wrote a detailed description of all that he had seen. With a hint of malice and jealousy he quoted their mother's remark that Beatrice's wardrobe looked just like a sacristy fitted with ecclesiastical vestments. Beyond, a series of small rooms contained cabinets of Murano glass, porcelain dishes, maiolica, ivories, crystals, enamels, perfumes, and hunting implements.[25]

Isabella did not have as much money available as did Beatrice. Nevertheless, her desire to possess a wardrobe of sumptuous garments and novel accessories was greater than any concern about falling into debt. In November 1490, Isabella wrote to Giorgio Brognolo, ordering:

> a beautiful lining of *zebellini* for an *albernia*. We
> wish you to buy eighty beautiful best quality ones,
> even if it means you have to search through all
> Venice. And would you try to find one to wear as a
> muff, with the head; and if it costs ten ducats, as
> long as it is a good one, do not worry about the
> price. In addition, would you send eight *braccia* of
> crimson satin of the very best that you can find in
> Venice, for it is needed to make the said *albernia*. I
> leave you to use your own judgement . . .[26]

The following year, Isabella wrote a letter to Ziliolo, who was on his way to France, sending him 200 gold ducats and a list of things to buy. It included engraved amethysts, paternosters of gold and of black amber, some of the best *tela rensa*, pale blue cloth (*panno celeste*) for a *camora* and black cloth to make an *albernia* 'of a quality that cannot be equalled; and do not think about the price, even if it does cost as much as 10 ducats for a *braccio*'. Isabella did not require any change from the money, but should there happen to be a little left over, would he spend it on some small novelty.[27] Isabella had admirable taste, and on many occasions was imitated by Beatrice, who in one letter asked her sister whether she could borrow the bodice (*pecto*) of the *camora* with a motif of tears, made of gold brocade, so that she could have a similar one made for herself.[28] Whether the tears were made by pearls and other stones embroidered to the bodice, or whether all the motifs were incorporated in the woven pattern of the brocade, we cannot tell: the former is more likely.

Though many new ideas were conjured up by the protagonists of fashion, they did very much depend on weavers, embroiderers and jewellers for their skilful interpretation of themes. Beatrice's letters to her mother and sister make several references to a Spanish embroiderer, Maestro Jorba, who was in the service of the Duchess of Ferrara. Much to the annoyance of Isabella, he was left by Leonora at Vigevano in 1493, to design hangings and gowns for Beatrice. After his return to Ferrara, Leonora sent Beatrice a new design for a *camora* which the Spaniard had invented. Beatrice acknowledged:

> I have tonight received the design of the *camora*
> made by Jorba, which I admire very much, and
> have just shown to my embroiderer, as your
> Highness advised. He remarks that the flowers of
> the pattern are all the same size, and since the
> *camora* will naturally be cut narrower above than
> below, the flowers ought to be altered in the same
> proportion. I have not yet decided what will be the
> best thing to do, but thought I would tell you what
> Schavezi says, and wait to hear what you advise,
> and then do whatever you think best.[29]

Occasionally, other names appear which may relate to artist–designers employed at court, though most of the work put into the making of clothes was done so anonymously. Seven years after the betrothal of Alfonso d'Este to Anna Sforza, Leonora Duchess of Ferrara still had not met her promised daughter-in-law, but she sent her a gift of a beautiful doll with a wardrobe of clothes designed by the best artists in Ferrara. Also anonymously conceived was that 'new trimming made of grey lamb's wool' noticed by Teodora degli Angeli at the celebrations following the birth of Beatrice's first son, Ercole in 1493.[30]

However, a certain Niccolò da Correggio is mentioned in 1493. Beatrice, who was industriously arranging the wedding celebrations for Bianca Sforza and the Emperor Maximilian was prepared to abandon her mourning clothes after only a fortnight's confinement of grief, following the death of her mother. Eager to determine what new outfit she might stun her audience with at the occasion, Beatrice wrote to her sister, asking permission to use a particular design for a *camora* suggested by Niccolò da Correggio:

> I cannot remember if your Highness has yet carried out the idea of that pattern of linked tracery which Messer Niccolò da Correggio suggested to you when we were last together. If you have not yet ordered the execution of this design, I am thinking of having his invention carried out in massive gold, on a *camora* of purple velvet, to wear on the day of Madonna Bianca's wedding. . . .[31]

This pattern was described as a '*fantasia dei vinci*', almost certainly a pun on Leonardo's name, and as a motif it probably owes its invention to the court painter. It is found in the original ceiling decoration of the great hall in the Castello di Porto Giova, where Gian Galeazzo's marriage celebrations had taken place, and also on the vaulting of the sacristy of Santa Maria delle Grazie in Milan. One month after the ceremonial procedures of the marriage between Bianca Sforza and Maximilian, Beatrice recalled the events in a letter to her sister. Bianca rode in the triumphal car which had been given to Beatrice by Leonora at Ferrara. It was drawn by four snow-white horses. The Queen of the Romans wore a gown of crimson satin, embroidered in gold thread and covered with jewels. Her train was immensely long and the sleeves were made to look like two wings, which had a very fine appearance. On her head she wore an ornament of magnificent diamonds and pearls. Messer Galeazzo Pallavicino carried the train, and Count Conrado de' Lando and Count Manfedo Torniello each supported one of the sleeves. The Duchesses Isabella (of Aragon) and Beatrice sat on either side of Bianca. Isabella wore:

> a *camora* of crimson satin, with gold cords looped over it, as in my grey cloth *camora* . . . and I [Beatrice] wore my purple velvet *camora*, with the pattern of the links worked in massive gold and green and white enamel, about six inches deep on the front and back of my bodice, and on both sleeves. The *camora* was lined with cloth of gold, and with it I wore a girdle of Saint Francis made of large pearls, with a beautiful clear-cut ruby for clasp.[32]

The Duchesses' triumphal car was followed by twelve more chariots containing noble ladies of Milan, and the ladies of the queen, who wore livery of tan *camore* and mantles of bright green satin.

The layer of looped gold cords over Isabella's crimson *camora* relates to the dress depicted on Beatrice's tomb in the Certosa at Pavia. The same design idea was probably worn at the birth celebrations of Ercole Sforza. A description written by Prosperi on that occasion described Beatrice's dress in some detail, for the benefit of Isabella d'Este:

> Your sister had a *veste* made for her of alternating horizontal bands of gold tissue [*tela d'oro*] and of crimson velvet. And over the velvet she had a *zellosia a mandoli* of silver threads, and from the lower edge of each band of velvet fell long strands of the silver over the bands of gold cloth, in such a way as to give a very graceful effect.[33]

No matter to what extent the designers at court worked at inventing new patterns and ideas, the ultimate word always lay in the hands of the employer. Beatrice and Isabella were particularly imaginative in their ways of dress. But they stand out because only from their letters have historians been able to glean some particularly illuminating clues about their search for new ideas. However, whilst they represent a frequently extreme form of fashion, the methods by which they were introduced to novel techniques, structures and motifs, must compare with those available to other women of high fashion at the same date.

Beatrice and Isabella, daughters of Ercole d'Este, had inherited both the good breeding and the more superficial, theatrical lifestyle from the many splendid spectacles which were held at the court of Ferrara. Such qualities were readily absorbed by the courts in Milan and Mantua after each had married. Yet the extravagant ways, especially of the Sforza court, somehow lacked that honest generosity and sense of refinement which had been a feature of the Este family as a long-established ruling household.

There is a strong contrast between the deserved blessing by the Pope of Borso d'Este, Duke of Ferrara, and the pretentions of his contemporary, Galeazzo Maria Sforza, Duke of Milan. A visit made by Emperor Frederick III in 1473 gave Galeazzo the opportunity of cladding himself in more and more presumptuous garments as the ceremonies progressed. It was not long before he was beheaded that Cicco Simonetta witnessed the meeting of Duke Galeazzo Maria with the Emperor. The Duke was dressed in a *turcha* of gold with a wonderful stone (a diamond?) and pearls on his hat, and with a fine brooch (*fermaglio*) on his leg. Then, after the ceremonial entry of the Emperor, on the fourth day of his visit, Duke Galeazzo was clothed 'as a duke, that is, in a *turcha* of black and silver *zetonino*; and over this he wore a *mantello* of cloth

84. The tombs of Ludovico il Moro and Beatrice d'Este at the Certosa in Pavia, ordered from the sculptor Cristoforo Solari in 1497, the year of Beatrice's death. The bands of latticed metal threads finishing in tassels are a feature of the dress worn by Beatrice for the birth celebrations of their son Ercole in 1493.

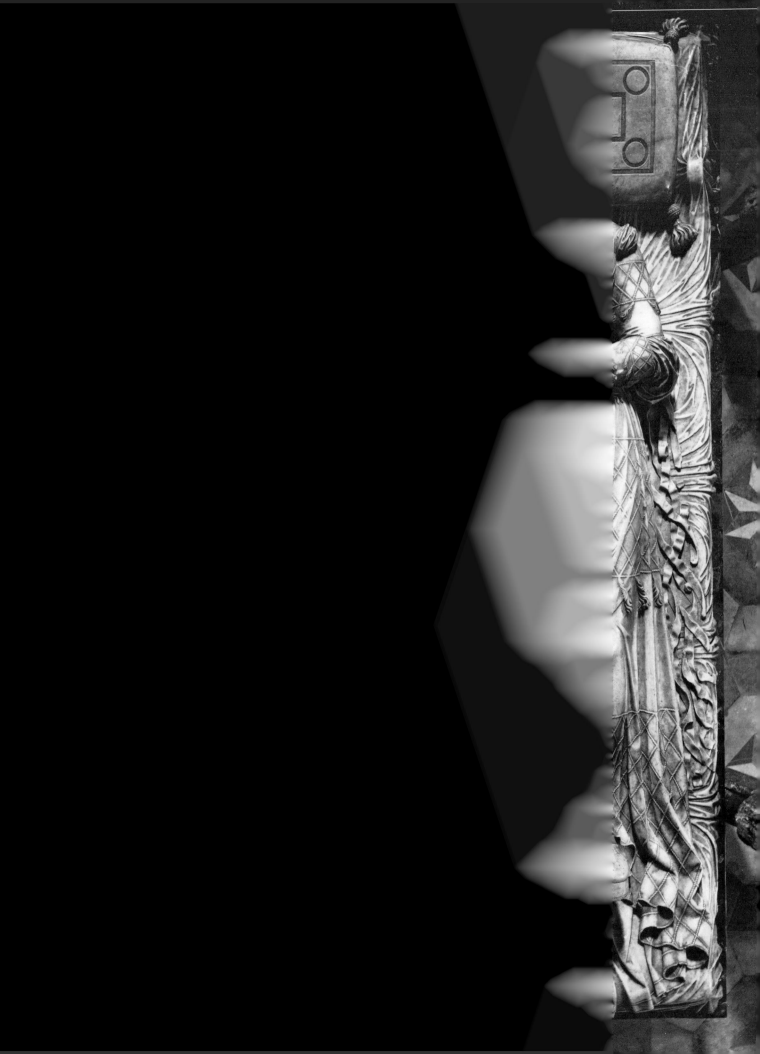

of gold [*drapo d'oro*] with a hood [*capuzo*] lined with ermine, rather like a cardinal's cloak, and on his cap [*boneto*], a fine sapphire and a *ballasso* with a diamond and a huge pearl'. On the eighth day, the Duke wore three *veste*: 'the first was a *mantelina* denoting '*quod est dechanus XII Parum Francia*'; the second, a *mantello d'oro in habito ducale* worn over the first; and the third layer was a royal one'.[34] The style and shape of his cap are ambiguous, but perhaps correspond to the ducal hat worn by Federigo da Montefeltro, Duke of Urbino.

That there was a recognized form of ducal clothing is supported by an entry in the Ferrarese diary for Easter Day, 1471.[35] The Pope took Mass in Saint Peter's, and presented the Duke of Ferrara, Borso d'Este, with a sword and spurs; the Pope blessed him, and Tommaso Paleologo, despot of the Morea, girded him with the sword, while Napoleone Orsini and Costanzo Sforza fitted the spurs to his ankles. The Pope also gave him a fur-lined *manto* of gold brocade which reached down to the ground, a *bereta a la ducale* with *orechie* (ear-pieces), also fur-lined, a neckchain of gold with precious stones and a ducal staff of gold. The following day, Borso was given by the Pope a *rosa*, made of 500 ducats' worth of gold, a *manto*, *colana* and *scofia*, which he wore as he rode through Rome from Saint Peter's to Saint Mark's. Borso was much loved and respected by the people of Ferrara: '. . . he never took a wife, and was the most magnanimous *signore* that ever lived, being very generous in giving to whoever demanded something of him'. And he always went about clothed in '*panno d'oro arrizado*, both in town and in the country, when he stayed at home, and when he went hunting; and he held a great court'.[36]

Borso d'Este died in 1471, and was succeeded as Duke by the very popular Ercole who, two years later, married Leonora of Aragon. The name of the Palazzo Schifanoia reflects the keen interest of the Este family, their courtiers and their subjects, in jokes and pageantry. An occasion such as the Festival of Saint George had traditionally included an enactment of the slaying of the dragon. The patron saint's Feast Day, 24 April, also set the scene for the *palio*, the name given to a great horse race and equally to the precious length of cloth awarded to its winner. In 1496, the main race of the day, run for a piece of gold brocade, was followed by the more comic races of donkeys, men and women. The latter were won with prizes of white, red and green *palii*—the heraldic colours of the house of Este. The runners-up of the women's race were given token cloths of little value; the second prize was some *pignolato* for a *guarnello*, the third received *bambasina*, and the fourth had material for some *scuffie*, and a pair of shoes.[37] Such trophies were not always provided by the Duke, but also by the guilds of Ferrara. In addition, Ercole's subjects enjoyed the many other street entertainments and carnivals realized by him, some of which occasioned the wearing of masks about the street. During periods of violence, these were

85. (opposite) Detail from The Flagellation, by Piero della Francesca. The figure on the right is grandly dressed in a *veste* of luxurious blue velvet brocaded with gold, fit to be worn by a duke or a king on ceremony.

86. (pages 146–7) The Triumph of Venus and the Sign of Taurus, an Allegory of the Month of April, by Francesco del Cossa, c. 1470. The lightheartedness and allegory of the Schifanoia frescoes correspond to the pageantry and festivity enjoyed through the streets of Ferrara.

forbidden—but permission to wear the masks was always restored in better times, because such carnivals were considered a public right.

Generous acts were not purely selfless; for the introduction of the Maundy Thursday ceremony of the washing of feet, performed by the Duke and his brothers, was not merely a tradition imported from Spain through the marriage of Leonora of Aragon with Ercole d'Este in 1473, but was a productive exercise in public relations. Acts of kind hospitality to foreign visitors have made their way into diaries and chronicles, too. The travels of Pero Tafur in the 1430s had included a visit to Gubbio, where the Spaniard had encountered the exceedingly pious Guid'Antonio da Montefeltro, Count of Urbino and Montefeltro, who had offered Tafur sets of his own clothing with which to continue the journey.[38] However small or great was the act of generosity, it was essential that every man's actions be the outward reflection of his education, manners and character. Each man and woman was acutely conscious of his or her own image.

6 The Image of Beauty: 1450-1480

With improvements in travel and the publication of printed books (from 1465 in Italy) the spread of ideas was assisted. From the mid-century, more artists were settling in the courts around Italy, amongst them Mantegna and Piero della Francesca who were employed by the Marquis of Mantua and the Duke of Urbino respectively. Approaching more nearly to the ideals of perfect proportion, mathematically planned on paper before construction, the architectural monuments to the Renaissance were being erected in increasing numbers. Leon Battista Alberti designed the facade of Santa Maria Novella in Florence in 1470, and in 1478 Bramante's drawings for San Satiro, Milan, were being realized. In addition to the investment in the arts for public display, there was a passion for collecting jewels, manuscripts and paintings—partly for financial security, but also for private enjoyment. Hand-in-hand with the technical advances made in the fine arts and architecture, literature and music flourished. The interaction of all the art forms, for a long time an integral part of Church art and of court life, was particularly strong in this period which, not surprisingly, has been christened the beginning of a Golden Age.

The establishing of the portrait as an art form in the latter part of the Quattrocento allowed painted costume to be seen from a new angle and at closer proximity than before. However, the profile portrait as a work of art was only of secondary importance. Its principal purpose was to establish an image of identity. The development of portraiture, despite its consonance with an increased interest and skill in rendering anatomical form, owes its existence to men's desire for self-advertisement.

During the course of the century there was a gradual concentration of power and money into the hands of fewer people. In 1459, because of the uncontrollable expenditure made on women's and girls' dress and accessories, restrictions were imposed on those women who were no longer content to go about 'as wives and daughters of merchants and private citizens', but who wished to clothe themselves 'as wives and daughters of great princes and *signori*' instead.[1] The development of a 'modern' class structure involved the rise of the new bourgeoisie.

On entering Bruges in 1468, Charles the Bold was accompanied by a group of foreign merchants, amongst whom was the extravagant Tommaso Portinari, manager of the Bruges branch of the Medici bank:

> First rode the Venetians, wearing costumes of red velvet. Then came the Florentines, with an advance guard of 60 torchbearers clad in blue and pages clad in cloth of silver and with short cloaks of red velvet. The horses wore covers of white silk with borders of blue velvet and the merchants themselves were dressed in black silk damask with red cloaks. Their leader, the powerful Tommaso Portinari, was as finely arrayed as the Duke himself.[2]

Not everyone had the aspirations of Portinari to become a Duke. However, dress remained as important as ever, if not more so. The principal layering and terminology of Italian dress in this period remains consistent with that in the earlier half of the Quattrocento. Also invariable is the attitude towards clothing; in particular, when a garment was worn at home, it did not matter if it was somewhat worse for wear. There are several direct references to used or 'sad' garments in inventories. When Alessandra Macinghi Strozzi died in 1470, she left three *gamurre*— one *mormorina*, one of old black silk and one of new black *rascia*. The five *cioppe* left in her wardrobe were all of black, and comprised a mixture of good and worn ones, one being of 'sad' *guarnello* to wear at home.[3]

The shapes of clothes worn by the majority of the population could not have altered very quickly in Florence (or probably elsewhere, for that matter), for a law of 1464 asserted that dresses had to be worn for a minimum of three years before they could be traded in; and in listing his wife's bridal outfit, Luca Landucci makes a special point of mentioning when a garment is new—presumably the exception rather than the rule.[4] The law of 1464 stated that women could have one overgarment dyed with *chermisi*, whether it be a *cioppa* or *giornea*.[5] It reinforced an earlier statute of 1456, which declared that women were allowed up to two overgowns of silk at any one time—one for winter, the other for summer—be they *cioppe* or *giornee*, whichever was preferred.[6]

However, there was always the clause which Alberti had written: that is, in a wardrobe comprising three sets of clothes it was permissible and morally acceptable that one should be new, for best wear.[7] Indeed, the wardrobes of the arbiters of fashion were filled with apparently limitless sets of clothes. Around the middle of the fifteenth century, various changes in the structure of garments are detectable. Particularly apparent were the closer-fitting bodices of garments, and the gradually lowering point

87. Portrait of a Young Lady, attributed to Antonio del Pollaiuolo, *c.* 1470. Attention is drawn to the face framed by the strings of pearls, ribbons, a brooch and a veil. The last is stretched over a fine wire understructure which curves round the front of the ear.

88. Miracles of Saint Vincent Ferrer, detail, by Ercole de' Roberti. In the 1460s the sleeves were set at a much higher point over the shoulder, and were cut narrower down the arm, often with slits which revealed the underlying chemise. The torso was moulded by padded doublets, carefully arranged folds, and a slim waistline set slightly higher at the back than the front.

Colour plate 9 (opposite) Detail of The Coronation of the Virgin, by Filippo Lippi. The grouping of figures at all angles gives an opportunity to show the various styles of arranging veils and hair. There is much fanciful painting of gold over the young women's otherwise fashionable clothing; these superficial references to the tabs of Roman armour add a historical feel to the picture. The young boys dressed as angels wear *gonnelle* (see page 119).

Colour plates 10 and 11 (overleaf) Battista Sforza and Federigo da Montefeltro, by Piero della Francesca, c. 1465. The Duchess of Urbino's jewellery and sleeves demonstrate how much money was invested in gems and clothing. Her lavish gold brocaded sleeves with the pattern picked out in red silk velvet pile form a strong contrast with the unexpected black of her bodice. The Duke is dressed in best quality *chermisi*. His hat is of a particular shape designated to the highest ranks; it is also worn by Ludovico Gonzaga in the Camera degli Sposi frescoes (see page 144).

across the chest from which pleats and folds neatly fall. The sleeves became tighter, until they finally 'split under the strain', as Leonardo put it,[8] to allow the chemise to puff through. Most sleeves, except those of men's doublets and of ample over-garments, were not sewn, but laced in at the shoulders, and the shoulderline by the 1460s was considerably higher than before.

Some of the most detailed pieces of documentary evidence for clothing in the period 1450–80 are the letters of Galeazzo Maria Sforza.[9] They are dated 1475, and are mainly addressed to Gotardo Panigarole. They are of interest, for rather than providing descriptions of the most lavish costumes worn for a special ceremony at court, they offer insight into the day-to-day acquisition of clothing within the Duke's household.

The general clothing supplied to Galeazzo for his own use between 17 February and 26 September of that year included several *zuparelli*, mostly made of *zambelotto* in black or a shade of red. An interesting entry is that of *bredoni e maneghetti* to put on a *zuparello d'armare*. Other general items of clothing are *vestiti*, *guardacori*, *gheleri*, *mantelli*, *turche*, *zupponi* and *mongilli*. A strong foreign flavour pervades the list, particularly in terms of

PERFECIT OPUS

PERFECIT OPUS

overgarments (*vestiti*), some of which are made in the Spanish fashion, and one of which is *a la franzesa*. To wear on his head were ordered some black hats (*capelli*), a crimson *berretta* for the daytime, and a few *berrette da nocte* to wear in bed. As in most inventories and accounts, there are no references to shoes, although pairs of *zibroni* made of *zetonino raso cremexino* and lined with *zendal rosso* may constitute some form of foot- or leg-wear. Sleeves at this period, except in the case of some overgowns, were nearly always made separately, and tied in at the shoulders: Galeazzo's orders therefore include pairs of sleeves for his *gheleri*. The occasional unusual item also appears, such as the scarlet cloth (*panni de scalata*) for a *stomaco*, and a *redena da bottono* of *brochato d'oro*—not to mention a pair of gloves for dancing (*guanti da balla*) made from *pelle di camozo* and lined with *scarlata*, and 400 handkerchiefs (*panicelli da naso*).

Duke Galeazzo was also responsible for clothing members of the court, who were variously supplied with *mantelli*, *vestiti*, *zuparelli* and *turche* but mostly were distributed *zuponi*, *zornee*, and *gheleri*. A certain Turcheto, listed both as *cameriero* and *sotto cameriero*, was apparently in need of six *camise* with several pairs of

Colour plate 12 (opposite) Detail of The Family and Court of Ludovico Gonzaga, by Mantegna, *c.* 1471–4. Conspicuous consumption, indicated here through the presence of more gold thread than silk in the textiles, was a demonstration of wealth and power. Some men attached to the court each wear one white and one red stocking, a feature of livery purchased as part of the Duke's household expenses.

89. Another detail from the Miracles of St Vincent Ferrer, by Ercole de' Roberti. To the right of the picture, the man in a conical hat and pointed shoes, with an eccentric angular line to his doublet, is a Burgundian. He forms a distinct contrast with the more sober Italian standing slightly behind and with the orientals and timeless old men elsewhere in the scene.

underpants (*mutande*), two pairs of hose (*calze*), and a cap (*bareta*). One *cameriero*, Antonio Carazola, was given an interesting *zornea de la moscharole*, the folds of which appear to come from the waistline, and not across the chest (*tuta afaldata et non da petto e sia recamata da cavalero*). In addition, the court organist, Giorgio de Gerardo, was supplied with a *zupone* of velvet, together with a knee-length *mantello* with side openings to put his arms through. The most common colours mentioned in the letters are *morello* and *cremesino*, though there are garments of *alexandrino*, *verde*, *berettino*, *turchino* and one of *pelo de lione*. *Bruno* is mentioned, but only with reference to mourning, not as a colour: and interestingly, *pavonazzo* is not mentioned at all in these accounts, despite its common usage in Italy at this time. Perhaps it was being reserved for mourning.

The letters do not include any garments for the Duchess, for presumably she must have had her own wardrobe. However, these documents are not without references to ladies' garments, for there are several entries destined for '*uno nostro segreto*' ('a little secret of mine')—meaning, of course, the Duke's mistresses. His favourite, the Countess of Melzo, is mentioned quite openly; she received gifts mostly of *mongini* and *zupe* that year. Mostly made of fine gold brocade, the list does also include one or two more humble *zupe* made from *terzanello*, *sandale* or *bombaxine venetiane*. She was also given a saddle, cushion and other possessions, including jewellery. Some of the clothing specified as '*per uno*

90. Lovers, a detail from The Triumphs of Venus by Francesco del Cossa, *c.* 1470. The regular folds of the tunics and dresses were probably kept in place by means of ties on the inside of the garments.

91. The Interior of a House, detail, attributed to Fra Carnevale. The women walking in the foreground demonstrate how they handled the long skirts of their dresses in movement.

92. The Proof of the True Cross, by Piero della Francesca, c. 1452–66. The twisting and wrapping of narrow veils about the hair and the folding back of the sleeves onto the shoulder in a toga-like manner is a conscious reference to the classical past.

nostro secreto' may also have been intended for her, especially as those entries mainly refer to *camorre* and to pairs of sleeves of very rich cloth, which the Countess would have needed to wear under the *mongini* and *zupe*.

Though horned understructures were often worn by ladies, and the shape of the hairstyle continued to be built out with twists and piles of false hair, the particularly large garlands and *balzi* were disappearing. Women's hair (whether real or not) was more tightly wrapped round the head, and often bound with fine strips (*bende*) of silk or linen veiling, strings of pearls and braids or ribbons. Their necklines were becoming a little décolleté, leaving flesh bare enough to accommodate fine necklaces and pendants. As the necklines of dresses dip lower, so the lengths of the men's doublets creep upwards. How much of the body should one reveal? Moralists attempted to answer this question, but men and women of fashion continued to pursue their own images of identity and ideal beauty.

What was considered attractive about young women of marriageable age? Marriage was the result of a financial agreement, indeed: nevertheless, the descriptions of prospective wives speak not only of manners, but of deportment, the colour of hair and tint of complexion. Few sumptuary legislations were adhered to; but should they be enforced, how were young women, at their most beautiful, marriageable, and potentially fashionable age, to stun the eligible bachelors? For this reason, there were some cases of concessions being made to young unmarried women; occasionally they were extended to cover the first three years of marriage.

The ideal beauty of Simonetta Vespucci is now legendary, immortalized in the writings of Lorenzo the Magnificent. In talking about the source of inspiration for the love expressed in his verse, Lorenzo recalled a lost Florentine beauty. He observed that:

> amongst other excellent gifts, she had a sweet and
> attractive manner [*maniera*], and that all those men
> who knew of her or had made her acquaintance
> believed themselves to be fervently in love with
> her. And women, even those of the same age as
> her, were not in the least envious, but highly
> respected and praised her beauty and kindness. And
> yet it seemed impossible to believe that so many
> men should adore her without jealousy, and that so
> many women lauded her without envy.[10]

Lorenzo wrote of Simonetta's physical appearance in the following terms:

> Her beauty, as I have said, was wonderful: she was
> of an attractive size and ideal height; the tone of
> her complexion was white yet not pallid, fresh yet
> not glowing. Her face was grave yet not proud,
> sweet and pleasing, not frivolous or light-hearted.
> Her eyes were animated and motionless, with no
> trace of conceit or meanness. And her whole body
> was so well proportioned that, compared with
> other women, she displayed dignity . . . in walking
> and in dancing . . . and in every move she made she
> was handsome and elegant. Her hands were so
> beautiful, more so than all others created by

Nature. She dressed in those fashions which suited a noble and gentle lady, in offering dignity and grace: she spoke truly, sweetly in clear sentences . . . the words and the pleasantries were witty and sharp, yet without offense, softy penetrating; and her intellect was quite marvellous, perhaps rather more than other ladies wished. She accomplished all this without ostentation or presumption, whilst avoiding a particular vice found in most women; and that is in thinking they know a great deal, they become insupportable in always wishing to pass judgement, thereby gaining a reputation for being know-alls.[11]

The freshness of youth spoken of in descriptions of processions and dances performed by young men and women is often accompanied by remarks on the magical charm of jewels, rich textiles and deep colours. Yet Alberti's poem about the love of his youth is the complete antithesis of reality. She was a brunette; she did not wear *balzi, scuffie* and *gorgere* on her head, but instead only a garland of grass. Her light step, sparkling eyes and charming smile spelt a freshness and grace accomplished with no artificial embellishments:

My dear brunette, with the water from the fountain, each morning washes her brow and her serene breasts. She does not wear *balzi, scuffie* and *gorgere* like you, haughty proud women. A garland of grass adorns her golden head; and she goes about light-footed and naturally, and with sparkling eyes she always smiles.[12]

The moralists had their views on cosmetics, and as usual Leonardo had something to say about the subject:

Do you not see that of all human attractions, it is the beautiful face, and not lavish ornaments, which causes the passers-by to stop in their steps? And this I say to you who adorn yourself with gold or with other rich decorations. Do you not see the resplendent beauties of youth diminish with the use of excessive and over-cultivated ornaments? And have you not seen the poor mountain folk wrapped up in their rude clothing possess much greater beauty than those who are lavishly adorned?[13]

93. Simonetta Vespucci, attributed to Piero di Cosimo; a posthumous portrait of the idealized beauty.

Similarly, Savonarola expressed the belief that women should allow the beauty of their souls to shine forth. San Bernardino had

also expressed this view in religious terms, but he did not refrain from making some strong-worded references to men. The friar recognized a somewhat feminine narcissism in the way that men wore perfumes and dyed their hair. It was not an illusion, he warned: sodomy was rife, even amongst married men.[14]

The use of perfumes and potions therefore was practised by both men and women. Despite this fact, warnings against the use of artificial embellishments were normally issued by men and directed towards women. One verse of the *Canto della Pinzochera* (*Song of the Devotee*) mocks the potentially ruinous effects of 'aids' to beauty:

> Musks, lavenders, and other scents have caused
> looking-glasses to shatter; our brows, now
> plucked, are but flesh, and our teeth decay.
> Cosmetics, sponges, perfume and beauty spots,
> filled with wondrous properties, together with
> balms and unguents to anoint the face, have
> irreversibly changed the skins they have touched.
> And then to wash clean away all blemishes, scum,
> and ashen tones, you are offered remedies
> manufactured in Heaven—distilled waters of
> various kinds to clarify the skin, smooth the
> wrinkles and firm the breasts.[15]

The recipe book of Caterina Sforza[16] includes hundreds of

94. Barbara of Brandenburg, wife of Ludovico Gonzaga (detail), by Mantegna. The Germanic origins of the Marchioness may have caused her to introduce foreign ways of arranging her hair to the Gonzaga court. However by this date her style of dress would be recognized as primarily Mantuan.

95. A Miracle of San Bernardino, by Fiorino di Lorenzo. According to the individual, tunics would be worn with or without belts. Hanging sleeves could be tucked into the belt at the back of the waist for reasons of both practicality and affectation.

161

remedies for washing the face and rinsing away the wrinkles and blemishes, for blonding the hair and making it grow down to the ankles, and for firming the breasts. The recipes were compiled probably around 1480, for Caterina died in 1509, a widow vowed nun; the various concoctions therefore would not have applied to the last years of her life, but to a more youthful interest in beauty. Solutions were made from boiling fruits, eggshells, egg whites, the roots of plants, and many other ingredients. Some may have possessed genuine chemical powers of transformation; many were founded on magic and superstition.

The majority of recipes for women were to be applied to their complexion, and are generally listed as *acqua da far bella*. Some of these consisted of diverse forms of distilled water; others were a little more extraordinary:

> Take a white dove, pluck it, and remove the wings, the head, the feet and the intestines and throw them away. Then take equal amounts of grape-juice and sweet almond oil, and as much dittany as you need for two doves, and wash this well. Then distil all these things together, and with this solution wash the face.[17]

Another recipe was guaranteed to dye anything which was immersed in this solution:

> Take some rain- or well-water, and urine from a child of about five years old, followed by white vinegar, live lime and oak-ashes. Mix them together and boil them until the liquid is reduced by a third; then strain it through a piece of felt. Afterwards, fetch some alum and throw it into the solution. When you wish to dye something, take what colour you want, and grind it, and put the amount you think best in the liquid for as long as you consider necessary; then put it in a glass vessel. After this, immerse the items you wish to dye, and they will come out the colour you see inside the glass. By boiling it for some time, or by putting it in a dung-bath for six or eight days, this will tint *corni*, feathers, furs, skins, hair, and other things.[18]

Many potions turned women's hair blond and rendered men's hair darker. Washing hands and face in nettle juice whitened the skin; while sparrow's brain added aphrodisiac qualities to any medicament. And finally the solution to a domestic crisis was a good dose of coral—for coral comforts the heart, and helps attract husband and wife together again.

Caterina Sforza was not the only collector of recipes, and as

96. Portrait of a Lady in Yellow, by Alesso Baldovinetti, *c.* 1470–5. The left sleeve of her dress is embroidered with a heraldic device (as yet unidentified).

one might expect, Isabella d'Este was eager to learn new secrets of beauty. In a letter written to Baron Bonvesino of Milan in July 1496, she expressed an anxious desire to know whether Gian Galeazzo, or any of his courtiers who also dyed their hair black, had a remedy to then make hair return to its pristine colour:

> because I remember, when I was last in Milan, having seen Count Francesco Sforza one day with dark hair, and the next wearing his natural colour. If you can find out how this is done, would you please let me know: and then write to me about it immediately, because I am dying to use it myself. You will be doing me a great favour.[19]

The fashion for dyeing men's hair darker had become a generally desired effect, so that a treatise by Teodore Trivulzio ensued, the *Tractatus de nigredine capillorum*.[20]

Musks and perfumes were also regularly used, many of them originating from the Orient. Barbers often doubled as perfumiers, and the court of Ludovico in Milan made sure that it was well served with scents. In 1486 a barber of Ludovico, Giuliano de Imeratici di Alessandria, was provided with a space in the clock tower of Vigevano both for accommodation and to open up a shop.[21] It was in Milan that the perfumiers joined up with the glovemakers to form one corporation,[22] which suggests that perfumed gloves were being used by the end of the fifteenth century.

One extremely proud Filippo da Napoli had arrived in Milan in 1474, advertising himself grandiosely as *magistro de profumi*. At that time, the Duke, Galeazzo Maria, was one of the most indulgent users of perfumes and other potions. A sign of great refinement, Galeazzo liked to take baths; and he also enjoyed keeping his hands well groomed, and having his hair cut into waves.[23] His interest in scents, balsam, musks, sweet waters, and other perfumes which possessed singularly revitalizing qualities was stimulated by informants. One was his ambassador in Venice, Leonardo Botta who, in a long letter, told Galeazzo of some particularly interesting examples of these things, which constituted a gift sent from the Sultan of Egypt.[24]

The Milanese court was not alone in enjoying the use of such exotic, perfumed recipes, although the Sforza men had something of a reputation in this field. It is said that Francesco Sforza's own example encouraged even his army to a certain resourcefulness in their style of dress: so much so, that Braccio di Montone's soldiers—who had often been defeated by the Milanese forces—disparagingly referred to them as 'that perfumed Sforza lot'.[25]

However, the moralists had spoken of men tinting and scenting themselves in a more general context, which suggests that such indulgences were practised elsewhere. But these variously concocted beauty products were not the only artificial adornments of which the critics spoke. The natural qualities of the face had for a long time been overshadowed by large and extravagant headdresses and, not least, by the glitter of jewels.

7 Jewellery and Embroidered Devices

I have had a splendid jewel made like that emerald one which was given to Your Illustrious Ladyship about three years ago. It consists of a square-cut table spinel of utter perfection, clear and of a good colour; and above it there is a table emerald and a beautiful pearl, with a crown and sidepieces of perfect diamonds. And I have arranged for letters in diamonds to go on the reverse, with the name of Your Illustrious Lady, worked in the same way as on the emerald jewel. I hope that it will be delivered within a few days, and that it will delight Your Ladyship when you see it. With regard to the reverse of the jewel, I can arrange for some motto or initials to take the place of the lettering, according to your wishes. For the same jewel there is a Saint George, made entirely of diamonds, and beneath his feet a pearl, formed by Nature to resemble a dragon. Never before was there made a jewel of such quality.[1]

It will come as no surprise to learn that Her Ladyship was Isabella d'Este. The richness of detail and quality of workmanship in Italian jewellery of the Quattrocento is almost legendary. Very few examples have survived, for despite the skill of the early Renaissance goldsmith and gem-cutter, pieces of jewellery were mostly regarded as composite arrangements of individually valued stones. It is known that Isabella d'Este, in order to purchase one marvellous jewel, was obliged to part with one or several others in exchange. And she was not alone in considering jewellery for the current price of its gold, silver and stones, rather in the way that the metal content of a coin was assessed.

Although there is comparatively little extant jewellery from the period, paintings and documents attest to its importance. Some was sought by serious connoisseurs for their collections; other items were regarded as frivolously as fashion, and were therefore broken up or melted down once the decorative style or thematic treatment was considered obsolete. The apparently more modestly conceived jewels which do survive were either tokens of love, or were held for some other special significance with a more lasting value.

The range of techniques applied to jewellery developed considerably during the period. Engraving became very popular, following the minor role it had previously played in the Middle Ages, when the decorative effect relied on the details of enamelling and filigree. There were many improved methods in gem-cutting, for it was realized that the clarity and colour of a stone could be enhanced greatly by the cutting of more and more faces. For a long time, the natural octahedron of the diamond had been cut in two, to yield a pointed diamond. In the fourteenth century, the very tip of this was sometimes cut off, to create a table form. Now, in the fifteenth century, experiments in much more elaborate methods of cutting gems were taking place.

The complexity of technique called for a bolder arrangement of form. In this respect, the development of the jeweller's art coincides with that of the weaver of figured brocades and velvets. The technique employed and the natural qualities of the material used are enhanced through the absorption and reflection of light, and take precedence over draughtsmanship and narrative content. This relationship between jewellery and textiles is a very important aspect of costume.

There is a logical balance in the arrangement of the stones, giving jewellery an architectonic quality. This is suggested in the following description of a pendant, 'a very beautiful jewel, which has a fine diamond above, and immediately beneath it is a large and impressive emerald stone, below which are three enormous drop pearls: this jewel cost 10,500 ducats'.[2]

The 1568 edition of Vasari's *Lives*[3] states that the gem-engraver's art owed its renewed importance primarily to the interest of collectors like Lorenzo de' Medici and his son Piero. His claims that Roman cameos were found daily in the catacombs and amongst other classical ruins are an exaggeration of the truth. Certainly, the interest in discovering antique cameos and other gems, as with manuscripts, was very strong. It did not take long for news to spread about 'the most beautiful emerald in the world today, which was discovered in the tomb of Marcus Tullus' daughter'.[4] The avid collector and dealer Niccolò Niccoli at one time bought a piece of chalcedony, reputed to have been carved by Polycletus, for five florins; he subsequently made a considerable profit by selling it to Pope Paul II for 200 gold ducats.[5] The same chalcedony later found its way into the hands of Lorenzo the Magnificent, who bought most of the Pope's and Niccoli's collections after their deaths. Other conscientious collectors included Pope Martin V, Leonello d'Este, Francesco Gonzaga, and the brothers Piero and Benedetto Dandolo of Venice (bankers, who had held, and probably kept, many of the

98. Portrait of a Young Woman, by Sebastiano Mainardi, *c.* 1490. The little devotional book, brooch and ring on the shelf behind may well have been presented as betrothal gifts.

167

patriciate's jewels as security).

In some cases, medieval and earlier engraved gems were recut (*ritocchi*) which made the identification of genuine antique cameos particularly difficult. Naturally, engravers must have taken advantage of this confused situation, and of the vogue for cameos and ancient cabuchons: some consequently forged examples of what they knew the collectors to be looking for. But apart from fraudulent copies of antique stones, there were also genuine commissions for replicas. In about 1428, Lorenzo Ghiberti was asked by a member of the Medici family to copy a cameo with an inscription of Nero's name and three figures, originally cut by Pyrgoteles or Polycletus. In addition, there were new jewels made *all' antica*, such as three belts (*coregie*) of gold, which Ludovico il Moro presented to Beatrice, in the year of their marriage, 1491.[6] Ludovico also had a cameo portrait of himself, made by Domenico dei Cammei, whose name suggests that he was a specialist in this art.[7] Further imitations were probably made from glass paste, a technique practised by several jewellers in Milan.

However, Renaissance jewellery cannot be called a direct revival of classical prototypes. And in spite of these discoveries of ancient objects, the art of the Italian gem-engraver and goldsmith was developing distinctive traits of its own; it was no more associated with the classical spirit than were sculpture, architecture, painting and literature. The architectural frames of devotional pendants and the like comprised classical columns in place of Gothic pinnacles; nymphs and satyrs became the subjects of engraved gems, and some illuminators of manuscripts included classical medallions and cameos in their decorative borders.

The engravers and goldsmiths were generally regarded as artisans in the way that a weaver or a painter might be. In fact, several painters and sculptors of the fifteenth century, especially in Florence, began their working lives by serving a goldsmith's apprenticeship. Amongst them are Ghiberti and Brunelleschi, Botticelli, Ghirlandaio, Lorenzo de Credi, Antonio del Pollaiuolo and Verocchio. Some of them continued to produce pendants and other objects whilst also developing their skills as painters. The most highly valued engravers and goldsmiths gained reputations by name, and some were offered residence and employment at the famous courts. Vasari claimed the two greatest masters of gem-engraving were Giovanni delle Corniuole, who worked for Lorenzo the Magnificent, and his rival, Domenico dei Cammei, who was employed at the court of Milan. In Mantua, the Mint was supervised by Bartolommeo Meliolo, one of Francesco Gonzaga's medallists; another position was given there to Giovanni Francesco de' Roberti. It was the latter who presented the Marquis with a golden parrot, once a novelty and much appreciated, but only four years after its acquisition, the gem was sent off to pay for new pieces of silver for the Gonzaga

99. Barbara Pallavicino, by Alessandro Araldi, *c.* 1495. This portrait shows how effective the simplicity of cut and size of each gemstone could be in creating an impact. The generous use of metal cords and lacing was influenced by fashions from outside Italy.

169

collection.[8]

Isabella and Francesco would sometimes order work from outside Mantua: in her hometown of Ferrara, there were three goldsmiths in particular whom Isabella patronized—Michele Orifice, Ercole Fedeli and, the most famous, Caradosso. But for many items of jewellery, the precious gems were bought in from dealers and gem-cutters elsewhere, and made into wearable pieces by the Mantuan goldsmiths. To this end, Isabella often wrote to Giorgio Brognolo, who acted as mediator between herself and the jewellers. She was very particular about his choice, and would return a stone posthaste had it the slightest flaw or were it not of the precise size.[9] Some of the instructions laid down by Isabella in letters to the jewellers were extremely explicit, leaving the artist's hand little room to manoeuvre; on one occasion, she even enclosed her own sketch of the jewel she wanted.[10]

The particular affinity between the painter's and goldsmith's art is reflected by a thorough understanding of jewellery and other metalwork in the paintings of the Quattrocento. This relationship would suggest that the painted sources offer reliable information about the forms and uses of jewellery. Most jewels were uncomplicated in design, because a great deal of importance was attached to the quality and value of the stones themselves. The use of extremely ornate jewels in Botticelli's paintings might, at first glance, appear to be imaginative products of the artist's license. However, to remember that Botticelli himself was apprenticed in a goldsmith's shop, and that he was also responsible for designing embroideries, may reinforce the genuine existence of the goldwork painted by him.

The Pollaiuolo brothers, Antonio and Piero, were responsible for one of the most successful *botteghe* in Florence in the latter half of the fifteenth century. Their name became associated with several media—painting, sculpture, engraving, goldsmithing and embroidery design. Like Botticelli, they frequently included certain stylistic forms and motifs in jewellery. The regular appearance of some designs probably represents the current trends in linking and mounting jewels, and may well have been real advertisements for their own workshop. One such feature is the chain of alternating palmettes and roses, used in separate ways, whether for a hatband, or for a gold collar, in a painting by Antonio and Piero del Pollaiuolo of Saints Vincent, James and Eustace.

The range of jewelled objects was extremely varied: however, contemporary documents do not contain much detailed information about the more usual stylistic categories of jewellery and are inclined to describe only the most astounding and valuable objects. Many items are recorded simply as 'jewels', suggesting their ambiguous form and diverse functions. Some gems recorded in inventories of the period were set in gold, but many were cut stones, remaining unmounted. Like Isabella d'Este, other lovers of jewels would purchase or be presented with gifts of precious

100. In this portrait attributed to Botticelli the woman wears a cameo depicting Apollo and Marsyas. A famous lost antique cornelian of the same subject was in the Medici collection.

171

stones, ready to be made into an appropriate ornament as the occasion required. The fact that those collectors searched far and wide for the best gem-cutters and engravers, but had many jewels mounted by the goldsmith nearest to hand, partly explains both the simplicity of the mounts and the speed with which some items of jewellery were prepared.

One of the most outstanding collections of the day belonged to Leonora of Aragon, Duchess of Ferrara. Even her daughters Isabella and Beatrice had difficulty in competing with her! The goldsmith Caradosso nevertheless came to Beatrice's rescue, by supplying a quantity of rubies and diamonds, which Ludovico bought for 2000 ducats. These were then strung into necklaces so that she, like her mother, also had a fresh supply of jewels to hand out to her lady companions on their famous visit to Venice in 1493.[11] Conversely, Leonora often patronized the excellent

Milanese goldsmiths, for she had a particular fondness for gold and silver metalwork. A constant flow of silver boxes and belts, chased and engraved, poured into her collection, whilst her husband Ercole d'Este had a passion for gems and cameos. One interesting item was a beautiful chain of gold hearts linked together, sent to Leonora by Francesco Francia, the goldsmith and painter.[12] The necklace won the admiration of the court, as she desired. But it may not have been worn by Leonora, as it was possibly intended as a wedding present for Elisabetta Gonzaga, sister of Isabella's fiancé. Elisabetta was due to call at Ferrara in the spring of 1488, on her journey to Urbino for the celebrations of her marriage to Guidubaldo da Montefeltro.

A jewel was a very convenient, easily transportable form of gift, and was often presented on the occasion of a marriage. But the betrothal ring would have been handed to the bride in a separate ceremony before the *nozze*.[13] Many rings held a significance, but of those which have survived, it is difficult to say with certainty what their meanings were. It has been suggested that the painting of A Man and Woman at a Casement, is probably a marriage portrait. The couple both wear rings, but the fingers on which the rings are worn, and the types of rings, cannot conclusively explain the significance of the painting. However, a ring 'with the stone made in the form of a heart',[14] listed in the inventories of the Este palaces, was almost certainly given as an offer of love. Other love tokens took the form of *fede* rings, characterized by a representation of clasped hands. As a symbol of love, this kind of ring derived from at least the Roman Empire, and continued to have the same significance in the fifteenth century. The placement of the wedding ring as we know it today is relatively recent, a custom probably conventionalized in the nineteenth century.[15] More often than not, rings were worn on whichever fingers they fitted best; and it can be seen that several rings were worn at one time, as a statute issued in Florence in 1415 proves: a woman 'cannot wear on one or more fingers more than a total of three rings. And across all the rings and fingers she may not have more than one pearl or another precious stone. These restrictions apply to both hands'.[16]

The inscriptions found on some surviving rings offer a closer idea of their meaning and function. Lettering and other linear representations were often rendered in *niello*, a technique for which the Florentine master Maso Finiguerra (1426–64) became justly famous. *Niello* produced a strong black-and-white contrast in the design; it was a black substance consisting of metallic alloys, which was used to fill in engraved designs, particularly those worked on silver. Extremely popular on both rings and pendants, *niello* was used to delineate the profiles of lovers, and sometimes their initials or motto as well. There are some very roughly executed pieces of nielloed silver, which suggest that the technique was much sought after, and popularized as a result.

101. (opposite, left) Details a) of Saint Eustace and b) of the hat at the feet of Saint James, from a panel by Antonio and Piero del Pollaiuolo, 1466–7. A chain of alternating rosettes and palmettes is used for the saint's collar and as a decorative band round the hat. The same motifs and style of metalwork are found in other paintings by the Pollaiuolo brothers, probably indicating the type of jewellery produced in their workshop.

102. (opposite, right) Portrait of a Young Man, attributed to Baldassare Estense.

103. (top) A Man and a Woman at a Casement, by Filippo Lippi.

104. (above, left) Two rings of silver with *niello*, north Italian, fifteenth century.

105. (above, right) A thumb ring, gilt metal, set with a crystal. Late fifteenth century.

Signet rings usually retained the stirrup shape which had been used in Roman times: there was not a revival of the style, but an increase in the production of the form, which had continued to exist throughout the Middle Ages. Set into the mount appears an intaglio, either antique or contemporary, bearing the owner's initials, arms or a device. As well as signet rings, many papal rings survive. These were souvenirs, presented by the Pope to pilgrims of the fifteenth and sixteenth centuries. They are usually very large but are not of great value, being made from a crystal or some semi-precious stone, in a heavy gilt-bronze or gilt-copper setting. Some have papal insignia and the Evangelists' symbols decorating the shoulders; others bear the arms of a bishop, cardinal or king. Because they are so cumbersome they were probably not worn as rings, but possibly used as badges, or as credentials by an envoy or official sent from the person whose arms and initials are born on the ring.

Some rings were thought to hold magical properties which may have been on account of the stones set into them. There was a considerable amount of superstition attached to gems and it was believed that their miraculous qualities were based, though with some alterations over the centuries, on a form of lapidary science. This theory of the properties and powers of stones was formulated after Pliny the Elder had written his Natural History. The variations on these theories differed from one century to the next, and between countries. By some, it was believed that diamonds offered protection in battle, and from ghosts and witchcraft. Rubies were meant to guarantee love and good fortune, peace and happiness; whilst turquoises prevailed against accidents, especially when riding a horse.[17]

It is doubtful whether there was one generally recognized vocabulary of jewels. Nevertheless, the mystical powers of some are implied in contemporary descriptions, such as Isabella d'Este's request to Brognolo for 'one of those stones which makes fountains spring in one night'.[18] And when Lorenzo de' Medici was treated by the physician Lazarus of Pavia shortly before he died in 1492, he was prescribed a dosage of pulverized diamonds and pearls. That one Pope, Clement VII, should have consumed as much as 40,000 ducats' worth of powdered gems towards the end of his life speaks highly of the belief in the medicine of jewels!

On the other hand, the consumption of jewellery was invariably far more conspicuous. Some jewels of the Quattrocento were so large or had such extraordinary properties that they were christened with pet names such as *il Lupo* or *il Spico*. These titles referred to two jewels in the collection of Ludovico il Moro: the former was wonderfully formed, with three pearls and a great diamond, valued at 12,000 ducats; the latter was a fiery balas, estimated at 25,000 ducats.[19]

The display of precious stones was a means of expressing great

106. The Madonna di Senigallia, by Piero della Francesca, *c.* 1470; detail of the Child's coral necklace. Corals were meant to ward off evil spirits, and safeguard the health of the stomach and heart.

wealth. Despite the devotional origins of some forms of jewellery, their use in the fifteenth century was usually profane. Rosaries and paternosters took on a new importance. Women began to wear their rosaries as necklaces, whilst their paternosters were hung from belts, wound around necklaces, or even transformed into love tokens. What Isabella d'Este did after the completion of an order for 50 paternosters of gold, 70 of amethyst, and others of black amber, is not stated.[20] Perhaps the 100 paternosters of *berettino* ordered in 1495 were to be worn with mourning.[21]

This transitional use of jewels was not due to a conscious lack of devotion, but rather to an increase in material display. As happened with items of dress, the Church and the local governments repeatedly attempted to check the lavish displays of jewels. However sumptuary legislations, in condemning the wearing of most ornaments, allowed rosaries and paternosters up to a certain value. In determination, feminine ingenuity won the day, and the ladies adapted the manner of wearing whatever jewels were permitted. Paternosters and rosaries were not totally abandoned; and some pendants did retain a prophylactic character. Reliquary pendants continued to be worn by some women; and the ex-Queen of Cyprus, Caterina Cornaro, was painted wearing as a pendant a piece of unicorn's horn, considered particularly efficacious against poison.

The custom of burying a corpse with jewels was probably practised quite commonly. Bianca Maria Sforza was placed in her coffin, wearing a black velvet gown. On her fingers were two rings, and wrapped four times around the right hand was a rosary of corals with each bead as big as a nut. On her head she wore a crown of gilded silver surmounted by a cross; around her waist, a belt of gold, and at her neck, a string of pearls.[22]

Changes in fashion in the fifteenth century bore a considerable influence over the wearing of jewellery. Costume was not complete without jewels, either in the form of independent pieces or as an integral part of trimmings and embroidery. Jewels effectively underlined the separate parts of dress and, the ladies believed, added to their beauty. The introduction of lower necklines and less draped, more closely-fitting bodices in the later part of the century did much to enhance the jewels and their wearers. The idea of showing off necklaces and pendants against the golden hair and a natural complexion allowed a very different display of the colour and crystal structure of jewels than had ever been seen before, for previously most had been worn with higher necklines and against less resplendent textiles.

The wearing of jewels was by no means confined to women. It was an accepted feminine custom to wear jewels daily; men, on the other hand, tended to wear their jewels on particularly grand occasions. When Galeazzo Maria Sforza donned his somewhat pompous ducal outfit, wishing to impress the Emperor

107. A presumed portrait of Caterina Cornaro ex-Queen of Cyprus, by Gentile Bellini. Transparent veils worn about her head and neck are edged with pearls, commonly used in embroidery. Less usual is the piece of unicorn's horn mounted in a pendant; it was meant to guard against poison.

108. Portrait of a Lady, sometimes called Beatrice d'Este, attributed to Ambrogio de Predis. There was a fashion for coifs and nets (*rete*) richly garnished with pearls and gemstones later in the century.

Colour plate 13 (opposite) Female portrait by Antonio del Pollaiuolo. The lavish angel brooch worn on her overdress is decorated with enamel, diamonds, probably a central spinel, and smaller stones of sapphire. The popularity of pearls is shown by the *frenello* in her hair, and those forming the necklace and drops from the attached pendant. Little metal ornaments, such as the spangles of the trim to her *giornea*, were also a common detail of fashion.

Frederick III, his costume included some magnificent jewels: on his cap he wore a wonderful sapphire and balas with a diamond and an enormous pearl.[23] The Duke of Ferrara's representative at the Sforza court, Giacomo Trotti, described Ludovico receiving a Genoese ambassador. Ludovico wore 'a *vesta* of the most beautiful cloth of gold, lined with ermine, open down one side'. Trotti added, '. . . he had a fine balas with a wonderful large pearl in a gold chain round his neck, and on his *beretta* he had a beautiful diamond with another huge pearl . . . he seemed a heavenly angel'.[24]

The forms of jewellery worn on the head fall into a variety of

categories, both technically and iconographically. Hat badges and aigrettes (plumes of silver or gold) were pinned to textile headwear. Sometimes, coloured real plumes would be set into a special hatpin of gold. In other forms of headwear, jewels were an integral part of the structure. This was particularly true of the *rete*, knotted nets of silk or gold threads, which often incorporated pearls and sometimes other gems. Amongst the list of jewels and clothes given to Ippolita Sforza on her marriage with Alfonso of Aragon in 1465 was a *legame da testa* (probably corresponding to the *rete* of later in the century), made with 89 rubies and 464 pearls.[25]

The fashion for these nets probably originated in Spain, and was often worn by the ladies of the Aragonese line in the later fifteenth century, but they were far more widely used in the

Colour plate 14 (opposite) Detail of Mary Magdalen from a polyptych by Carlo Crivelli. The phoenix embroidered in pearls and metal thread evokes the legendary richness of that extravagant sleeve listed in the inventory of Bona of Savoy (see page 185).

109. Sacra Conversazione, detail of two angels, by Piero della Francesca.

110. (above) Saint Catherine; detail from The Virgin and Child with Saints and Angels, by Piero di Cosimo. Pendants and brooches were worn in a versatile fashion – on the shoulder, in the hair, as pleased the wearer.

111. (opposite) A Female Saint with a Donor and two Women, detail, by the Master of the Baroncelli portraits, c. 1490. Elaborate enamel work, such as these swan and angel brooches, either came from or was technically influenced by the jeweller's art of northern Europe.

Cinquecento. Other strings of jewels, particularly pearls, were not formally arranged into a structure, but were trailed through the loops and twists of real and false hair. Brooches and pendants were also popularly worn on headdresses. In Florence, according to a letter of 1472, there was a flourishing industry making 'light and elegant gold and silver wreaths and garlands, which are worn by young maidens of high degree, and which have given their names to the artist family of Ghirlandaio'.[26] But except for a theatrical context, crowns and coronets were reserved for ladies of royal or imperial stature: for this reason the consort of the Emperor Maximilian, Bianca Maria Sforza, was placed in her coffin wearing one.[27] For her journey in 1473 to Ferrara, as young wife of Ercole I, Leonora of Aragon, daughter of King Ferrante, was accompanied by Sigismondo d'Este, the Duke's brother. When she greeted him in Naples, she was bedecked with 'a golden crown decorated with pearls and jewels', embracing him 'with such gentleness and such a noble *maniera* that many people, so touched, were reduced to tears'.[28]

Sometimes worn on the head, the pendants and medallion brooches were very versatile jewels. The *fermaglio*, as the brooches were generally termed, were originally functional, but now mostly decorative. They were still being used in the Quattrocento to fasten cloaks, but more frequently were worn for effect, on a bodice, or a shoulder, as well as on headwear. The inventories of Piero de' Medici list a *brocchetta da pecto* and a *brocchetta da testa* as two separate things.[29] And the trousseau of Elisabetta Gonzaga[30] demonstrates how the form of the *fermaglio* was very similar to that of the pendant. One in a gold mount with a table-cut balas in the middle, two faceted diamond points and three large pearls, was worth 600 ducats. Another of a table-cut diamond with a rounded (*cugolo*) ruby and two large pearls was estimated at 700 ducats. In each case, the pearls would probably have been drop-pearls, used in a similar way to those attached to pendants. A *fermaglio* was presumably normally quite large, for in Elisabetta's trousseau, it is explicity stated when there is a small one; for example, that with a pointed diamond, three table rubies and four pearls, which was only worth 100 ducats. Possibly used as brooches or pendants, but simply listed as *zoglieli* is a series of enamelled jewels in the Este inventories of 1494.[31] They are all described as being made *ala todescha*, indicating that they employed a technique derived from north of the Alps. The subjects rendered in these enamels are quite enchanting, such as one 'with a half-woman, half-fish, blowing a horn' (surely, the scribe had never seen a mermaid sounding a conch shell!). In the same inventory there are other medallions, including cameos, one of which was engraved with a half-goat, half-fish, and another cameo with a head of a jester in relief. More often, however, medallions were incised with portrait heads, in a loosely classical manner. The Este collection of jewellery included several

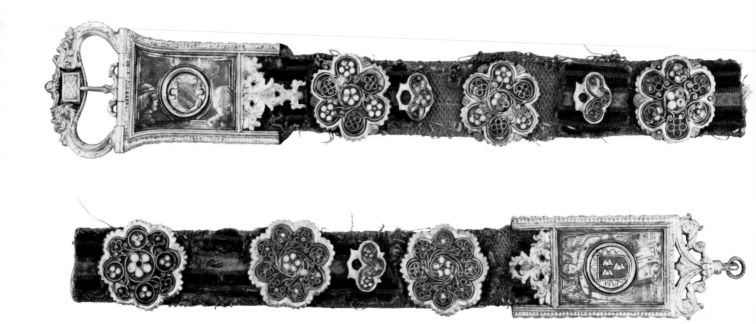

examples, portraying the heads of successive dukes and other members of the family.

Gold and jewelled belts were an important complement to the *gamurra*. Some were made entirely of linked metal pieces, perhaps with an enamelled or jewelled buckle and clasp. Others were made of textile, invariably a brocaded velvet, and fitted with a buckle of gold. The belts had no function except to be novel in form or in the detail of jewels used. A reference in the correspondence between Isabella and Beatrice d'Este throws light on the imaginative translation of a traditional object into fashion. Isabella had evidently seen her sister wearing a jewelled belt purchased in France, made to imitate a *cordone di San Francesco* and her letter requested a pattern from which she would have the belt copied.[32] Sometimes belts had a ceremonial value: every trousseau included one, and invariably the bride was formally girded with it, in memory of the *cestus* given by Vulcan to Venus.[33]

Not only were there freshly discovered ways of wearing jewellery, but also some forms of jewels were new to Italians. The fashion for wearing earrings was not adopted until the close of the fifteenth century. During the Quattrocento there are few references to earrings; however, a clause in a Sicilian sumptuary legislation of 1425 stated that while other items of jewellery were permissible, all ear ornaments were forbidden.[34] There is a record of a pair of earrings in the north of Italy, but since the rings are listed as two separate items the compiler of the inventory may not have appreciated the fact that they could be worn together.[35] The other form of jewellery which was beginning to come into vogue during the century was the bracelet. Few are mentioned, except that one with ten pearls, seven rubies and four diamonds made into leaf-shapes was given to Ippolita Sforza.[36]

112. (above) Two ends of a velvet belt; Venetian, late fifteenth century. The male and female busts and the shield of arms, incorporated with the initials 'LB' in the sunken medallion of the silver-gilt buckle, are all nielloed. The belt-end which would hang down, and to which a pendant might be attached, has on the reverse a shield surrounded by cherubs and inscribed above 'Con el tempo' ('With Time'). The presence of the facing profiles and the motto suggests that the belt was a betrothal gift. The arms are probably those of the Malatesta of Rimini. The north Italian interest in enamel is shown by the decorative sexfoils in filigree enamel, applied to the (remounted) velvet of the belt.

113. (opposite) The Miracle of the True Cross at Ponte S. Lorenzo, detail, by Gentile Bellini, 1500. The figure in the foreground resembles the portrait identified as Caterina Cornaro (plate 107). The fashion for earrings spread in the sixteenth century.

114. (above) Two Sicilian women wearing earrings; detail from *The Triumph of Death*, *c.* 1450.

115. (opposite) Mary Magdalen, by Carlo Crivelli, *c.* 1476–8. In addition to individually mounted jewels and necklaces, the gilt *maglie* fastenings, belt buckles and embroidery were an integral part of fashionable dress.

The metalworker's art was applied not only to individual pieces of jewellery worn as glittering display but also to the more practical details of dress, such as the metal points (*punte*) at the ends of ribbons or laces, or the gilt *maglie*, which were eyelets for the openings of a garment.[37] Pearls, and sometimes other gems, were used for buttons, and the *doploni* around the neck of a rich velvet *veste* mentioned in the trousseau of a noble lady of Friuli[38] were probably applied decorative golden discs. Fringing and purses also worked in metal added to the expenses of an outfit. Although each town had its own craftsmen in metal to satisfy the tailors' and weavers' needs, some places must have produced identifiable styles of these objects. *Borse* were made in the Ferrarese style, both *rize* and *de diverse guise*; other variations on the theme include a *borsoto d'oro facto a la genovesa*.[39]

The use of embroidery on women's dress appears in various forms, and designed in different scales. Some embroidery did cover the whole of a garment, with the advantage that it could be

scaled up and down in proportion with the volume of textile. Thus a floral motif would appear smaller and more tightly spaced on a bodice, and could gradually broaden out and increase in size towards the wide hem and train of the dress. In April 1493, Leonora, Duchess of Ferrara, sent to her daughter Beatrice a new design for a *camora* which her Spanish embroiderer Jorba had just devised; when acknowledging receipt of the design, Beatrice reported the reaction of her own embroiderer to Jorba's idea, 'He remarks that the flowers of the pattern are all the same size, and since the *camora* will naturally be cut narrower above than below, the flowers ought to be altered in the same proportion'.[40] A *vestito* belonging to Bianca Maria Sforza had just the top part (*busto*) covered with 80 little jewels, with a ruby and four pearls surroundings each one.[41] Most frequently however, embroidery with jewels, especially pearls, was confined to the edges of the neckline, hem and openings. An extremely rich example of jewels used in this way is mentioned amongst the gifts presented by Galeazzo Maria Sforza to Bona of Savoy—a *vestito*, em-

116. Saint Ursula, detail from The Meeting of the Betrothed Couple and their Departure, by Carpaccio, 1495. The saint's coif and the bodice of her dress are an example of the general fondness for pearls with which to trim garments and accentuate the fashionable line of dress.

broidered with pearls and rubies, and around the lower edges (*balzane*) of the dress were placed six huge balas rubies, the whole garment being valued at 50,000 ducats.[42]

The most effective use of jewels in embroidery was on the sleeve. In cases of extremely elaborate sleeves the detailed embroidered motifs were sometimes confined to one arm; this was always the left. For this reason, there appear entries for one single sleeve in the contemporary wardrobe accounts. Probably the most famous of all of them is a sleeve belonging to Bona of Savoy, a *mongino* sleeve embroidered with a phoenix in balases, diamonds and pearls, which was valued at 18,000 ducats in 1468.[43] It is significant that this sleeve was not recorded amongst a general list of clothes, but is entered under Bona's collection of jewels. Many other embroidered sleeves incorporate fanciful themes, emblems or heraldic devices. They were similar in subject matter to the numerous badges worn in the fifteenth century.

Badges very often were not like the simply mounted, carefully balanced jewels, with subtly and skilfully cut stones found in pendants, necklaces, rings and other small-scale jewellery. Rather, these items were a form of 'costume jewellery'. It was appropriate to the function of a badge—for instance, one with a complex battle scene—that it should be carved in high relief on a gem measuring three centimetres across. Worn on the shoulder, or on a hat, such a jewel was intended to create an effect from a distance: the engraved surfaces had to be large enough for the subject matter to remain legible.

From this slightly distant viewpoint an anonymous Florentine poet of the first decade of the Quattrocento saw a procession of young men and women wearing a form of livery quartered with red and white, with gold plumes in their hats. Each one wore a *fermaglio*. Some of these badges were made with pearls; and all of them stood out beautifully in relief, their gold mounts reflecting the light around them. One young man wore a ship, and his neighbour's badge represented a little boat. The observer saw castles, towers, columns, and even a bear under a pavilion. Lions appeared, sitting or rampant, and one young man, just for pleasure, wore an elephant and a castle. Various species of birds, a unicorn, a leopard and a winged griffin appeared too.[44] Such *fermagli* were entirely ornamental, although they may have originated from the more significant medieval pilgrims' badges. However, there were also badges in the form of a medallion which bore the initials or arms of the wearer.

There was, during the course of the century, a growing interest in and importance attached to emblems and mottoes. Some were suitably devised for a particular occasion, possibly never to be employed again. Others became family emblems, such as the *A bon droit* motto, possibly suggested by Leonardo da Vinci. Used by the Sforza family, in combination with the dove and sun's rays motif, the device was used not only on clothing but

117. Two young men in a boat; detail from The Meeting of the Betrothed Couple and their Departure, by Carpaccio, 1495. Hat badges were like costume jewellery – large in scale in order to be noticed from a distance. Embroidered emblems on sleeves such as the sitting figure wears, were invariably confined to the left arm.

is featured on an altar frontal in the Poldi Pezzoli Museum, Milan. The range of Sforzesca devices was wide and complex with different ones allotted to each brother in the family. A manuscript illumination which portrays the presentation of a book to Filelfo incorporates a device of three diamond rings, and next to it a mulberry tree. Ludovico il Moro, using the pun on his name and the landscape feature of mulberry trees in Lombardy, not only used the 'Moro' device but often the colour *morello* as well. Another play on the word 'Moro' appeared in the device of a Moorish head, and the wearing of Moorish costumes at masquerades and other festivities.

On several occasions, Beatrice d'Este wore the embroidered motif of the towers of the port of Genoa on her dress. In 1493, she entered Ferrara, wearing a *camora* of *tabbi cremexino* embroidered with the device, bearing two towers on each sleeve, two more on the front of the bodice and a further pair on the back. The response to her clothes on the continuation of her visit to Venice was one of amazement, despite the reputedly majestic and highly extravagant uses of jewellery worn by the Venetian ladies themselves.[45] The motif was related to the Milanese dominion over Genoa. However, it is difficult to comprehend in retrospect how the mottoes and devices should be read and in what spirit they were first used.

Most Italian devices, though they may in time have come to bear considerable significance, were the products of whimsical notions. In 1480, the Duke of Ferrara was presented with the Garter by the King of England.[46] Worn by the Duke at Mass in the Duomo and in the following year on the Feast of Saint George, the Garter was probably viewed as something com-

118. Uberto de' Sacrati with his wife and son, Ferrarese School, *c.* 1490. The little boy wears a gold aigrette on his cap, attached to a brooch; the drop pearl was a common feature of both brooch and pendant design.

parable with the embroidery and badges worn on hose in a half-heraldic, half-fashionable way. There was no Italian equivalent of the highest Order in the land, and therefore there was no appropriate term in the Italian vocabulary to describe the Garter. The wearing of the Garter was confined to the most valiant men of the Realm, symbolizing the unity of chivalrous virtue. However, it must be remembered that the spirit with which the motto and the form of the Garter was created probably resembled the depth of meaning behind the Italian devices. The adoption of the motto '*Honi soit qui mal y pense*' ('Evil to him who evil thinks') is taken from the comment of reproval made by Edward III to his court. It happened when, at a ball in Calais, the garter belonging to the attractive Princess Joan of Kent fell to the ground when she was dancing. Edward picked it up, and tied it round his knee, whilst declaring the words of his motto.

It is not certain what the badge or device was called in Italy in the fifteenth century, but the term *impresa* was authoritatively used by Giovio in the next century.[47] Apart from the device, one means of formal identification was by the colour of clothing. The parti-coloured livery appropriated to a particular house or individual was described as *a divisa*. Clothes bearing military or family badges or symbols were often referred to as *a le armi*. When it was specified that the clothing had been presented, it was then called *a livrea*.

The effect of uniformly coloured livery and of devices is depicted in a Florentine chronicle of 1464 which describes the entry of a gentleman into the city:

> . . . he was mounted on the most beautiful horse,
> with trappings and a bridle and saddle all of *chremisi*
> embroidered in silver as richly as could possibly be.
> The cavalier wore a doublet [*giubbone*] of em-
> broidered pearls and jewels, with a wing of gold
> and other colours on each shoulder. And
> surrounding this gentleman were fifteen fine young
> men on foot. They all wore *gonnellini* of *raso chremisi*,
> lined with ermine, with *pavonazzo* hose, all of which
> this gentleman had presented to each one. And in
> addition to this suite of fifteen, the gentleman had
> 150 young men, all clothed in one of his liveries;
> that is, they were in *gonnellini* and *calze* of green,
> with falcons on the breast and back, whose plumes
> spread over the *gonnellino*. Each one of these
> 150 young men was holding a lighted torch.[48]

The passion for devices covered everything from horsecloths to little silver boxes. Some were passed from one generation to the next: for example, the diamond ring, of significance to Ercole d'Este because his ancestor had given it to the *condottiere* Muzio

Attendolo in 1409, became his chief device. This diamond is spoken of in almost mystical terms in a eulogy on Ercole.

The giving of devices from one house to another sometimes happened in recognition of services rendered, or as a declaration of affinity between two houses. The three-ring device associated with the Sforza was granted by them to other Milanese families such as the Borromeo, as a detail in the Zavattari frescoes at Monza records.

The three-ring device (and sometimes four-ring) was also associated with the Medici, for it had been adopted by Cosimo. As happened with most important Italian families, several emblems were used by the Medici. Another important Medici device was *palle* (balls), seven of which appear surrounded by cherubs' wings and cloud forms in a brocaded textile in Paris.[49] Allied to the Florentine style for smaller-scale motifs in regular repeating patterns, some silks produced there incorporated heraldic devices. Several examples of a red velvet figured with gold 'spots' at first sight hardly looks like a textile with devices, but in fact the dimension of the discs corresponds precisely to the florin and half-florin pieces, the emblem of the *Arte del Cambio* in Florence.

The disadvantage of woven emblems, however, was that they had to conform to repeats. Nothing quite as fanciful as the magnificently embroidered phoenix rising up the sleeve of Bona of Savoy would have been woven even by the best figured velvet weavers. Such an object epitomizes both the ingenuity and the forthright ostentation of the Quattrocento. Although mottoes and devices continued to be created and worn in later periods, they became conventionalized and never regained the extraordinarily dramatic and narrative power they held in the fifteenth century.

8 The Diffusion of Foreign Dress: 1480-1500

T he beginning of the High Renaissance in Italy, the era of Leonardo, Michelangelo and Raphael, coincides with the stark exposure of political and social weaknesses of the fifteenth century. The economic equilibrium of highly successful trading and commercial enterprizes was beginning to crumble. Nevertheless, there remained an indulgent display of wealth in dress, jewels and artists' commissions—the splendid reflections of a corrupt society.

Savonarola's call for Church reform involved not the coming of some spiritual saviour, but that of a foreign power. Such a political and physical intervention would, he believed, disentangle the unscrupulous habits into which the Italian rulers (including the Pope) had fallen. Italy, thus shattered, would have to begin all over again, but in a reformed state. In 1494 the armies of Charles VIII, King of France, invaded Italy and pushed their way down through Milan to Florence, and through Rome to Naples. Savonarola's dream had come true.

The French penetration of Italy marks the obliteration of the borders of Europe. Suddenly, Italy, though still very regionalized, found the influence of her trade and culture spilling out of her hands. As the century progressed, there had been an increase in the number of visits from artists, scholars and ecclesiastics from abroad, and after 1490 much artistic and humanistic influence spread north and west to the remainder of Europe. At the same time, the Mediterranean was no longer the richest and most vital stretch of sea in the world. In 1487 the Portuguese sailor Bartolomeu Dias succeeded in rounding the Cape of Good Hope, thus encouraging further exploratory attempts, and in 1497 Vasco da Gama's ship was the first to reach Calicut in India. Many Genoese seamen were involved in these ocean voyages, not the least Christopher Columbus, who sailed off from Castile on his most famous expedition to America, on 3 August 1492.

In the latter half of the fifteenth century in Italy, the wearing of costume in foreign styles becomes increasingly diffuse. This does not imply that influence from abroad had not previously been felt. However, improvements in communication and political events did assist the knowledge of foreign dress. Subsequently, foreign

119. (overleaf) Groups of figures in the Piazza San Marco; detail from the Procession of the Reliquary of the Cross, by Gentile Bellini, 1496.

120. (top) *The Meeting of the Betrothed Couple and their Departure,* detail; by Carpaccio, 1495. The silhouettes of distant background figures demonstrate the contrast between the tightly fitted hose and doublet and the wide sleeves and collars of the gowns worn on top.

121. (above) *Ladies approaching San Marco;* detail from *The Procession of the Reliquary of the Cross,* by Gentile Bellini, 1496. The last decade of the Quattrocento witnessed, particularly in Milan and Venice, the décolletage of women's dress.

Colour plate 15 (opposite) Detail from *The Visitation,* by Domenico Ghirlandaio, 1485–90. The *giornea* worn by Giovanna degli Albizzi (wife of Lorenzo Tornabuoni) bears heraldic devices woven into the textile. The contrasts in styles of hair and headdresses are indicative of differences in the ages and ranks of the women.

styles were very much in vogue; and many of those garments described as being in the French, German, Spanish, or Turkish style, may not be genuine exotica, but the Italians' own version, founded on a much more informed idea of foreign clothing. Concurrent with the more cosmopolitan and international fashions, there remains within the Italian peninsula convincing evidence for distinctive regional differences in dress.

The fashionable silhouette in the final decades of the Quattrocento was almost precocious. To be most effective, it depended on a youthful body which, by wearing extraordinarily close-fitting garments, though clothed, appeared naked. Never before had young men gone about in such tight doublets and hose, openly wearing them without a tunic, as part of general fashion. Nor had the necklines worn by Italian ladies ever reached so low, in some cases barely supported by the shoulders. Older members of society and most official and academic dress remained

more or less unchanged, taking the form of soberly tailored gowns. But the layers of the most fashionable dress were beginning to play a different role from before. Rather than a logical build-up, layer upon layer, we find a strong contrast between the particularly close-fitting dress or doublet, and the comparatively loose overgarment or cloak. Young men of fashion tended to abandon the intermediate layer of the tunic, and the doublet developed an apology of a short skirt at the back.

Always acting as a reliable gauge, the sleeves worn by both men and women highlight the mood of dress, and betray the sources of influence on clothing. Earlier in the century, the fundamental sleeve (that usually used on men's doublets) had been constructed of two parts, but the upper had been gathered and sewn to the lower part of the elbow. Towards the end of the fifteenth century, sleeves were slit and split, the upper and lower parts becoming separated. The various parts of the arm were held together only by means of eyelets and laces. Much show was made of this type of sleeve. The relatively recent fashionable use of sideless mantles allowed at least one arm to reveal little sleeve, but a great play of chemise and laces. Coinciding with this use of lacing on the arm, both men's doublets and ladies' dresses no longer discreetly concealed the laced openings down the main body of the garment which had once been a purely practical means of allowing the clothes to be put on and the seams to be drawn together to achieve the required fit. The display of lacing, both down the centre front and at the back of garments, is now exploited as a fashionable detail.

This general trend in the shape of the silhouette coincided with, and possibly encouraged, the development of new under- and upper-layers of clothing. One, the chemise, during the latter half of the fifteenth century, became an interesting garment in its own right. At the beginning of the Quattrocento, the chemise had constituted a practical shift which acted as an easily laundered layer between the hidden flesh and the visible garments but with its exposure, it became necessary to embellish it at the neck and wrist. The quality of linen used for such chemises was not only felt, but noticed. Both the style of the chemise and the materials from which it was made became dependent on skills from abroad.

Stylistic intercourse between the various countries of western Europe had always existed in fashion. However, the influences from outside Italy appear to have strengthened in the later fifteenth century. Whilst a current fashionable shape is detectable throughout the Italian peninsula during the period, the extremes of fashion appear in the north. They are particularly evident in the paintings of Venice, and the documents associated with Ferrara, Mantua and Milan. That so much fashion should revolve around the inspired use of clothing and the luxury of Isabella and Beatrice d'Este, is not merely an historian's bias. It is indicative of the

Colour plate 16 (opposite) Two Venetian Ladies on a Balcony, by Carpaccio, c. 1495–1500. The extremely low necklines of Venice and Milan are features of northern Italian costume which contrast with the more conservative styles of the Florentines. The two women have often been called courtesans, but there is no evidence in their manner of dress to support this theory.

infiltration of stylistic and decorative details in fashion from Spain. The Aragonese Kings of Naples, Alfonso and Ferrante, were reputedly austere in their style of dress.[1] Yet their wives and daughters appear to have enjoyed the excesses of fashion. Through a series of marriages,[2] the Aragonese female line was to bring a Spanish flavour to Milan, Mantua and Ferrara especially, and further marriages between members of the Sforza family[3] and other Italian houses caused some of the initially Spanish styles, with adaptations and modifications, to filter into more courts. In the detailed correspondence of ambassadors, agents and interested individuals, news was regularly conveyed about new or unusual ideas in dress. The links of trade and politics also caused a confrontation of differing styles and cultures with varying consequences in the rejection and acceptance of foreign dress. For a long while, since the thirteenth century, Genoa had close contacts with Castile and also received a wide range of goods from north and west Africa. In addition, the political influence over Genoa fluctuated between the Milanese dukes and the French kings, thereby causing a considerable diffusion of styles. Milan itself, so well-placed at the foot of an important trade route through the Alps, was quite familiar with the fashions of France and Burgundy. Germanic dress would also have found its way into Lombardy. But, due to considerable numbers of Germans in Venice, the best-placed outlet for the products of south German towns, its influence on fashion was felt particularly forcefully in the Veneto. Venice, therefore, as a long-established thoroughfare to and from the Orient, combined the excesses of Germanic dress with the exoticism of Eastern styles.

Within Italy, customs, politics and geography affected the many variants on a theme of dress. It was not only a matter of the degree of influence from abroad but also the anti-cosmopolitan attitudes of the more conservative members of society and areas of the country which contributed to a form of regional Italian dress. The manner of wearing veils, and the underlying structure, were probably the most noticeable indications of the wearer's origins. In Bologna, there was apparently a special fashion for wearing a type of *fazzoletto* around the neck. In 1474, the Duchess Bona decided she would like to introduce the style to Milan, so she sent a letter to Ginevra Bentivoglio, requesting 50 of those fine beautiful silk *fazzoletti* to be sent.[4] The fashion appears not to have caught on in Milan. The silk veils themselves, however, may have been used in a similar way in Florence, for the art of making *veli crespi* had been introduced to the city.[5] The Florentines, like all Italians, were intrigued by these regional differences; in 1467 Lucrezia Tornabuoni Medici had written to her son Piero, describing the amazing style of Mantua of arranging the hair in the form of a sugarloaf (*acconciature a pane de zucaro a la guisa et figia Mantuana*).[6] The confusion of styles is therefore complicated by their adoptions as fashion. To what extent the non-fashionable

122. (opposite) The Martyrdom of the Pilgrims and Funeral of Saint Ursula, detail, by Carpaccio, 1493. The archer, a somewhat eccentric German with long fair hair, wears the latest style of doublet reaching only to his waist, except for the small fluted skirt at the back.

123. (above) Isabella Aldobrandini, mother of Pandolfo and Carlo Malatesta, and Violante Bentivoglio Malatesta (who married Pandolfo in 1489) in an altarpiece by Ghirlandaio, the figures having been completed by a Bolognese artist, *c.* 1490. There was once a special fashion of wearing fine silk veils in Bologna, similar to those illustrated here. The younger woman, on the other hand, wears her hair in a *coazzone*, a style with Spanish origins which spread into North Italian fashion from Naples through the daughters of the house of Aragon.

Italians adhered to a recognizable local style is difficult to assess. For surely, particular people in the backwater hilltowns and the peasants working on the land, had some protected traditional features. A pair of peasant girls in the Sistine Chapel frescoes wear interesting examples of chemises with embroidered bands. These are probably romanticized forms of peasant dress, but it is impossible to say whether they are based on actual peasant clothing used in Italy during the period or whether the garments were convenient artist's props.

The use of embroidered chemises was becoming a prominent feature in fashion. The Greek woman 'who produces such delicate work with a needle', recommended by Costanza d'Avalos, went to work for Isabella d'Este in 1491.[7] She had presumably been taught the traditions of Greek embroidery and worked in fine geometrical patterns. Such details would have looked particularly appropriate around the decorative edges at the neck and the wrist of a chemise. That Isabella should employ

124. The daughters of Jethro in The Temptation of Moses by Botticelli, 1481–2. They wear a romanticized form of peasant dress.

the woman suggests that her art was particularly well adapted to the needs of current Italian fashion. Also appreciated in Italy was the use of Spanish embroidery, Spain being the country from which blackwork probably originated. Towards the end of the fifteenth century, examples of narrow bands of embroidery appear, which relate to the chemises mentioned in contemporary documents. By the time (1501) the Contessa di Mesocco's inventory was compiled, a variety of chemises was in existence. The Contessa's everyday chemises are recorded together with the rest of the household linen, while others, with embroidered details, are mentioned separately.[8] Two chemises of *tela di renso* with *petti fati a la Napolitana* were worked with embroidery in gold thread and black silk. Another, constructed from *tela de Cambrai* with a *busto facto a la Castiliana* had the hem, and the edges of the sleeves and the collar, worked in the Moorish style (*a punto*

125. A portrait by Raphael, *c.* 1500. The lowered necklines and slits in sleeves through which the chemise was drawn coincided with an interest in embroidered edges. The blackwork is probably of Spanish origin.

moresco) in black silk, with additional groupings of gold thread stitchery. A further example was trimmed with green silk and with gold fringing *a la Napolitana*. And the list ends with two *camisi moreschi* made from *tela de Cambrai*.

The new forms of overgarments in the later fifteenth century are derived from a variety of sources. The *mongile*, defined as a mantle with sleeves, probably of monastic origin, is long, elegant, opens down the front, and was worn by both men and women. This may be one of the overgarments which originated in Spain. The *sbernia* is another overgarment which features quite frequently in this period. It is lined, often with fur. In 1490, Isabella d'Este asked Jacopo Trotti to look out for ten *gatti di spagno*, of the largest and best he could find in Milan, for lining an *albernia*.[9] The range of furs available was wide, and many, like the *vaio* and the *zibelline* and the *gatti di spagno* were imported from

126. (opposite) Pandolfo and Carlo Malatesta, detail from an altarpiece by Ghirlandaio, *c.* 1490. The forms of overgowns and mantles were as diverse as the ways of wearing them.

127. (left) Men of various nationalities in The Return of the Ambassadors to the King of England, by Carpaccio, *c.* 1496–8. The German, whose backview is shown, contrasts with the sober Venetian officials behind and the Armenian (wearing a brimmed hat) in the right distance.

199

Spain. Also possibly introduced from Spain was the novel trimming of brown lamb's skin, which an intrigued observer saw worn by Beatrice d'Este.[10]

The exact nature of many overgowns is very often made ambiguous by the generic term *vestimento* or its variants. Such gowns appear described *a la castiliana*, *a la tedesca*, or *a la francese*. The degree of accuracy in such descriptions is variable. Sometimes the chronicler or diarist has something genuinely foreign in mind, but in many cases such documentary evidence relates to the Italians' concept of a style from the country in question.

The national costumes described at the celebrations of the marriage of Gian Galeazzo Sforza and Isabella of Aragon in 1490 may well have been fanciful. The Polish dancers wore their hair long and wavy with leafy garlands worn on their heads, decorated with feathers, with short capes of black silk, mulberry-coloured hose and shoes with long-pointed toes.[11] The longer hairstyles of men were considered in the most general way to belong to a fashion from beyond the Alps. Germanic people were often characterized by long-pointed shoes, long hair, and a very expressionist use of slashing. The crowd scenes in Venetian paintings of the period often include these Germans.

Late Quattrocento Italian dress possessed a tendency towards exaggeration, verging on that elongated Germanic silhouette. However, some men within Italy found such excesses to be over-indulgent, immodest and quite undesirable. The word '*tedesco*' came to be used as a term of abuse, whether or not the person or object was actually German. A sonnet written in the last years of the century pokes fun at the rather gross ladies of Milan who insist on wearing the current fashion for extremely low necklines. Everything about them makes them look like walking advertisements of all that is German:

> They have beautiful women in Milan; but, as you
> have probably heard, they are far too gross. You
> know that they have a pale complexion, are slim in
> the middle, and well proportioned below. But
> from the waist upwards, they resemble the plumpest
> of capons. They wear a particular line in *giornee* and
> *gioppe* [*cioppe*] which makes them look even fuller in
> the breasts. They go about wearily in low-heeled
> slippers [*pianelle*], overfilled at the brims of their *veste*
> of silk and *rosato*, with their caps [*scoffie*] of gold, a
> jewel at the breast, and sleeves embroidered or
> brocaded. Each one bears a rich and beautiful balas
> on her shoulder, the neck covered in links of pearls
> with a pendant, engraved or nielloed; and every
> finger has a ring. Then when you see them eating at
> their platters, they all look like German shop-
> fronts [*botteghe da Thedeschi*].[12]

Conversely, Italian fashions sometimes received criticisms from abroad. Matteo de Coucy remarked that the Italians wore tight-fitting clothing of a type you would dress a pet monkey in, '*ainsi comme l'on souloit vestir les singes*'.[13] But for the most part, foreign dress, if not beautiful, was at least different, and the fashions of the day were designed to create a visual impact by means of surprise.

Antonio Calco, the Secretary of the Milanese mission to Charles VIII of France in 1492, sent back detailed words about the costumes worn by the royal couple when out hunting in the forest of Saint Germain. Anne of Brittany's headdress consisted of a black velvet cap with a short gold fringe hanging over her

128. A Female Saint with a Donor and two Women, by the Master of the Baroncelli portraits, *c.* 1490. The left woman is dressed in the Italian fashion, while the figure behind wears the squarer neckline and French hood with black velvet facings more common to France and Burgundy.

forehead and over her head she wore a hood. This covered the top of her head, reached down over her ears and was lavishly decorated with large diamonds. The news of this fashion so fascinated Beatrice d'Este and her lady companions that Ludovico wrote to Calco, demanding a drawing of the French Queen's costume, 'in order that the same fashion may be adopted here in Milan.'[14] Later in the same year, Isabella had also taken to incorporating elements of French fashion in her dress. Furious with the tailor Alberto da Bologna for making a bad job of one dress, she demanded that he should cut from the redundant textile a *camora* with *bande al pecto a la francese, fodrate de velluto negro*. She wished Alberto to face the sleeves also with black velvet, and to attach to them *stringhe nere* like the long ones on a black velvet *camora* in her possession.[15]

Two years later, a French eyewitness account of what Beatrice wore when Charles VIII visited her at the castle at Annona, was despatched to the King's sister, Anne of Bourbon. Beatrice wore:

> a robe of gold and green brocade, and a fine linen *gorgerette* turned back over it, and her haid was richly decorated with pearls, and her hair hung down her back in a long coil with a silk ribbon twisted round it. She wore a crimson silk hat, very much like our own, with five or six red and grey feathers. . . .[16]

The next day, the King visited Beatrice again; but this time, the eyewitness was struck by the diamonds, pearls and rubies, decorating both the front and the back of the bodice of her dress. He also commented on the very tight sleeves, slashed down the length of the arm, to show the chemise worn underneath it; they were then tied with wide grey silk ribbon, which trailed down almost to the ground. Beatrice's jewels, on the other hand, were not very different in shape from some in Anne of Burgundy's possession—they were only larger.[17]

Mentioned in the Frenchman's description, the long roll of hair hanging down Beatrice's back and bound with latticed ribbons is exactly the hairstyle worn by her in the Pala Sforzesca (plates 12 and 151). Known as a *coazzone* in Lombardy, the fashion for wearing the hair in this manner came from Spain and was often worn in conjunction with the *reta*, a form of knotted net headdress, which was also of Spanish origin.

The use of Spanish headdresses in Milan was probably, by the very late Quattrocento, no longer associated with Spain, but was seen as a Lombard fashion instead. It was, after all, a generation old, for Leonora of Aragon had aroused considerable interest by wearing her hair in that *coazzone* on her arrival at Ferrara in 1473. Mounted on a white horse, she was dressed in black velvet; even her hat and *baviera* were black, 'except for the fine plumes worn on one side. They looked as white as snow as they waved lightly in the breeze.' The pearls and rich jewels which hung round her neck 'seemed that much more splendiforous, being set against the dark shade of her clothes and the long roll of hair which, in the style peculiar to the noble young ladies of Naples, hung freely from the nape of the neck'.[18] Particularly Milanese, however, was the decorative use of ribbons (*stringhe*) hanging down from the dress worn by Beatrice in the Pala Sforzesca.

Compared with most other Italian towns and states, there was in Milan and Lombardy a general absence of sumptuary laws. Led by Beatrice's example, the Milanese incorporated a profuse quantity of detail in their dress. Baldassare Castiglione's memory of the time spent in the court of Ludovico il Moro gives authenticity to his remark about the Milanese way of dress. '*Chiassoso*' is the word he used in *Il Cortegiano*, meaning loud and showy. However, there was a legislation passed in 1498 which prohibited women from using a *faldia*,[9] an underskirt of linen, held firm by horizontal bands padded with cotton wool or linen fibre. The existence of such a clause in the law would suggest that this fashion for such an underskirt was well established by that date.

The court was a haven for dreaming up fantastic clothes and

129. A group of kneeling women; detail from The Madonna and Child with Saints, by Cima da Conegliano. In humble devotion, the younger women also cover their heads and shoulders with veils — be they fine ones, barely disguising the décolletage and hairstyle identical to those worn by the two women in plate 130.

applying more and more details through the skilful art of tailors and embroiderers. One wonders how much contact there was between the members of a court or some elite household in the republics, and the general citizens. The former, being to some extent involved with the 'international set' were usually eager to experiment in new ideas for dress. Adhering less to local custom, therefore, they were capable of causing considerable sensation amongst the onlookers of the general public. Ludovico il Moro, when writing to his sister-in-law Isabella, related an incident which Beatrice encountered.

Isabella and Beatrice, both having experience of the customs of the ruling house of Aragon in Naples, decided to go out shopping. It was raining, and the two duchesses and their lady companions decided to go out wearing *pannicelli*, linen towels, on their heads in the customary manner of the women of Naples. But such a style of headwear was not readily accepted by the women of Milan who began to pass rude comments, and the duchesses and the women of the town nearly came to blows over the matter![20] Clearly, duchesses were meant to look like duchesses; they were much better admired when wearing horned headdresses in the French fashion, with jewels and long silk veils dripping off them, as was the case on 1 May 1492.[21]

Conforming to the general trends and changes in fashion, but to a more conservative degree, the ladies of Florence in the 1480s and '90s look very sober by comparison with Milan and Venice. The very low necklines, slipping off the shoulders, do not appear to have been worn in Florence; and probably the *pianelle* were not built up as high as the exaggerated versions on the ladies' feet in the north. Nonetheless, no fashion-conscious man or lady would ignore styles found elsewhere in Italy or abroad. The letter from the highly observant Lucrezia Tornabuoni to her son Piero de' Medici confirms this point.[22]

The diffusion of foreign styles was not simply confined to the late fifteenth century, nor to women. Early in the Quattrocento, a verse attributed to Sanguinacci, describing the elegant lady-killers of Venice, remarked that 'It would seem as if the youth had all come from France or Catalonia, or from other foreign places; for there are so many variations in their different styles of dress'.[23] However, the styles—or at least the names given to them—were that much more cosmopolitan at the close of the century. The clothing worn by Agostino, the twenty-year-old son of Lodovico da Campofregoso, constituted:

A black hat in the German style. An Italian *zipone*. A dark coloured *vestito*, reaching only half-way to the hips [*curta a meza braghetta*], lined with fur and made in the Burgundian fashion. A larger floor-length overgrown [*tabarone*] of London cloth, Burgundian style. A rather long Lombard sword. A

130. Two Venetian Ladies on a Balcony, sometimes called courtesans, by Carpaccio. A pair of tall *pianelle* lie on the ground beside the peacock.

pair of boots [*stivali*] in the German style, with pointed toes. A pair of dark *morello* hose [*calce*]. A Catalan style belt [*cento*] with a little purse [*taschetta*].[24]

131. The Resurrection of a Child, by Ghirlandaio, completed in 1485. The Florentines tended to dress much more conservatively than the Milanese and Venetians.

The diaries of Mario Sanuto, beginning in the year 1496, give a lively picture of the comings and goings of many nationalities in many guises at Venice, and he reports the news as it is received from elsewhere. The documents are spiced with comments about the Marquis of Mantua's latest mistress, or the most recurrent question of 1496, was the Queen of France pregnant? One poor tailor of Venice, having cut *cape* (*cappe*) and *gonelini* for Octoviano de Vicomerato, the unmarried orator of Milan in Venice, found his work had been abandoned without payment; for his client had retired to a monastery on the island of Termidi, where he would dress as a monk, and no longer needed the order. The case was reported to the Signoria.[25]

Sanuto's diaries include copies of letters, such as one written by the Venetian ambassador to Milan. The following description of the entry of the King of France into Milan offers an image of a sumptuous version of the current late Quattrocento fashion for men. His Majesty was:

Dressed with a cloak of white damask [*manto de damaschin biancho*] lined with grey fur, over a *vesta* of

205

cloth of gold with an ermine collar [*bavaro de armelini*]. On his head he wore a cap [*bareta*] of white damask, also lined with grey fur; and he rode upon a white steed decked with cloth of gold. . . . His Royal Highness rode alone under a gold canopy [*baldachin d'oro*], lined with fur, supported by eight horses . . . around the *baldachin* was the entire college of doctors, clothed in scarlet with their collars [*bavari*] and caps of scarlet lined with fur . . . the streets were completely covered with woollen cloths of various colours . . .[27]

132. (above) Portrait, possibly of Francesco di Bartolomeo Archinto, by Giovanni Ambrogio Preda, 1494. Wide lapels of fur and dropped shoulder-lines, giving a cloak-like loose fit to the overgowns, were common in the last decade of the century.

133. (right) Thunderstruck figures in The End of the World, by Signorelli, 1499. As men's doublets fit only to the waist, their hose are necessarily constructed in one garment and worn with a codpiece (*braghetta*).

134. (opposite) The Daughter of Benvegnudo is Miraculously Healed, by Giovanni Mansueti, *c.* 1500. There are some extremely colourful, highly patterned men's hose shown in the picture. These were always considered fashionable throughout the century; it is difficult to say when they have definite heraldic significance.

The use of fur features very prominently in the overgowns worn by both men and women in this period. Collars and facings of fur and of velvet distinguish the lines of the various layers of clothing and emphasize the contrast between the full outer garments and the more tailored clothes beneath. As a result, the neck and shoulderline is probably the most prominent element in late Quattrocento dress. Simultaneously, the figured textiles lose their importance in fashion. No longer does the organic presence of large pomegranates dominate the rich figured velvets of silk, silver and gold. Rather, a much bolder contrast of colour and texture is used, and the figured textile motifs are reduced in size, although the pomegranate, now a tradition, lingers on in the larger-scale textiles for furnishing and ecclesiastical vestments.

And so what had happened to dress in the Quattrocento? Why should Italy and the fifteenth century have been singled out? For surely dress, and particularly fashion, continues to follow its usual path, sporadically bursting into noticeably new shapes and styles, without regard for the beginning and end of a century. The answer is probably that we have been conditioned to history by the historians of the nineteenth century. However, one cannot ignore the splendour of dress during the Renaissance and the important part it played in art and society. In retrospect, the glamour and glitter of the dresses, jewels and textiles stand out as masterpieces; technically superb, incomprehensibly expensive, and the epitome of good—or perhaps bad—taste.

Glossary of Renaissance Dress and Textile Terms

The entries suffixed by 'M' and 'F' indicate whether they are garments worn by men or women. 'Z', 'c' and 'g' are often interchangeable ('z' being used in the north). The 's' may or may not appear at the beginning of a word, e.g. *sbernia/bernia*, *scuffia/cuffia*. 'S', 'x' and 'z' may be interchangeable. Double consonants may appear as single ones. Most of the vowels are variable in the spelling, also. In some documents the hard 'c' and 'g' (i.e. those followed by the vowels 'a', 'o', 'u') are followed by 'h'; e.g. *ghamurra = gamurra*.

ADOGATO/ADDOGATO. Particoloured with broad stripes of cloth. An inventory of 1414 registers a tunic *addogata* with green and *monachino*.

AFFALDATO. Arranged into neat folds. Particularly from the mid-century on, garments were cut with far greater precision of tailoring, the arrangement of folds from the shoulders down being a very important factor in defining the fashionable silhouette. The letters of Galeazzo Maria Sforza of 1475 include an entry for a '*zornea de la moscharole*' which was '*tuta afaldata e non da petto*'; this suggests that the bodice fitted smoothly, whilst the folds came from the waist (Porro, *op.cit.*, p.663).

AFFRAPPATORI. See FRAPPATURE.

AGHETTO/AGUGELLO. See PUNTA.

ALESSANDRINO. A vivid violet blue colour, achieved by dyeing the cloth with *oricello*, a form of lichen, before immersing it into the *vagello*.

ALLUCCIOLATI. The sparkling loops of silver or gold which stand out above the silk velvet pile (see VELLUTO).

ALTOBASSO/ALTO E BASSO. See VELLUTO.

APPICCIOLATO/PICCIOLATO. A kind of silk, generally damask, possibly with a pattern arranged in stripes or detached flowers.

BALDACCHINO. A silk textile, possibly originating in Baghdad (vocabolario della Crusca). *Baldacchino* is not registered very often as a textile used for clothing, though an inventory of 1417 records a *cotta* of red *baldacchino*, and another of 1452 lists a *gamurra pavonazza* with sleeves of *baldacchino* (Polidori Calamandrei, *op.cit.*, p. 126). Alternatively, the word *baldacchino* is used for a hanging or canopy.

135. Miracles of Saint Vincent Ferrer, detail; by Ercole de' Roberti. The men's *giornee* are *affaldate*.

BALZANA/BALZA.   Trimming around the hemline of a gown, e.g. jewelled ornaments around the hemline of a dress, or a border of contrasting textile or fur.

BALZO (F).   A large headdress, rising up in a rounded form from the forehead, completely hiding the female wearer's hair (the hairline having been plucked back to create an artificially high forehead). The shape of the headdress is founded on an understructure, probably of willow, which is covered by a rich textile and alternatively by false hair of white or yellow silk, or by real hair (*capelli morti*). The *balzo* then may be decorated further with ribbon or braid. The fashion for *balzi* is peculiar to Italy, and to the first half of the Quattrocento.

BAMBAGIA.   A linen or cotton textile used for interfacing garments. It is invariably sold by weight, rather than the length of *braccia*.

BECA/BECCA (F).   Probably a belt of silk to which the hose are attached. A trousseau listed in 1493 included two *beche* of velvet, with gold laces (G. Biagi, *Due corredi nuziali fiorentini, 1320–1493*, Florence, 1899).

BECCHETTO.   The long hanging part of the *cappuccio* which is sometimes draped over the arm or shoulder, or wrapped about the neck (see CAPPUCCIO).

BENDA/BINDA (F).   A length of silk or linen veil used for covering, wrapping round or intertwining with the hair.

BERETTINO.   A shade of grey, verging on black, favoured by Isabella d'Este apparently because it suited her complexion extremely well, but probably also because of her Spanish origins. In other circumstances, it was sometimes worn as a colour of mourning.

BERRETTA (M/F).   Any form of cap or hat of rounded or semi-conical shape. Usually fitting closely to the head, the *berretta* could be brimless, or turned up around the edges. The woman's *berretta* was rather like a coif (*cuffia*), and was often decorated with

embroidery, or was made of a silk textile such as damask or satin. The man's *berretta* could also be made of a similar silk textile; but it was made usually of felted woollen cloth, and was frequently worn with a hat badge (*fermaglio*). There were some *berrette* of distinguishing shapes, e.g. *berretta ducale* or the *berretta alla capitanesca*.

BIANCHERIA.   A composite term for all white linen goods, personal and otherwise, belonging to a household. *Biancheria* therefore covers sheets and towels, as well as shirts, kerchiefs, coifs, collars and the occasional *guarnello*.

BIANCHETTA.   A kind of white cloth, possibly woollen.

BIGIO.   A shade of grey.

BOCCACCINO.   A modest textile of cotton or linen used for lining sleeves (M. Giuliani, *op.cit.*), or for simple versions of garments, e.g. the black *giornea* of *boccaccino* recorded in a trousseau of 1459 (Polidori Calamandrei, *op.cit.*, p. 126).

BOMBASINA.   A cheap cotton, or cotton and linen fabric, equivalent to fustian. It was regularly used for lining doublets or for interfacing. *Bombasina* has also been used as the name of a garment made of that fabric (Malaguzzi Valeri, *op.cit.*, p. 225).

BORSA/BORSETTA.   A purse, usually attached to the belt. Many were decorated with embroidery, sometimes with pearls or gems.

BOTTONI/MASPILLI.   Buttons. With the advances in tailoring during the fourteenth century came the use of buttons for fastenings. Whilst being practical, buttons, like ribbons, cords and laces, became important decorative details on garments, sometimes being made of or covered with silk, or of silver or silver-gilt.

BRACHE/BRAGHE (M).   In the fourteenth century long balloonish versions of these were worn by laughable caricatures in the novelle related by Boccaccio and Sacchetti. As underpants, they are listed in the fifteenth century under entries for *panni di gamba*. More frequently, however, underpants are referred to as *mutande*.

BRAGHETTA (M).   Codpiece; a kind of pouch devised to hide the genitals. *Braghette* began to be worn at the end of the century as doublets grew shorter and shorter.

BREDONE.   A pair of *bredoni* appears in the letters of Galeazzo Maria Sforza. They probably are pieces which hang down from the back of the shoulders, perhaps vestiges of fuller hanging sleeves.

BROCCATO.   Brocade, a textile usually made of silk, in which the patterning is introduced with one or more supplementary wefts. In a true brocade, the brocading weft is confined to the area of the pattern where it is needed, and then turns back on itself at the end of a motif, i.e. the patterning weft is not carried across from selvedge to selvedge. In the fifteenth century, the term is used in this strict sense; it rarely appears on its own as a noun, but qualifies a description of the cloth, e.g. *velluto chermisi broccato d'oro e d'argento*.

BRUSCHINO.   A shade of dark red, verging on *pavonazzo*, often used for *cioppe*.

BUSTO/PETTO (M/F).   The top part of the main body of the garment, probably referring to the area from shoulder to waist. It was becoming more and more common in the Quattrocento for garments to have the bodice and skirt cut separately.

CALCETTO.   A light short sock of linen, providing a washable layer between the foot and the *calza* of wool or silk.

CALZE (M/F).   Hose or stockings, usually made of woollen cloth, but also of silk. The men's *calze* are conveniently attached to the *farsetto* by means of laces and eyelets. There is no definite indication as to how the women's *calze* were supported, though a reference to a *beca* in 1493 provides a clue. Some form of harder footwear (*botte*, *scarpe*, *stivali*) is often worn over the *calze*. But when *calze*

136. (opposite, above) Portrait of Francesco Brivio, by Giovanni Ambrogio Preda. He wears a *berretta*, and the neck and front opening of his *vestimento* are trimmed with fur *filetti*.

137. (opposite, below) Francesco Sassetti and his son, by Ghirlandaio. Sassetti wears a *borsa* attached to the belt (*cintola*) worn round his *vesta*.

138. (left) Saint Roch, by Carlo Crivelli. To the *calze* are attached laces, which can be fastened through eyelets in the *farsetto* or doublet.

constitute the only layer of legwear, a piece of leather or felted wool would be attached to the sole of each foot.

CAMBELLOTTO/ZAMBELLOTO. Woollen cloth, probably quite hardwearing, originally made of camel's or goat's hair. A gown for wearing in the country, made of *zambellotto*, is listed in the letters of Galeazzo Maria Sforza (Porro, *op.cit.*, p. 129). In 1469 in Florence, it is recorded how a group of people jointly sent '*un cambellotto pavonazzo e broccato pagonazzo e d'ariento per un paio di maniche*' as a gift to a new-born child (Strozzi, *op.cit.*, p. 599). The exact meaning of the term is difficult to ascertain for there are also in the fifteenth century examples of *cambellotto* of silk.

CAMICIA/CAMISA (M/F). The chemise, made usually of linen, but occasionally of cotton or silk. In the earlier part of the century, the *camicia* is a functional washable layer of clothing worn between the skin and the outer woollen or silk garments. However, as the Quattrocento progresses, the chemise, revealed through slits and slashes down the sleeves and the bodice, and around the neckline, becomes more decorated with embroidered bands around the collar and cuffs. The cut of the shirt was different for men and women. There must have been regional variations also; e.g. men's shirts '*a modo di Firenze*' (Strozzi, *op.cit.*, p. 100).

CAPPA (M). A garment with sleeves, associated with the *roba*.

CAPPELLO (M/F). A hat with a substantial brim, often made of straw. Considerable quantities of straw hats were exported to France (and presumably elsewhere in the north of Europe) from the late fourteenth century (J. Evans, *Dress in Medieval France*, Oxford University Press, 1952, p. 51). These hats were sometimes lined with black silk or velvet, and trimmed round the brim with black or gold fringing (Polidori Calamandrei, *op.cit.*, pp. 126–7). Such hats were probably used when travelling, and appear in paintings worn by riders and grooms.

CAPPUCCIO (M). A hood, often with a rolled brim round the crown of the head, which then hangs down. It is composed of three sections: the *mazzocchio*, the padded rolled base; the *foggia*, a shorter fuller hanging end; and the *becchetto*, the long end which is conveniently and effectively wrapped or draped over the arm or shoulder.

CAPPUCCIO (F). The women's version of the male *cappuccio* remains in fashion in the early years of the century. But generally, throughout the Quattrocento, the feminine *cappuccio* is simply the hooded part of a garment such as the *mantello*.

CHERMISI/CREMISI. Kermes. The word applies both to the dyestuff itself, the colour it makes, and woollen cloth dyed with kermes. Considered the best quality dye for reds available, yielding the greatest intensity of colour per ounce, *chermisi* came from the East, usually transported via Constantinople. The brilliant red dye was obtained from the dried bodies of pregnant females of the kermes shield-louse, *Coccus*

139. (above) The Discovery of the True Cross, detail; by Piero della Francesca, *c.* 1452–66. The *camicia* is worn directly under the *farsetto*.

140. (right) A group of men in The Resurrection of a Child by Ghirlandaio, completed in 1485. The nearest figure wears a *veste togata*, and on his right shoulder a *cappuccio*. Against his back hangs the *foggia* from the *mazzocchio*; the *becchetto* passes over the shoulder and hangs down in front, perhaps to be supported with a gesture of the right hand.

141. (opposite) The Three Graces, detail from Primavera by Botticelli, 1478. They wear imaginatively draped silk *camicie*, which correspond in substance – though not precisely in form – to the finely embroidered women's chemises of the latter part of the century.

illicis. The same insect found around the Mediterranean was also used for dyeing; it was not of such a good quality, however, and was known as grain, *grana*. *Chermisi* was used for the finest textiles. The most expensive silk velvets brocaded and decorated with a looped pile in silver and gold (*broccati* and *allucciolati*) were always dyed with kermes. In 1464, it was decreed by Pope Paul II that *chermisi* should be used as the cardinals' purple (*purpura cardinalizia*); for there had been a considerable decline in the dyeing, and therefore use, of purple murex. A statute of 1464 forbids the possession by women of Florence of more than one overgarment, *cioppa* or *giornea*, dyed with kermes.

CINTOLA/CINTURA/CINGOLA (M/F). The belt, worn by men and women,

was used less as a means of drawing a gown into folds at the waist or the hips, than as an often lavish piece of ornamentation. Belts were invariably made of precious metals, sometimes incorporating jewels, and often with rosaries, strings of pearls or metal ornaments hanging off them. Other belts, particularly those worn by women, were made of precious brocaded textiles, and finished with an enamelled or jewelled silver or gold buckle.

CIOPPA (M/F). A type of overgown. The word is used in Tuscany and the Naples region, and is the equivalent of *pellanda* (north of Italy), and the *veste* or *sacco* (Bologna and elsewhere). Towards the end of the century, the terms *pellanda* and *sacco* disappear, and are replaced by *vestito*, which refers to

something rich and fashionable. The *cioppa* is a generous garment, often with long hanging sleeves, which appear in a variety of forms. It is worn by women over the *gamurra*; except in the case of a poor young woman who, in an impecunious state when she had to mend her *gamurra*, was forced to wear her *cioppa* directly over her chemise (*camicia*) (Strozzi, *op.cit.*, p. 548). In general, the longer, fuller, sweeping sleeves are worn in the north of Italy, whilst in Tuscany and the south, the sleeves of this overdress are more conservatively cut. The *cioppa* is often lined with fur or silk, depending on the season, the lining being turned back at the hem. Invariably, a richer or more valuable fur is used around the facings, whilst the majority of the *cioppa* is lined with more modest skins.

COAZZONE (F). A broad plait or roll of hair, often decorated with ribbon or braiding, which hangs down the back. It is sometimes worn with a *trinzale*.

CORDELLA/CORDELLINA. A cord, used for lacing up the opening of a garment or shoe, or for lacing in sleeves. The *cordella* often has a little metal point (*punta/agugello*) at each end, to stop it from fraying, and to assist the threading through the eyelet (*maglia/maglietta*).

CORNA (F). Literally, horns; meaning the horned headdress which enters fashion in Italy towards the middle of the century. The style originates in the gothic north of Europe.

COROZOSO. *Colori corozosi* were the colours prescribed for mourning. Many of them were worn daily as a matter of course. They were dull dark colours, shades of mulberry, blue, green and brown, as well as black.

CORPETTO (M). See FARSETTO.

COTTA (F). Probably the summer version of the *gamurra*, being made of silk rather than woollen cloth. Some *cotte* were quite elaborate, such as that which appears in 1466 in the trousseau of Nannina de'Medici which was a *cotta* of white *damaschino* brocaded in gold with flowers, with sleeves embroidered with pearls; and another *cotta* was of silk, with sleeves of *cremisi* and gold brocade (*con maniche di broccato d'oro cremisi*). As in the case of the *gamurra*, the *cotta* could have sleeves of a textile different from the main body of the dress. Whilst it was considered extremely informal to go out wearing a *gamurra* and nothing over it, the *cotta* could be worn alone on quite formal occasions in summer. The relative fullness of the *cotta* compared with the *gamurra* is difficult to determine. Marco Parenti noted in 1465 that 18 *braccia* were sufficient to make a *cotta* of *zetani vellutato di chermisi* for his wife (Strozzi, *op.cit.*, p. 445). Because silk has less give than wool, silk garments probably needed to be cut more generously than woollen ones.

CREMISI. See CHERMISI.

CUFFIA/SCUFFIA (M/F). A coif, i.e. a close-fitting cap or bonnet, sometimes covering the ears and with ties which pass under the chin. It may be made of linen, in which case it is either worn under other kinds of headgear, or worn alone at night.

DAMASCHINO. Damask, a monochrome figured textile with a ground of satin (warp-faced) and a pattern in sateen (weft-faced). The origins of the textile are commonly ascribed to Damascus.

A DIVISA/DIVISATO. Parti-coloured. The hose (*calze*) are often worn *mi-parti*, sometimes as fashion, sometimes as part of a livery.

ALLA DOGALINA. A description of sleeves which, like those worn by the Doge and the highest-ranking Venetian officials, are wide all the way down.

DOSSI. Skins of fur from the back of an animal.

ERMELLINI. Ermine, a highly prized fur, rarely used to line an overgarment throughout, but rather reserved for areas—necklines, sleeves and hems—where it will be shown off. All references to this and other

142. (opposite, above) Bust of Beatrice d'Este, by Cristoforo Romano. The back of her head is covered with a *trinzale*, whence her hair hangs down in a *coazzone*.

143. (opposite, below) Figures before the Madonna of Mercy, detail; School of Romagna. The women wear their hair *a corna*.

144. (above) A small boy observing The Annunciation, by Carlo Crivelli, 1486. He wears an embroidered *cuffia*, and over a *gonnellina* a practical linen or cotton pinafore.

145. A soldier in The Victory of Heraclius, by Piero della Francesca, c. 1452–66. The construction of the *farsetto* is clearly shown; to its upper sleeves are attached laces, for tying on the pauldrons (shoulder-pieces) of armour.

furs are made in the plural, thus not merely indicating the type of fur, but the fact that many skins must be used to make up a substantial area of fur.

FALDIA (F).   An underskirt of linen held out by means of horizontal bands padded with cotton wool or linen fibre. The fashion appears in the later part of the century.

FARSETTINO (F).   Related to the *farsetto*, doublet, of men's dress. A *farsettino da donna* with 16 silver buttons appears in the inventory of Riccardo del Bene of 1411. It was probably a kind of undergarment, the buttons of which would show, its collar rising above the neckline of the fuller garments worn on top. (Polidori Calamandrei, *op.cit.*, p. 128.)

FARSETTO (M).   The generic term for a man's doublet, which is also known by the names *corpetto*, *giubetto*, *zuparello* and *zupone* (*giubbone*). This type of garment is made by a professional *farsettaio*. The doublet is a close-fitting garment, stuffed and quilted. It has a low-standing collar and usually sleeves. Worn over the shirt, and beneath a tunic and/or other forms of overgarment, the *farsetto* offers warmth and protection, and defines the outline of the torso, finishing around the hipline. The shape of the doublet varies from one decade to the next, depending on the fashionable silhouette. In the earlier Quattrocento, the doublet is nearly always hidden by some form of tunic or gown, the exception being for sporting activities. Later in the century, as clothes worn by the fashionable young become more revealing, the doublet is shortened and is generally much more in evidence, worn with a loose cloak or gown as opposed to a closed tunic with sleeves. It has been suggested by Levi Pisetzky that some forms of doublet (the *corpetto*, the *giubetto* or *zuparello*) were meant to show, whereas others (the *farsetto* or *zupone*) were always concealed. It is the richness of the textile from which the doublet is made which indicates the nature of the occasion for which it is worn, and implies the degree with which the garment is to be shown off.

FAZZOLETTO.   A kerchief had various uses. Worn by women, the fine silk or linen *fazzoletti* were tucked into or worn over the lower necklines of their dresses.

FERMAGLIO.   A brooch or hat badge, also known as a *brocchetta* or *medaglio*, depending on its form and use. A versatile piece of jewellery worn on the shoulder, on a headdress, the sleeve, or the bodice of a garment. Invariably made on a large scale, the *fermaglio* was effective from a distance. Some brooches bore figures or emblems in relief, sometimes with heraldic significance.

FILETTO.   The very edge of a border or hem, which was sometimes trimmed with narrow strips of fur. A Florentine sumptuary legislation of 1471 allowed women's *veste* to have *filetti*, *garzi* or *orli* of fur (C. Mazzi, *Provvisioni suntuarie fiorentine, 29 novembre 1464, 29 febbraio 1471*, Florence, 1908, p. 10).

FINESTRELLA.   The opening at the front of the elbow of a sleeve, through which the arm passes, leaving the remainder of the sleeve to hang down independently. Thus a contrast is shown between the textile of the main body of the overgarment and the upper part of the sleeve, and the lower arm, which reveals the textile of the closer-fitting sleeves attached to the layer of clothing beneath. Sometimes, if the sleeves of the overgarment are detachable, those sleeves hang loosely direct from the shoulder.

FOGGIA.   Part of the male *cappuccio*.

FRAPPATURE/FRASTAGLI.   Dagged hems, i.e. edges of cloth which have been decoratively cut into scallops, leafy shapes or some other kind of pattern. A feature of both masculine and feminine dress, the *frappature* may be an eccentricity, criticised by moralists; but they are a sign of a sophisticated culture and indulgent lifestyle. Once dead as fashion, vestiges of dagging and fringing are sometimes found worn as livery by young men and commonly by fools and jesters.

FRENELLO (F). A hair ornament—a string of pearls, which is entwined round the twists of real and false hair and fine silk veil.

GABBANO (M). A heavy cape with sleeves, used especially for protection against bad weather, but also as an elegant ceremonial overgarment.

GAMURRA/CAMMURA/CAMORA (F). The Tuscan term for the simple dress worn directly over the woman's chemise (*camicia*). In the north of Italy, it is known by the terms *zupa*, *zipa* or *socha*. The *gamurra* is worn by women of all classes. It is both functional and informal, being worn on its own at home, and covered by some form of overgarment such as the *cioppa*, *mantello*, *pellanda* or *vestimento* out-of-doors or on a more formal occasion. Following the contour of the body, it is usually unlined, and made of wool or occasionally silk. Earlier in the century, the sleeves are attached; but later they are more commonly

separate, and often of a different, richer textile.

GARANZA. An alternative term for *robbia*, madder, a dyestuff obtained from the roots of the madder plant *Rubia tinctorum*. Like all the red dyes, it produced a range of reds through to purples and black, depending on the mordant used and whether it was under- or over-dyed with a different colour (notably blue or yellow).

GHELERO. A type of garment frequently mentioned in the letters of Galeazzo Maria Sforza. It must have been an overgarment, because there are several examples lined with fur; and it did have detachable sleeves, for three pairs were ordered for a *ghelero* at the court of Galeazzo Maria Sforza (Porro, *op.cit.*, p. 642).

GHIRLANDA/GRILLANDA (F). Literally, a garland, which is worn as a headdress by women. It often takes the form of a padded roll, covered with some elaborate textile.

146. The Judgement of Paris, Tuscan School. In addition to the shoulder tabs resembling a detail of Roman armour (thus conjuring a classical flavour into the picture) there hang decorative *frappature*.

217

147. (right) The head of Ilaria del Carretto; detail of the tomb sculpture by Jacopo della Quercia, 1406. She wears a *ghirlanda* made from textile, and decorated with spiralling flowers finely worked in metal.

148. (below) Federigo da Montefeltro in a Sacra Conversazione by Piero della Francesca. The duke wears a *giornea* with his armour.

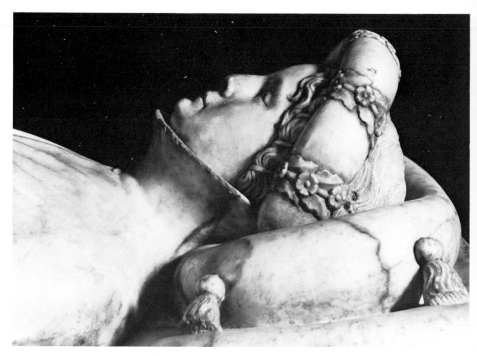

Garlands of flowers or grass are worn by the young innocent beauties of whom the poets sing. Sometimes the *ghirlanda* is covered with gems or with feathers. A decree published in Siena in 1412 forbade all embroidery and pearls, except for a *grillanda* on the head worth a maximum of 25 gold florins (Giuliani, *op.cit.*).

GIORNEA (F). An overdress, open in front and down the sides, to allow the textile of the *cotta* worn underneath to show through. The *giornea* is quite often longer at the back of the hem, offering a sweeping profile in movement. It may or may not have detached sleeves. It is a summer garment, worn more often in Florence than further north, where the *pellanda*, with open or closed long sleeves, is more suitable for most of the year. Sometimes, however, the *giornea* is lined with fur, in which case it may be worn during the cooler months. It appears to be a garment normally worn by the young. In a law of 1456, the *giornea* is associated with the *cioppa*, both being garments worn directly over the *cotta*. It was stated that women were allowed up to two silk overgarments—to be worn at separate times—one for winter, the other for summer. It could be a *cioppa*, or a *giornea*, whichever was preferred, with one *cotta* for wearing underneath (Polidori Calamandrei, *op.cit.*, p. 44).

GIORNEA (M). An open-sided overgarment which, as with the women's version, takes the place of the fourteenth-century *guarnacca*. But it is shorter than the *guarnacca*, and is sometimes worn in a military context. It is worn directly over the *farsetto* or *zupone*. San Bernardino despised the *giornea*, likening it to a horsecloth trimmed with fringes down the sides and about the hem. The *giornea* often bears embroidered devices, such as the three *zornee de raxo cremisino*, embroidered with beautiful pearls and the symbol of a clock, suggested by Ludovico il Moro.

GIUBETTO (M). See FARSETTO.

A GOMITO (M/F). A form of sleeve, bulbous in shape, but narrow at the wrist.

GONNELLA/GONNA/SOTTANA (F). The fourteenth-century term for the fifteenth-century *gamurra*.

GONNELLA (M). The fourteenth-century version of the *veste* or *vestito*, and in the fifteenth century, a relatively short form of gown worn by men. The *gonnellino* is a shorter version still, worn by younger men.

GORGERONE (M). The part of a suit of armour which protects the neck and shoulders.

149. Members of Ludovico Gonzaga's court, by Mantegna, *c.* 1471—4. The men wear *gonnellini,* each with an *orlo* of fur.

150. (above) Portrait of Smeralda Bandinelli by Botticelli, *c.* 1470. Over a *gamurra*, she wears what may be termed a *guarnello*.

151. (opposite) Beatrice d'Este in the Pala Sforzesca, Lombard School, *c.* 1495. She wears her hair in a *coazzone*. Her dress is decorated with *liste*, the sleeves being tied in and decorated down the arm with *stringhe*.

GORGIERE (F).   The equivalent of the French *gorgerette*; it is a silk or linen veil which covers the neck.

A GOZZO (M/F).   Likened to a bird's crop, the sleeves described in this way are of a bulbous shape, fitting closely at the wrists. A common form of sleeve at the beginning of the century, by 1446 *gozzo* was probably so widely accepted that it alone came to describe a large sleeve; thus Lorenzo Strozzi's description of *cioppe* with *gozzi a trombe*—the word *maniche* is understood. (Strozzi, *op.cit.*, p. 29).

GRANA.   Grain, the red dye obtained from the kermes (see CHERMISI) found around the Mediterranean. It was cheaper, being inferior to the *chermisi* imported from the East. As with other red dyes, *grana* was used as the basis of many colours and shades ranging from pink and scarlet reds through to purples and black.

GRIGIO.   As a colour, it means grey. However, as in English, the word is also used to denote 'grey' cloth, i.e. untreated cloth.

GUALESCIO.   A plain fabric, probably of silk, invariably used for lining, e.g. Marco Parenti's wife's *cotta* of *zetano vellutato* was lined with red *gualescio* (Strozzi, *op.cit.*, p. 445). In a sumptuary law published in Siena in 1412, it was stated that sleeves could be lined modestly with *gualescio* or *panno lino*, *bocchaccino* or *taffeta* (Giuliani, *op.cit.*, p. x). In the Pucci inventory are listed horsecloths of *gualescio*, as well as men's *sopravesti* for riding.

GUANTI (M/F).   Gloves. In the second half of the century, *guanti di camoscio* (chamois leather) are quite frequently mentioned. Galeazzo Maria Sforza ordered a pair for dancing, lined with scarlet. The gloves made in Milan were quite highly prized in other cities.

GUARDACORE (M/F).   Possibly worn as a nightshirt, for the young Isabella d'Este possessed '*uno guardacore overo camisia da portare la nocte*' of *rosato* cloth (Levi Pisetzky, *La Storia del Costume*, *op. cit.*, p. 285). The 1445–6 registers of the Court of Ferrara note that the Marquis Leonello ordered two *braccia* of *cetanino* (*zetanino*) *raso crimisino* to have a *guardicore* made for wearing in bed.

GUARNACCA (F).   The term continues to be used in the fifteenth century, but is more commonly called a *giornea*. A statute issued in Perugia in 1445 permitted a *guarnacca* as part of a bride's outfit, provided that its value did not exceed 30 florins, and that if it were made of velvet or silk, it was not decorated with embroidery.

A GUARNAZZONE.   A style of full sweeping sleeve found on male and female overgarments similar to those like wings (*ad ale*). This type of sleeve was worn by Bianca Maria Sforza for her wedding celebrations in 1493.

GUARNELLO (M/F).   Both a kind of linen or cotton textile, and the feminine garment constructed from such a fabric. The *guarnello* probably has the same significance as a *rascia*. It is a simple, reasonably loose-fitting dress, similar to the *cotta*, but sometimes worn without sleeves. *Guarnello*, being cotton or linen, may be registered in inventories with the rest of the *biancheria*—chemises (*camicie*), towels and kerchiefs. The *guarnello*, *rascia* or *saia* is the standard form of dress for angels. It is worn by children as a simple, washable garment, and possibly also by pregnant women. There are also examples of *guarnelli* listed under items of male clothing.

GUAZZERONE.   A border of a hemline, sometimes made from a contrasting fabric.

INDISIA.   A type of lining material, possibly of wool.

INFERRIATO/A INFERRIATA.   See VELLUTO.

LACCA.   Lacquer, a resinous substance born from the branches of some trees in the Euphorbia family through the activity of certain parasites. It was imported from India and Indo-china. As a red dye, it was rather precious, and appears to have been used infrequently.

LENZA.   A ribbon or braid tied round the crown of the head, and often decorated with a jewel over the forehead.

LISTA.   A strip of cloth applied to a garment to give a bold striped effect, such as is found on the dress worn by Beatrice d'Este in the Pala Sforzesca.

LUCCO (M/F).   A form of long gown worn in Florence, initially as part of official or academic dress, and subsequently in a more general context. It was open in front and fastened at the neck; it also had slits at the sides to allow the arms to pass through.

MAGLIA/MAGLIETTA.   A metal eyelet or little loop through which laces are threaded, sometimes made of silver or silver-gilt.

MANICHE.   Sleeves come in all forms of shape and construction. Although the sleeves of overgarments are sometimes short, or hanging open, the arm is always covered to the wrist. Even peasant women working in the fields had to respect this rule of modesty. During the early decades of the century, the sermons of San Bernardino and the sumptuary legislations passed by the local governments reflect disapproval of the devilishly monstrous sizes of sleeves, in an attempt to check the width of the hemlines. The sleeves of overgarments are invariably ample and long; whilst those of the clothes worn beneath (*gamurra, farsetto, cotta, gonnella*) fit the arm more closely. In the first half of the Quattrocento, the cut of the sleeve, like the cut of the rest of the garment, becomes more sophisticated; instead of being cut in one piece from shoulder to wrist or to hemline, the sleeve is much more finely tailored once the upper (often slightly gathered) and lower sleeves are joined at the elbow (see DOGALINA, FINESTRELLA, GOZZO, GOMITO, GUARNAZZONE.)

MANTELLO (M/F).   Traditionally a practical cloak worn over all clothes for warmth and protection against inclement weather, especially when travelling. It is draped over the shoulders and, in the case of the elderly or widowed women, over the head. San Bernardino (*op.cit.*) alluded to the volume and drape of the *mantello* in describing the vast size of the sleeves of ladies' *cioppe*: 'You could say that the *cioppa* has one *mantello* on each side'. Because of its simple shape, and since it is both a practical and a classless garment, the *mantello* is often used as a convenient theatrical prop for figures in paintings. The Madonna nearly always wears a *mantello* over a *gamurra*; it is significant that she often covers her head with a cloak—a sober gesture—being the prerogative of widows and older women. Saints, too, are invariably donned with *mantelli*; their appearance is thus related very closely to that of pilgrims. Although the cut and construction of the basic *mantello* barely changes, fashion demands that it be worn in different ways, e.g. turned back over the shoulder, or fastened over one shoulder instead of under the chin.

152. (above) Presumed portrait of Lucrezia Crivelli, known as La Belle Ferronière, by Leonardo. Mounted with a jewel over the forehead, a *lenza* is worn about the crown of her head. The details closely correspond to those viewed from behind in plate 142.

153. (right) The Madonna della Rondine, detail of the Virgin, by Carlo Crivelli. Little metal eyelets, *maglie*, appear at the laced seams of sleeve and bodice.

MASPILLI.   See BOTTONI.

MAZZOCCHIO (M/F).   A stuffed roll covered with fabric which is worn on the head. It forms the basis of the men's *cappuccio*, being the part of the hood which fits round the crown. By women, the *mazzocchio* is pinned to the hair, giving slight height and a rounded shape to the veil worn on top. The *mazzocchio* continued to be worn by veiled older women long after new taller fashions in headdresses had been introduced to the fashionable younger women.

MONACHINO.   A shade of brown with a reddish tint. It is a modest colour, occasionally worn in mourning or by widows; it is also used quite generally for a functional garment not of great value.

MONGILE/MONGINO/MONZINO (M/F).   A form of cloak with sleeves, possibly of monastic origin, which may have originated in Spain. It is worn open in front, and long to the ground. Between 1478 and 1485, 40 are listed in the wardrobe of Leonora of Aragon some described as '*ala moresca*' (in the Moorish style), many without sleeves attached.

MORELLO.   Literally, mulberry-coloured. It is equated in treatises on dyeing and painting with *pavonazzo*. A red dye formed the basis of *morello* and *pavonazzo*, the resulting quality being dependent on the type of dye used (*chermisi, grana, garanza* or *verzino*). Being a dark shade, *morello* is one of the *colori corozosi* worn by widows and in mourning. It is also commonly worn for everyday civic dress.

154. The Interior of a Church, detail, attributed to Fra Carnevale. The younger women go about with their heads uncovered, each wearing a *cioppa* over a *cotta* or *gamurra*. Other women, for reasons of age or bereavement, drape themselves in *mantelli*.

MUTANDE (M). Underpants, confused with *brache* at the beginning of the century, listed amongst the *biancheria* relating to men's attire. However, there are no known documented examples of *mutande* to be worn by women.

ORLO. The hem of a garment. Corazza in his Florentine diary recorded on 12 November 1435 the boys of a *brigata* wearing fur-lined tunics with the hems turned back on the outside (*con l'orlo di fuori*) by a third of a *braccio* (see also FILLETI.)

PANCIE. Skins of fur from the underside of the animal's belly, which are of finer quality than those from the back (*dossi*).

PANNICELLI. Cloths of linen, usually worn by women over the head and/or shoulders.

PANNO. A general word for cloth (often used in the plural). *Panno lano*: woollen cloth. *Panno lino*: linen cloth. When unqualified, it may usually be presumed that *panno* refers to woollen cloth.

PASSATEMPO (F). A short cloak, open at the sides, rather like some *giornee*.

PAVONAZZO/PAONAZZO/PAGONAZZO. Literally, peacock-coloured. However, it does not mean peacock-blue or -green, but rather relates to the colour of the peahen—a brownish tint of red. Red dye forms the basis of *pavonazzo*, the quality of which depends on the type of dye used, whether it be *cremisi* or *grano*.

PEDULE. The protective sole attached to the bottom of each *calza*—necessary when shoes or boots were not worn over the hose.

PELLANDA/OPELANDA (F). The word used in the north of Italy in the first half of the fifteenth century to denote an overdress; it is related to the *houppelande* of northern Europe. It is the equivalent of the Florentine *cioppa* (see CIOPPA).

PELLANDA (M). An ample overgarment, opening down the front, fur-lined, with full sleeves

often cut into decorative hemlines (see FRAPPATURE). Towards the end of the century, the term *pellanda* dies out, and is replaced by the equivalent *roba*.

PELO DI LIONE. A tawny yellow colour, resembling that of lion's skin.

PIANELLA. A form of shoe with a leather sole built up into a wedge, the foot being covered with a strap or band of silk textile. At its lowest, the *pianella* resembles a simple slipper or mule; however, it could also reach uncomfortable heights, for in 1480 in Venice the sole measured the equivalent of about half a metre (Molmenti, *op.cit.*, p. 262). The fashion for tall *pianelle* was not just a Venetian one; for on his journey from Milan to Genoa in 1480 Florentine, Giovanni Ridolfi, commented with surprise on the Genoese women going about with no, or at least very low *pianelle* (*senza pianelle o basse basse*). (Levi Pisetzky, *La Storia del Costume*, *op.cit.*, p. 219.)

PUNTA/AGHETTO/AGUGELLO. The point, sometimes of precious metal, which reinforces the tip of a ribbon or cord used for lacing up clothes. They pass through the eyelets (*magliette*) of silver or silver-gilt. The term comes to mean the whole lace, not just the metal tip.

RASCIA (F). A garment named after the textile from which it was made, rather in the way that the *guarnello* was.

RASO. Textile of satin weave (see ZETANO). As with *zetano*, *raso* may be used as a solid single-coloured textile; but it often constitutes the ground structure of a figured fabric, e.g. *raso vellutato*.

RENSA. Fine linen (probably originating from Rheims), used for the best quality *biancheria*.

RETA. A knotted net of silk or gold threads, which often incorporated pearls and sometimes other gems, worn over the hair.

RICCIO/RIZZO. See VELLUTO.

ROBA (M/F). Towards the end of the

155. (above) A figure in The Baptism of Christ, by Piero della Francesca. Men's *mutande* are recorded; but there is no known reference in contemporary documents to an equivalent for women.

156. (opposite) Saint Sebastian; detail from The Madonna della Rondine by Carlo Crivelli. The laces are tipped with *punte*. Presented as a fashionable young man of the later 1480s, his chemise puffs through the *finestrelle* of his sleeves.

century, *roba* signifies specifically a garment lined with fur, completely open in front—but closed in the following century.

ROSATO.   A shade of red (probably pinkish) often made from *grana*. Probably, *rosato* became so closely associated with a particular kind of cloth that the word is often used on its own, to denote the woollen cloth of the same colour. The solemn *rosato* appearance of Leonardo Bruni is described by Vespasiano da Bisticci (*op.cit.*). *Rosato* was not as highly prized as *chermisi*, for in a Florentine embassy to the Pope the eight ambassadors were clothed in *cremisi*, but their 72 companions wore *rosato*.

SACCO (F).   An overdress with sleeves, similar to the *cioppa*. There are examples made from velvet and others of woollen cloth.

SAIA.   Originally a type of woollen cloth; but alternatively, later in the century, *saia* may refer to a silk textile. The term often denotes a woman's garment, when it is probably related to the *cotta* and the *gamurra*; the 1464 Florentine legislation categorizes *saia*, *cotta* and *gamurra* together (see COTTA). A *saia doppia* is listed amongst the Pucci possessions of 1449, indicating that it was self-lined; because the entry specifies that it had sleeves of silk, this particular *saia* was probably made from woollen cloth. During the summer, Filippo Maria Visconti would wear a *saio* decorated in the military style; with it, he wore a lining of sable (*zibellini*) in winter, or of *vaio* or ermine in spring or autumn.

SBERNIA/BERNIA/ALBERNIA (M/F).
A short cloak, worn slung over one shoulder *a la apostolica*. Some suggest its name is a corrupted form of *burnus* (Arabic). (*Diario Ferrarese*, 1494.)

SBIADATO.   Possibly a shade of bluish grey; or the cloth of that colour. Used in combination with blue (*azzurro*) or grey (*bigio*), *sbiadato* might comply with this tonal range. (Polidori Calamandrei, *op.cit.*, pp. 131–2)

SCARLATTA.   Scarlet cloth; i.e. a woollen cloth, sometimes of a bright red scarlet colour.

SCARPE/SCARPETTE.   Shoes are not mentioned very frequently in inventories. Perhaps they were not even worn that often, for Lorenzo Strozzi remarked with delight at how in Spain he was wearing shoes, laced at the side of the foot (*scarpette colle cordelline dalla latora, colle punte lunghe tre dita*), thus removing the need to wear *peduli* on his *calze*. (Strozzi, *op.cit.*, p. 29) Shoes may be made of woollen cloth, perhaps with soles of felted wool; or they may be made of leather.

SCIUGATOIO/ASCIUGATOIO.   A towel; it has as many meanings as it does uses. As well as being a hand towel, it could be a cloth to cover a chest, or a pillowslip; it was equally commonly applied to the linen veil, worn over the head, usually by older women and widows. These *sciugatoi* look rather practical, plain and dense, compared with some of the light silk veils worn by the younger Italian women, or in Spain; the contrast is well described in a letter to Alessandra Macinghi Strozzi from one of her sons (Strozzi, *op.cit.*, p. 29). The *sciugatoio* was attached by means of hairpins and ribbons, in whatever manner best suited the wearer, and then fell down over the neck and shoulders. Certain religious orders, and possibly some widows, drew the towel under the chin, thus completely covering the neck.

SCUFFIA (M/F).   See CUFFIA.

SELLA (F).   A saddle-shaped headdress worn by women in the middle of the century, probably influenced by fashions from north of the Alps. Like the *corna*, the *sella* usually suspends a fine veil of silk.

STIVALI (M).   Boots. Footwear is not mentioned very frequently in contemporary documents. However, where *stivali* appear, they are often described as being made in a foreign style, e.g. *a la todesca con le poncte*, or of gilded leather (the gilding of leather being a speciality of Valencia, Spain).

157. (opposite) A Miracle of San Bernardino, detail; by Fiorino di Lorenzo. The second figure from the left wears what may be a *sbernia*.

158. (above) Study of a man doing up his shoe, by Antonio del Pollaiuolo. When walking outside raised *pianelle* or *zoccoli* were sometimes worn in addition to the *scarpe*, which were usually made of cloth or leather.

159. (above) The Princess; detail from Saint George and the Dragon, by Paolo Uccello. Attempts to restrict the length of the *strascico* were repeatedly enforced by sumptuary legislations.

160. (opposite) The Madonna and Child, detail; attributed to Piero della Francesca. A variety of different weights and styles of *veli* were worn over hair wrapped in *bende*.

STRASCICO (M/F). The depth of hem of a garment. It is difficult to determine exactly how the *strascico* was measured. In some cases, and perhaps most commonly, it refers just to the train of a woman's dress, often referred to as the *coda di veste*. At other times it signifies the depth of the border about the hem. Several sumptuary legislations included clauses restricting the size of the *strascico*.

STRINGHE. The ribbons or laces which hang decoratively from a garment, like those attached to Beatrice's sleeves in the Pala Sforzesca.

TABARRO/TABARRONE (M). A heavy overgarment, often lined with fur.

TAFFETA. A plain woven silk, used for lining sleeves, and for modest silk dresses.

TERZANELLO. A silk cloth, not of high quality, sometimes used for lining.

TOGA/TOGATO. A procession of scholars of the University of Bologna in 1431 was led by the rectors and public readers dressed in splendid *toghe* (see p. 123). The use of *toghe*, or the wearing of a *veste togato* probably bears a conscious reference to dress in classical Rome.

TREMOLANTI. Small pieces of decorative metalwork, often incorporated with fringing and chains, e.g. on headdresses.

TRINZALE (F). A piece of fine cloth covering the hair which, in the case

of Bianca Maria Sforza, covers both the back of her head and the long roll of hair (*coazzone*) hanging down her back, tied with ribbons and pearls.

TURCA (M/F). Corresponds to the *tunica alla turchesca*. Its name suggests an Oriental, possibly Turkish, origin. It is a long garment with sleeves, probably opening down the front, and perhaps with short slits at the sides as well. On knighting a Genoese nobleman, Ludovico il Moro adorned him with a *turca* (Malaguzzi Valeri, *op.cit.*, p. 233); it was probably an ample garment. In an inventory of 1491, Anna Maria Sforza is listed as possessing '*una turcha scarlatta fodrata de nocte*'. It is not certain whether this garment was meant to be a closed nightshift to be worn in bed, or an open lined dressing-gown.

TURCHINO. A colour, possibly a turquoise blue.

VAGELLO. A dye vat containing a solution of reduction dyes (woad and indigo).

VAIO. A general term for fur, used for lining overgarments but not often shown around the borders. For example, a *cioppa* may be lined with *vaio* and the more valuable ermine, the ermine being used around the facings down the front opening, around the hem and the sleeves, where it would show.

VALESCIO. See GUALESCIO

VELLUTO. Velvet, a textile with a ground structure of a plain weave, but which is characterized by a surface pile created by the use of an extra warp. In addition to plain single-colour silk velvets, there are many kinds of figured ones which incorporate a combination of weaves. *Velluto operato* is the general term for figured velvet. *Velluto inferriato/a inferriata* and *velluto raso*; voided velvet, in which the smooth ground weave contrasts with the apparently darker velvet pile: the pattern is traced in the voided areas where the pile, having been shaved away, allows the ground to show through. *Raso vellutato/zetano vellutato*: structurally similar to *velluto inferriato*,

for the pattern is dependent on the contrast between a satin ground and velvet pile; but in this case, the pattern is reversed. Much of the ground satin is apparent, and the figured pattern is defined by the velveted areas.
Velluto alto-basso/rilevato/controtagliato: two-pile velvet; the higher of the two cut piles absorbs more light and appears the darker shade.
Velluto cesellato incorporates cut (*tagliato*) and uncut (*riccio*) piles, the cut being higher than the uncut.
Velluto allucciolato: velvet which is highlighted by little loops of gold or silver, introduced in the weft of the textile, which stand out above the silk velvet pile.
Velluto riccio sopra riccio/rizo sopra rizo: velvet in which the areas of looped gold or silver threads stand out above the silk pile; the effect is much more solid than in the *velluti allucciolati*.

VELO/VELETTO DA TESTA (F). A veil; many are listed in inventories, and may be of fine linen or silk.

VERZINO. Brazil-wood, an important source of red dye, obtained from the trees of the *Caesalpinia* family, introduced to the West by the Venetians through their trading with the East; the country of Brazil was later named after its large number of indigenous trees of the *Caesalpinia* species.

VESCAPO (M/F). Recorded in the north of Italy, it is probably the type of cloak (*mantello*) worn over the head.

VESPAIO (F). Literally translated, it means a wasp's nest. In fact, it was a netted headdress worn by women, often made of strings of pearls.

VESTE/VESTA. Either the term corresponds to the *gonnella* of the fourteenth century, in which case it is a man's gown with sleeves, made from a variety of textiles; or it applies more generally to a suit of clothes.

VESTIMENTO (M/F). Later in the fifteenth century, the term which replaces the words *sacco* and *pellanda*, a regularly worn type of overgarment.

VESTITO (M/F). A general term, particularly during the latter part of the century, for an overgown with sleeves, probably a heavier version of the *veste*. In the splendid trousseau of Bianca Maria Sforza in 1493, there was just one *vestito*; but it was an extremely precious embroidered one (*di raso cremesino recamato*) with a hem (*balzana*) of embroidered *raso turchino*, and over the breast 80 little jewels with a ruby and four pearls in each one. Ludovico il Moro once gave 17½ *braccia* of *zetonino avvellutato morello* to Messer Mariotto da Reggio, *oratore*, to get himself made a *vestito* and a *zuppone* (Malaguzzi Valeri, *op.cit.*, p. 422).

ZAMBELLOTTO. See CAMBELLOTTO.

ZENDADO/ZENDALE. A very light silk textile of Oriental origin; but later, the term came to refer to textiles made from fibres other than silk.

ZETANO/ZETANINO. Satin, a plain fabric characterized by its smooth reflective surface. The term relates to the cloth structure, and not to the fibres from which it is made. However, it may be presumed that all satins in fifteenth-century Italian dress are of silk. Although plain satins were used in the fifteenth century, satin weave often appears as the ground of a textile figured in velvet, i.e. *zetano vellutato* (see VELLUTO).

ZOCCOLO (F). Venetian chopine, a tall version of the *pianella*.

ZORNEA. See GIORNEA.

ZUPARELLO (M). A form of doublet. At a tournament held in 1491, Annibale Bentivoglio was accompanied by 12 swordsmen wearing green satin *zuparelli* (Malaguzzi Valeri, *op.cit.*, p. 42). Galeazzo Maria Sforza, who was of course responsible for clothing members of his court, supplied several *zuparelli*. His letters also include an interesting entry of *maneghetti* and *bredoni* (protective shoulder and hip pieces) to put on a *zuparello d'armare*. The correspondence between armour and fashionable clothing was very strong; it is therefore probable that the *zuparello* as armour and as everyday dress made from silk or cloth both followed the same silhouette about the torso (see FARSETTO).

ZUPONE (M). See FARSETTO.

Notes

Chapter 1:
The Quattrocento

1. C. Guasti, ed., *Tre lettere di Lucrezia Tornabuoni a Piero de' Medici ed altre lettere*, Florence, 1859, pp. 9–10; letter of 28 March 1467.

2. G. Niccolini di Camugliano, *The Chronicles of a Florentine Family, 1200–1475*, Cape, 1933, pp. 109 and 112.

3. *ibid.*, pp. 110–12.

4. Baldassare Castiglione, *Il Cortegiano*, written 1508–16. Having trained first at the Sforza court in Milan, and then at the Gonzaga court in Mantua, Castiglione entered Guidubaldo da Montefeltro's court in Urbino in 1508, and left in 1513.

5. F. Malaguzzi Valeri, *La Corte di Ludovico il Moro*, vol. 1, *La vita privata*, Milan, 1913, p. 9.

6. L. Landucci, *A Florentine Diary from 1450–1516*, Dent, 1927, p. 1.

7. M. Baxandall, *Giotto and the Orators*, Oxford University Press, 1971, p. 1.

8. Eight prophets were sculpted by Donatello between *c.* 1416 and 1435, to complete a series begun in the fourteenth century, for the Campanile, Florence.

9. L. B. Alberti, *Della Pittura*, ed. L. Mallè, Florence, 1950.

10. The Italian lyric poetry of the fourteenth century was principally responsible for the development of the madrigal, the greatest composer of which had been a Florentine, Francesco Landini. During the earlier half of the Quattrocento, Italian music was largely dominated by foreign composers. But in the later fifteenth century there was a revival of this musical form; Lorenzo the Magnificent's words were set to music by Isaak.

11. M. Baxandall, *Painting and Experience in Fifteenth Century Italy*, Oxford University Press, 1972, p. 71.

12. J. Cartwright, *Beatrice d'Este, Duchess of Milan, 1475–1497*, Dent, 1899, p. 195.

13. J. Cartwright, *Isabella d'Este, Marchioness of Mantua, 1474–1539*, Murray, 1903, vol. 1, pp. 88–9.

14. D. S. Chambers, *Patrons and Artists in the Italian Renaissance*, Macmillan, 1970, pp. 94–5.

15. P. Burke, *Culture and Society in Renaissance Italy, 1420–1540*, Batsford, 1972, p. 83.

16. Vespasiano da Bisticci, *Vite di uomini illustri del secolo XV*, ed. P. d'Ancona and E. Aeschlimann, Milan, 1951, pp. 217–8.

17. G. R. B. Richards, *Florentine Merchants in the Age of the Medici*, Cambridge, Massachusetts, 1932, pp. 44–6.

18. Malaguzzi Valeri, *op. cit.*, p. 333.

19. Luzio and Renier, 'Il Lusso di Isabella d'Este, 1, Il Guardaroba di

Isabella d'Este', *Nuova Antologia*, ser. IV, vol. LXIII, 1 Guigno, 1896, p. 453.

20.   Cartwright, *Beatrice d'Este, op.cit.*, pp. 188–9.

21.   *ibid.*, p. 182.

22.   Luzio and Renier, 'Il Lusso di Isabella d'Este II, Gioielli e gemme', *Nuova Antologia*, ser. IV, vol. LXIV, 16 Luglio, 1896, p. 311.

23.   Cartwright, *Isabella d'Este, op.cit.*, vol. I, p. 116.

24.   Luzio and Renier, 'Il Lusso di Isabella d'Este II, Gioielli e gemme', *op.cit.*, p. 314.

25.   Cartwright, *Beatrice d'Este, op.cit.*, p. 19.

26.   N. Machiavelli, *Istorie Fiorentine*, book 7, chapter XXVIII.

27.   E. Verga, 'Leggi suntuarie milanesi. Gli statuti del 1396 e del 1498', *Archivio Storico Lombardo*, ser. III, vol. IX, Milan, 1898, p. 70.

28.   Malaguzzi Valeri, *op. cit.*, pp. 260–4.

29.   A. G. F. Howell, *San Bernardino of Siena*, Methuen, 1913, p. 245.

Chapter 2:
The Making of
Renaissance Dress

1.   L. B. Alberti. *Della Pittura, op.cit.*

2.   Levi Pisetzky, *Il Costume e la Moda nella società italiana*, Turin, Einaudi, 1978. pp. 6–7.

3.   *ibid.*, p. 187; the five black *cioppe* left, on the death of Alessandra Macinghi negli Strozzi, comprised a mixture of good and worn ones, one being of *guarnello trista* to wear at home.

4.   A. Macinghi negli Strozzi, *Lettere di una gentildonna fiorentina del secolo XV ai filiuoli esuli*, ed. C. Guasti, Florence, 1877, p. 445; letter of 26 July 1465.

5.   G. Marcotti, *Un mercante fiorentino e la sua famiglia*, Florence, 1881, p. 86.

6.   Strozzi, *op. cit.*, p. 18.

7.   C. Merkel, ed., 'I beni della famiglia di Puccio Pucci', in *Miscellania Nuziale Rossi-Theiss*, Trento, 1897, pp. 185–6.

8.   Strozzi, *op. cit.*, p. 548; letter of 25 January 1465.

9.   E. Polidori Calamandrei, *Le Vesti delle donne fiorentine nel Quattrocento*, Florence, 1924, p. 52.

10.   *ibid.*, p. 128.

11.   Levi Pisetzky, *Il Costume e la moda, op.cit.*, p. 193.

12.   Florence, University (exhibition), *L'Oreficeria nella Firenze del Quattrocento*, Florence, Studio Per Edizioni Scelte, 1977, pp. 101–17. A list of the professions of the inhabitants of Florence includes some *farsettai*.

13.   Bernardino (San) da Siena, *Le prediche volgari dette nella Piazza del Campo l'anno 1427*, ed. L. Banchi, Siena, 1880–8, vol. III, p. 189.

14. Merkel, *op. cit.*; and San Bernardino, *op. cit.*

15. San Bernardino, *op. cit.*, vol. III, p. 211.

16. Jan van Eyck, *The Marriage of Giovanni Arnolfini and Giovanna Cenami*, London, National Gallery, dated 1434.

17. B. Ghetti, *Di alcune leggi suntuarie recanatesi.* Fano, 1905, p. 6.

18. See above, note 2.

19. Ghetti, *loc. cit.*

20. *ibid.*, p. 4.

21. L. Chiappelli, *La donna pistoiese del tempo antico*, Pistoia, 1914, p. 25.

22. M. Giuliani, *La Prammatica Senese per le nozze del' anno MCCCCXII*, Siena, 1879, p. x.

23. San Bernardino, *op. cit.*, vol. III, p. 66.

24. Malaguzzi Valeri, *op. cit.*, p. 215.

25. Levi Pisetzky, *Il Costume e la moda*, *op.cit.*, p. 187.

26. C. dell'Acqua, *Della morte e funerali del duca Gian Galeazzo Visconti, 3 settembre–20 ottobre 1402*, Pavia, 1903.

27. Polidori Calamandrei, *op. cit.*, p. 114.

28. Florence, University (exhibition), *L'Oreficeria nella Firenze del Quattrocento*, *loc. cit.*

29. L. Brenni, *La Tessitura Serica attraverso i secoli*, Como, 1925, p. 100.

30. Polidori Calamandrei, *op. cit.*, p. 22.

31. L. B. Alberti, *Opere Volgari*, ed. C. Grayson, Bari, 1960, vol. 1, *I Libri della Famiglia*, book 3, p. 202.

Chapter 3: Cloth of Gold

1. A. C. Weibel, *Two Thousand Years of Textiles*, New York, Pantheon, 1952, p. 61.

2. I. Origo, *The Merchant of Prato, Francesco di Marco Datini*, Cape, 1957, pp. 70–1.

3. Richards, *loc. cit.*; letter by Benedetto Dei to a Venetian in 1472.

4. Sercambi, *Le Croniche di Giovanni Sercambi*, ed. S. Bongi, 3 vols, Rome, 1892.

5. Weibel, *op.cit.*, p. 61.

6. L. N. Cittadella, *Notizie relative a Ferrara*, Ferrara, 1864, p. 502.

7. Brenni, *op. cit.*, pp. 46–7.

8. According to the CIETA vocabulary (English version, 1964), the term 'lampas' refers to: 'Figured textiles in which a pattern, composed of weft floats bound by a binding warp, is added to a ground fabric formed by a main warp and a main weft. The ground may be tabby, twill, satin, damask, etc. The weft threads forming the pattern are normally pattern or brocading wefts; they float on the face as required by the pattern, and are bound by the ends of the binding warp in a binding ordinarily tabby or twill and which is supplementary to the ground weave.' The word *diaspro* was used particularly widely in the thirteenth century, but not usually later than the fourteenth, and nearly always indicated the lampas textiles attributed to Lucca.

9. A. Geijer, *A History of Textile Art*, Sotheby Parke Bernet, 1979, pp. 99–100.

10. *ibid.*, p. 104.

11. D. Devoti, *L'Arte del Tessuto in Europa*, Milan, Bramante, 1974, glossary, pp. 254–5.

12.   E. Verga, *Il Comune di Milano e l'arte della seta dal secolo XV al XVIII*, Milan, 1917, p. XII.

13.   Vespasiano da Bisticci, *op. cit.*, p. 60.

14.   O. von Falke, *Kunstgeschichte der Seidenweberei*, Berlin, 1921, p. 36.

15.   The clothes in the Imperial Wardrobe have been well preserved, for it was the custom to wrap up each one in a cloth envelope and label it with the name of the owner. However, we cannot be certain that every label remains attached to its appropriate kaftan. The dates of some of the Italian textiles do not comply with those of their supposed owners.

16.   N. A. Reath, 'Velvets of the Renaissance from Europe and Asia Minor', *Burlington Magazine*, vol. L, 1927, pp. 298–304.

17.   G. Arese, *L'industria serica piemontese dal secolo XVII alla metà del XIX*, Turin, 1922, pp. 6 and 78.

18.   F. Michel, *Recherches sur le commerce, la fabrication et l'usage des étoffes d'or et d'argent au Moyen Age*, Paris, 1852, vol. II, pp. 270 ff.

19.   Brenni, *op. cit.*, p. 61.

20.   P. Minucci del Rosso, 'Invenzione di ferri da tessere drappi di seta e di velluto', *Archivio Storico Italiano*, ser. V, vol. VI, 1890, p. 310.

21.   Brenni, *op. cit.*, pp. 98–100.

22.   *ibid.*, p. 100.

23.   P. Molmenti, *La Storia di Venezia nella vita privata*, Bergamo, 1905, part I, pp. 321–2.

24.   Malaguzzi Valeri, *op. cit.*, p. 165.

25.   Cennino Cennini, *Il Libro dell'Arte*, ed. F. Brunello, Vicenza, 1971.

26.   G. Gargiolli, *L'Arte della Seta in Firenze*, Florence, 1868, pp. 24–5. The Codice Riccardiano n.2580 which Gargiolli reproduces is not dated; but another copy (n.2412) is datable to 1450, and further copies appeared in the second half of the Quattrocento. However, Gargiolli is of the opinion that even the earliest version, reproduced by him, is probably a copy of a lost manuscript originating from the late fourteenth or early fifteenth century. The contents of the treatise are the results of proven techniques and materials used in the silk industry over a period of time; that such a treatise should continue to be copied for a whole century (or more) indicates the continued relevance of the methods quoted.

27.   A mordant is a chemical substance, often an acetate of a metal, which has an affinity for both the fibre and the colouring matter, and which forms, with the colouring matter, an insoluble colour, or lake.

28.   Gargiolli, *op. cit.*, pp. 78–9.

29.   F. Podreider, *La Storia dei Tessuti d'Arte in Italia (secoli XII–XVIII)*, Bergamo, 1928, pp. 89–90.

30.   *ibid.*, p. 89.

31.   Malaguzzi Valeri, *op. cit.*, p. 167.

32.   *ibid.*, p. 166; from *Archivio di Stato di Modena, Cancelleria Ducale, Carteggio degli Ambasciatori ed Agenti Estensi in Milano*.

33.   Luzio and Renier, *Delle relazioni di Isabella d'Este Gonzaga con Ludovico e Beatrice Sforza*, Milan, 1890, p. 78.

34.   Podreider, *op. cit.*, p. 84.

Chapter 4: Dress as Narrative

1.   Alberti, *Della Pittura, op.cit.*

2.   F. Zambrini, ed., *Trattato dell'arte del ballo di Guglielmo Ebreo Pesarese*, Bologna, 1873.

3.   W. L. Gundersheimer, *Ferrara: the Style of a Renaissance Despotism*, Princeton, 1973, p. 106; quoted from Angelo Camillo Decembrio's *De politia literaria*, Book I.

4.   Levi Pisetzky, *La Storia del Costume in Italia*, vol. II, Milan, 1964, p. 252; from Casa estense Amministrazione, 1448 marz. 26, in G. Pardi, 'La suppellettile dei palazzi estensi in Ferrara nel 1436', *Atti e memorie della R. Deputazione ferrarese di Storia Patria*, vol. XIX, extract, Ferrara, 1908, p. 119, note 1.

5.   Vespasiano da Bisticci, *op. cit.*, pp. 60-1.

6.   Levi Pisetzky, *La Storia del Costume, op.cit.*, p. 428; from 'Della Prammatica o sia regolamento sopra il sontuoso vestire degli uomini e donne, e sopra le larghe spese de i convitti e funerali, Ex. Decret. Amed. VII, 17 Juni 1430, car. 53', in *Editti antichi e nuovi de sovrani principi della Real Casa di Savoia*, pp. 677 ff.

7.   M. Manfredini, *Contro i superflui ornamenti delle donne, 12 maggio, 1460*, Padua, 1896, p. 13.

8.   Molmenti, *op. cit.*, part I, p. 292.

9.   Strozzi, *op. cit.*, pp. 15-19.

10.   Levi Pisetzky, *La Storia del Costume, loc. cit.*

11.   D. Catellacci, ed., *Ricordanza delle nozze di Francesco de' Medici con la Tessa Guicciardini*, Florence, 1880, p. 8.

12.   Strozzi, *op. cit.*, p. 29.

13.   Merkel, *op. cit.*, p. 172.

14.   A. Zanelli, 'Di alcune leggi suntuarie pistoiesi dal XIV al XVI secolo', *Archivio Storico Italiano*, ser. v, vol. XVI, 1895, p. 209.

15.   B. di Michele del Corazza, 'Diario Fiorentino, anni 1405-1438', ed. G. O. Corazzini, *Archivio Storico Italiano*, ser. v, vol. XIV, 1894, p. 290.

16.   *ibid.*, p. 277.

17.   Levi Pisetzky, *La Storia del Costume, op.cit.*, p. 428.

18.   *ibid.*, p. 430.

19. Vespasiano da Bisticci, *op. cit.*, p. 6c

20.   London, National Gallery Catalogue, *The Earlier Italian Schools*, by Martin Davies, 2nd ed., 1961, pp. 525-31.

21.   Baxandall, *Painting and Experience in Fifteenth Century Italy, op.cit.*, p. 89.

22.   Close examples of this are to be found in *Scriptores Historiae Augustus, Vitae diversorum principum et tyrannorum a diversis compositae*, Ms. E.III, 19, Turin, Biblioteca Nazionale; reproduced in G. Paccagnini, *Pisanello*, trs. J. Carroll, London, 1973.

23.   Gundersheimer, *loc. cit.*

24.   Levi Pisetzky, *Il Costume e la Moda, op.cit.*, p. 72.

25.   Levi Pisetzky, *La Storia del Costume, op.cit.*, p. 435.

26.   Merkel, *op. cit.*, p. 171, note 1.

27.   Levi Pisetzky, *Il Costume e la Moda, op.cit.*, p. 195.

28.   Merkel, *op. cit.*, p. 171.

29. Polidori Calamandrei, *op. cit.*, p. 13

30.   Merkel, *loc. cit.*

31.   Levi Pisetzky, *Il Costume e la Moda, op.cit.*, p. 72.

32.   W. Terni de' Gregori, *Bianca Maria Visconti, duchessa di Milano*, Bergamo, 1940, p. 192.

33.   Polidori Calamandrei, *op. cit.*, p. 130.

34.   Levi Pisetzky, *Il Costume e la Moda, op.cit.*, p. 197.

Chapter 5:
Extravagance at Court

1.   The writings of Guarino and others on Pisanello are discussed in detail in Baxandall, *Giotto and the Orators*, *op.cit.*, pp. 90–6.

2.   Baxandall, *Painting and Experience in Fifteenth Century Italy*, *op.cit.*, p. 77.

3.   *ibid.*, pp. 77–8.

4.   See above, p. 100.

5.   The condition of the portrait is such that there appear some discrepancies in the details of dress. Leonello is probably wearing the same layers of clothing as in the medal by Pisanello of 1444—that is, a sideless tunic (*giornea*), over a doublet (*farsetto/zuparello*) and shirt. However, closer scrutiny of the painted portrait will show how some outlines of the clothing do not make sense. For example, the black edging with its silver ornamentation, which follows a line down from the near shoulder, derives from no logical source of construction, finishing at a point in mid-shoulder. It neither completes the line round the back of the neck nor continues down the back of the shoulder to the hem of the tunic. A misunderstanding on the part of a restorer probably accounts for such inconsistencies.

6.   Red, white and green were definitely the colours of the Este of Ferrara (see p. 144), and of the three theological virtues. However, these colours do not appear to belong to the Gonzaga family at the court in Mantua, with which so much of Pisanello's work has been associated.

7.   Cartwright, *Isabella d'Este*, *op.cit.*, p. 71; and C. M. Ady, *The Bentivoglio of Bologna: a study in despotism*, Oxford, 1937, p. 171.

8.   G. Pozzo, 'Nozze di Beatrice d'Este e di Anna Sforza', *Archivio Storico Lombardo*, ser. 1, vol. IX, 1882, pp. 483 ff.

9.   'Tincti in mori' could mean either that the men had tinted their skin with mulberries, or that their clothes were dyed with mulberry. The meaning depends on the reason for Ludovico's name, 'il Moro'—that is, whether it was because of his dark complexion (although Giovio asserted that Ludovico was fair-skinned), or because of his association with the mulberry tree, one of his many devices, through the cultivation of silk in Lombardy.

10.   Cartwright, *Beatrice d'Este*, *op.cit.*, p. 171.

11.   C. M. Ady, *A History of Milan under the Sforza*, Methuen, 1907, pp. 138–9.

12.   Descriptions of the sequence of events appear in A. Dina, *Isabella d'Aragona, Duchessa di Milano e di Bari, 1470–1524*, Milan, 1921.

13.   E. Solmi, 'La Festa del Paradiso di Leonardo da Vinci e Bernardino Bellincione 13 gennaio 1490', *Archivio Storico Lombardo*, ser. IV, vol. I, 1904, pp. 75–89.

14.   The references to Spain and the wearing of Spanish dress in this context were intended as a compliment to the Aragonese line from which Isabella was born.

15.   The first-floor hall, in which the *Paradiso* by Leonardo took place, had a chapel at one end for everyday use. The presence of a *paradiso*, both as the representation of a heavenly place and as a theatrical device which opened up, was a well established feature of religious drama; see S. M. Newton, *Renaissance Theatre Costume*, Rapp and Whiting, 1975, pp. 49 and 130.

16.   Malaguzzi Valeri, *op. cit.*, p. 32.

17.   Levi Pisetzky, *Il Costume e la Moda*, *op.cit.*, p. 69.

18.   Levi Pisetzky, *La Storia del Costume*, *op.cit.*, p. 431; from F. Muralto, *Annalia*, chap. IX, 3, p. 54.

19.   Levi Pisetzky, *Il Costume e la Moda*, *op.cit.*, p. 6.

20.   Levi Pisetzky, *La Storia del Costume*, *op.cit.*, p. 431; from

237

P. Giovio, *Istoria del suo tempo*, trs. Domenichi, Venice, 1608, p. 11; Giovio described Beatrice as a '*donna di superbia e grandissima pompa*'.

21. Cartwright, *Beatrice d'Este*, *op.cit.*, p. 102; recorded from a letter of Ludovico Sforza to Isabella, Marchioness of Mantua, 12 June 1491.

22. Ady, *A History of Milan under the Sforza*, *op.cit.*, p. 139.

23. *ibid.*, p. 140.

24. Cartwright, *Beatrice d'Este*, *op.cit.*, p. 89.

25. *ibid.*, pp. 170–1; and Levi Pisetzky, *La Storia del Costume*, *op.cit.*, p. 433.

26. Luzio and Renier, 'Il lusso di Isabella d'Este I, Il Guardaroba' p. 455.

27. *ibid.*, p. 453.

28. Luzio and Renier, *Delle relazioni di Isabella d'Este Gonzaga con Ludovico e Beatrice Sforza*, *op.cit.*, p. 383, note 1.

29. Cartwright, *Beatrice d'Este*, *op. cit.*, p. 173.

30. A. Portioli, 'La nascita di Massimiliano Sforza', *Archivio Storico Lombardo*, ser. I, vol. IX, 1882, p. 332.

31. Cartwright, *Beatrice d'Este*, *op.cit.*, pp. 208–9.

32. *ibid.*, p. 213.

33. Portioli, *op.cit.*, p. 333.

34. Cicco Simonetta, 'I diari', ed. A. R. Natale, *Archivio Storico Lombardo*, ser. VIII, vol. II, 1950, p. 71.

35. G. Pardi, ed., 'Diario Ferrarese', by unknown authors, *Rerum Italicarum Scriptores*, vol. XXIV, part VII, p. 67.

36. *ibid.*, p. 66.

37. *ibid.*, p. 176.

38. P. Tafur, *Travels and Adventures*, trs. Malcolm Letts, London, 1926, pp. 44–6.

Chapter 6: The Image of Beauty

1. A. Municchi, *Una provvisione suntuaria della reppublica fiorentina*, Florence, 1909, p. 19.

2. Geijer, *op. cit.*, p. 142.

3. Levi Pisetzky, *Il Costume e la Moda, op.cit.*, pp. 185 and 187

4. Landucci, *op. cit.*, p. 6.

5. Polidori Calamandrei, *op. cit.*, p. 4

6. *ibid.*

7. Alberti, *I libri della Famiglia*, *op.cit.*, p. 202.

8. Levi Pisetzky, *Il Costume e la Moda, op.cit.*, pp. 6–7.

9. G. Porro, ed., 'Lettere di Galeazzo Maria Sforza, duca di Milano', *Archivio Storico Lombardo*, 1878–9.

10. Levi Pisetzky, *La Storia del Costume*, *op.cit.*, p. 227.

11. *ibid.*

12. Polidori Calamandrei, *op. cit.*, pp. 19–20.

13. Levi Pisetzky, *Il Costume e la Moda, op.cit.*, p. 23.

14. San Bernardino, *op.cit.*, vol. III, p. 205.

15. Levi Pisetzky, *La Storia del Costume*, *op.cit.*, p. 302.

16. P. D. Pasolini, ed., *Gli experimenti de la Exma S.^{ra} Caterina da Furlj*, Imola, 1894.

17. *ibid.*, p. 42.

18. *ibid.*, p. 30.

19. Luzio and Renier, *Delle relazioni di Isabella d'Este Gonzaga con Ludovico e Beatrice Sforza*, *op.cit.*, p. 635.

20. Malaguzzi Valeri, *op. cit.*, p. 253.

21.   *ibid.*, p. 247.

22.   Levi Pisetzky, *La Storia del Costume*, *op.cit.*, p. 363.

23.   B. Corio, *Storia di Milano*, Milan, 1857, vol. III, part VI, p. 313.

24.   P. Ghinzoni, 'Un ambasciatore del Soldano d'Egitto alla corte milanese nel 1476', *Archivio Storico Lombardo*, ser. I, vol. II, 1875, p. 166.

25.   Terni de' Gregori, *op. cit.*, p. 56.

Chapter 7:
Jewellery and
Embroidered Devices

1.   Luzio and Renier, 'Il Lusso di Isabella d'Este II, Gioielli e gemme', *op.cit.*, pp. 299–300; letter written in Venice from Domenico di Giorgio to Isabella, 24 November 1494.

2.   Malaguzzi Valeri, *op. cit.*, p. 382.

3.   G. Vasari, *Le vite de' più eccellenti pittori, scultori e architettori*, 3 vols, Florence, 1568.

4.   Luzio and Renier, 'Il Lusso di Isabella d'Este II, Gioielli e gemme', *op.cit.*, p. 296.

5.   A. Morassi, *Art Treasures of the Medici: jewellery, silverware, hard-stone*, trs. P. Colacicchi, London, 1964, p. 6.

6.   Levi Pisetzky, *Il Costume e la Moda*, *op.cit.*, p. 190.

7.   O. M. Dalton, *Catalogue of the Engraved Gems of the Post-Classical Periods in the British Museum*, London, 1915.

8.   Luzio and Renier, 'Il Lusso di Isabella d'Este II, Gioielli e gemme', *op.cit.*, p. 302.

9.   *ibid.*, pp. 296–7.

10.   *ibid.*, p. 303.

11.   Cartwright, *Beatrice d'Este*, *op.cit.*, p. 182.

12.   *ibid.*, p. 34.

13.   See above, p. 32.

14.   Levi Pisetzky, *Il Costume e la Moda*, *op.cit.*, p. 191.

15.   G. Taylor and D. Scarisbrick, *Finger Rings, from Ancient Egypt to the Present Day*, Lund Humphries, 1978, p. 23 on the wearing of rings.

16.   Florence, University (exhibition), *L'Oreficeria nella Firenze del Quattrocento*, *op.cit.*, p. 303.

17. E. Steingräber, *Antique Jewellery*, trs. P. Gorge, Thames and Hudson, 1957, p. 15.

18. Luzio and Renier, 'Il Lusso di Isabella d'Este, II, Gioielli e gemme', *op.cit.*, p. 299.

19. Malaguzzi Valeri, *op. cit.*, pp. 387–8.

20. Luzio and Renier, 'Il Lusso di Isabella d'Este II, Gioielli e gemme', *op.cit.*, p. 295.

21. *ibid.*

22. *ibid.*

23. Simonetta, *op. cit.*, p. 171.

24. Malaguzzi Valeri, *op. cit.*, pp. 344–5; from *Archivio di Stato di Modena Cancelleria Ducale—Carteggio degli Ambasciatori ed Agenti Estensi in Milano, Busta 5.*

25. E. Motta, *Nozze principesche nel Quattrocento*, Milan, 1894, p. 71.

26. Richards, *op.cit.*, p. 46.

27. Luzio and Renier, 'Il Lusso di Isabella d'Este II, Gioielli e gemme', *op.cit.*, p. 295.

28. Levi Pisetzky, *La Storia del Costume*, *op.cit.*, p. 433.

29. E. Müntz, *Les collections des Médicis au XVe siècle*, Paris, 1888.

30. Luzio and Renier, *Mantova e Urbino*, Turin, 1893.

31. G. Campori, *Raccolta di cataloghi ed inventarii inediti, dal sec. XV al sec. XIX*, Modena, 1870, pp. 5–6.

32. Cartwright, *Isabella d'Este*, *op.cit.*, vol. 1, p. 72.

33. See above, p. 28.

34. Levi Pisetzky, *Il Costume e la Moda*, *op.cit.*, p. 192.

35. *ibid.*

36. E. Motta, *op.cit.*, p. 72.

37. Landucci, *op. cit.*, p. 7; he spent 1 lira 2 denari on *maglie* for a *cotta* for his wife.

38. Levi Pisetzky, *La Storia del Costume*, *op.cit.*, p. 243.

39. *ibid.*, pp. 219, note, and 224, note.

40. Cartwright, *Beatrice d'Este*, *op.cit.*, p. 173.

41. Luzio and Renier, 'Il Lusso di Isabella d'Este II, Gioielle e gemme', *op.cit.*, p. 295.

42. E. Motta, *op.cit.*, p. 42.

43. *ibid.*, p. 51.

44. C. Guasti, *Le Feste di San Giovanni in Firenze descritte in prosa e in rima*, Florence, 1884, pp. 15–16.

45. Malaguzzi Valeri, *op. cit.*, pp. 220–1; a letter to Ludovico il Moro from Leonardo Botta, Milanese ambassador in Venice, refers to '*tanta lasività de pompe*' on the part of the ladies who went about, some of them bearing jewels and finery up to the value of 5000 ducats.

46. G. Pardi, ed., 'Diario ferrarese dall' anno 1476 sino al 1554', by Bernardino Zambotti, *Rerum Italicarum Scriptores*, vol. XXIV, part VII, appendix, p. 77.

47. P. Giovio, *Dialogo delle imprese militari e amorose*, Lyons, 1559.

48. F. Cappi Bentivegna, *Abbigliamento e Costume nella pittura italiana: Rinascimento*, Rome, Bestetti, 1962, p. 6.

49. Podreider, *op. cit.*, pp. 149–50. The textile is in the Musée des Arts Décoratifs, Paris. The same device of the seven *palle* appears on the doors of the Bargello in Florence, and around the base of the tomb of Giovanni de' Medici in San Lorenzo.

Chapter 8:
The Diffusion of
Foreign Dress

1.   Levi Pisetzky, *La Storia del Costume, op.cit.*, p. 435.

2.   1465 Alfonso, Duke of Calabria (later King of Naples), married Ippolita Sforza, daughter of Francesco; 1473 Leonora of Aragon married Ercole d'Este; 1489 Isabella of Aragon married Gian Galeazzo Sforza; 1490 Isabella d'Este (elder daughter of Leonora of Aragon) married Francesco Gonzaga; 1491 Beatrice d'Este, sister of Isabella, married Ludovico Sforza, 'il Moro'.

3.   In 1493, Bianca Maria Sforza married the Emperor Maximilian. A series of marriages through the century associated the Sforza with all the great Italian family names— Aldobrandeschi, Bentivoglio, Este, Farnese, Gonzaga, Medici, Montefeltro, Orsini, Sanseverino— among others.

4.   Malaguzzi Valeri, *op. cit.*, p. 219.

5.   See above, p. 87.

6.   A. Giulini, 'Nozze Borromeo nel Quattrocento', *Archivio Storico Lombardo*, ser IV, vol. XIII, 1910, p. 269.

7.   Luzio and Renier, 'Il Lusso di Isabella d'Este I, Il Guardaroba', *op.cit.*, p. 453.

8.   Motta, *op. cit.*, p. 19.

9.   Luzio and Renier, 'Il Lusso di Isabella d'Este I, Il Guardaroba, *op.cit.*, p. 455; letter of 28 November 1490.

10.   Cartwright, *Beatrice d'Este, op.cit.*, p. 169.

11.   Solmi, *op.cit.*, p. 83.

12.   Malaguzzi Valeri, *op. cit.*, p. 236; quoted from E. Percopo, *I sonnetti faceti di Antonio Cammelli*, Naples, 1908, LXX.

13.   Luzio and Renier, 'Il Lusso di Isabella d'Este I, Il Guardaroba', *op.cit.*, p. 443.

14.   Cartwright, *Beatrice d'Este, op.cit.*, pp. 120–1.

15.   Luzio and Renier, 'Il lusso di Isabella d'Este I, Il Guardaroba', *op.cit.*, p. 454.

16.   Cartwright, *Beatrice d'Este, op.cit.*, p. 235.

17.   *ibid.*

18.   Levi Pisetzky, *La Storia del Costume*, *op.cit.*, p. 435.

19.   G. Butazzi, *Il Costume in Lombardia*, Milan, Electa, 1977, p. 30.

20.   Levi Pisetzky, *Il Costume e la Moda, op.cit.*, p. 190.

21.   *ibid.*

22.   See above, note 6.

23.   Chiapelli, *op. cit.*, p. 25.

24.   Malaguzzi Valeri, *op.cit.*, pp. 199–200; from *Archivio di Stato. Miscellanea. Statistica. Busta 8.*

25.   M. Sanuto, *I diarii di Marino Sanuto*, vol. I, ed. F. Stefani, Bologna, 1879, p. 145.

26.   Sanuto, *op. cit.*, vol. III, ed. R. Fulin, Bologna, 1880, p. 24.

Appendix: Extracts from contemporary documents relating to clothing

(The spellings do not always correspond precisely to the original, but here and there are modified, in order to assist reference to the glossary. A suffix 'M' or 'F' denotes whether the garment is for masculine or feminine wear.)

The Inventory of Angelo da Uzzano[1]

Following the death of Angelo da Uzzano in 1424, the house at Via dei Bardi 28, in Florence, and its contents, passed into the hands of Angelo's brother, Niccolò. Niccolò made a list of all the household possessions, including the clothing found in each room. The inventory is probably datable to between Angelo's death and shortly after Niccolò made his will in December 1430. Amongst the clothes of Monna Bamba, the widow of Angelo, were:

1 cioppa di panno paghonazzo di grana con maniche aperte

1 cioppa bigia rotta[2]

4 cioppe monachine usate

2 mantelli grandi da cappa[3] monachini usati

2 gamurre scarlattine usate

2 guarnelli vecchi a cordellina[4]

3 foderi vecchi

7 camicie usate

3 paia di calze usate

2 cappelline di fodero per la notte usate

4 bende di panno lino per avvolgere al capo

8 benducci grandi usati[5]

1 cintola di seta nera fornita d'ariento[6]

1 mantello di panno travisato soppannato di bianchetta, che si dice una chiocciola[7]

The list of clothing belonging to Angelo da Uzzano included:

5 berette ad ago[8] all'anticha, rosse, nere et azzurre

braccia 4 di saia milanese o circha, nera

1 giachetta[9] rossa, soppannata[10] di valescio

1 guardacore di bianchetta foderato a pezzuoli di vaio

1 paio di maniche di scheriuoli[11]

1 cioppa paghonazza foderata d'indisia

1 cioppa bigia nuova foderata di martore

1 cioppa di panno paghonazzo foderata di scheriuoli

1 cioppa rosata foderata di dossi

1 cioppa di panno bigio vecchia foderata di martore et fodero

1 mantello di panno rosato, usato

1 mantello di panno rosato, nuovo

1 mantello di panno bruschino nuovo

1 mantello di panno scarlattino da cavalcare[12]

1 cioppetta rosata foderata di taffettà di grana, usata

1 cioppetta rosata foderata di terzanella di grana

6 paia di calze nere solate tra di saia e perpignano[13]

5 cappucci rosati

1 berretta rosata ad ago foderata

2 cappelline di fodero grandi

2 farsetti et 2 guarnelli

1 cappellina di fodero nuova

9 paia di panni lini tra nuovi e vecchi

1 gonella di panno bigio doppia

1 cioppa rosata scempia[14]

1. W. Bombe, *Nachlass-Inventare des Angelo da Uzzano und des Lodovico di Gino Capponi*, Leipzig, 1928.
2. *rotto* = worn out. The majority of clothing listed in household inventories and wills had been well worn. In some cases the adjectives *rotto, tristo, usato* and *vecchio*, do not necessarily refer to the age of a particular garment, but rather describe the sad state of the textile. There were many cases of garments being recut.
3. Cloaks with sleeves.
4. It is difficult to say exactly what *cordellina* refers to here; the entry may refer to dresses with drawstring necklines.
5. Note that this inventory was made when Monna Bamba was a widow; it is particularly appropriate, therefore, that she should possess plenty of smaller *bende* and larger *benducci* for covering her head, neck and shoulders.
6. The silver decoration on this belt probably constitutes the buckle, but possibly also refers to applied silver discs or some other form of ornament.
7. *chiocciola* literally means 'snail'; the type of garment so named may be a cloak, in this case lined, which is wrapped about the person many times, almost like the spiralling shell of a snail.
8. *ad ago* = made with a needle, therefore probably embroidered.
9. *giachetta*, a diminutive of *giacca*, meaning jacket; the word rarely appears in the fifteenth century, but presumably indicates an overgarment with sleeves, opening down the front.
10. *soppannata* = lined.
11. *scheriuoli* = squirrel fur.
12. *da cavalcare* = for riding; many riding garments were distinguished by the slit leading part-way up the front and the back of the skirt from the hem, for ease of movement.
13. *perpignano*, a type of low-grade woollen cloth, originating from Perpignan; here it is being used, together with *saia*, for the soles to some pairs of hose.
14. *scempio* = of a single thickness, as opposed to *doppia*, self-lined, or of double thickness.

Gifts presented on the marriage of Francesco de' Medici and Tessa Guicciardini in 1433[1]

The couple were betrothed in August 1432; and in June 1433 the presentation of the ring and the festivities of the *nozze* took place. Francesco began by recording the gifts received from various friends and relatives. Apart from a beautiful *telo di renso*, a silver-framed mirror in a little box, and a small bottle of musk, presented by Messer Batista da Champo Fregoso, most gifts came in the form of single jewels, of modest value. However, Francesco's parents presented some rather more expensive items (although they had not yet been paid for); his father Giuliano gave Costanza a length of *vellutato in chermisi*, and his mother Mona Sandra presented her with 100 *martore* (skins of marten). Francesco himself, on presenting the marriage ring, also gave Costanza two smaller rings, one of a table-cut diamond mounted with a pointed diamond to each side, and another with an emerald and two rubies, both set in gold. Piero Guicciardini, Costanza's father, presented Francesco with 200 florins' worth of dowry (*donora*), which consisted of the following valued items:

uno paio di forzieri dipinti,[2] di pregio di fiorini	f.	62
una peza di domaschino bigio di braccia 34[3]	f.	55
uno ucho[4] di panno biancho con richamo di perle	f.	25
una cioppa di panno verde bruno	f.	15
uno mazochio di chermisi con ariento	f.	8
una peza di sciughatoi	f.	10
una saia con maniche di seta	f.	8
una filza di choralli	f.	8
uno libricciuolo d'Uficio di Donna[5]	f.	8
	fiorini	200

Further uncosted items were then listed by Francesco; being of less value, they were not counted officially as part of the agreed dowry:

una ghamurra verde	17 chamicie
una cioppa di paghonazzo con arienti	30 benducci grandi
una giornea di ghuarnello	40 fazoletti

25 chuffie

una choffia (cuffia) di velluto biancho con oncie 3 d'ariento

una berretta di velluto azurro richamata con perle

una berretta verde di velluto con boctoncini[6]

una berrecta biancha chommessa[7]

una berrecta di velluto verde e nero

duo chappelline con ariento

tre borse

uno paio di chalze e scarpecte

nastri e refe di diversi cholori[8]

una coppia di sciughatoi grandi

uno velo di seta

1. D. Catellacci, *Ricordanza delle nozze di Francesco de' Medici con la Tessa Guicciardini*, Florence, 1880. In the documents, Tessa is frequently referred to as Costanza.
2. The painted marriage *cassoni*, into which the subsequent items would have been placed.
3. This may refer to the length of the piece of damask as it came off the loom.
4. *ucho* = possibly *lucco*.
5. A devotional book, perhaps of parchment and illuminated

with miniatures.
6. Little buttons (*bottoncini*) were often more decorative than practical; this is true of this case, for a *berretta* had no need for fastenings.
7. *chommessa* = made up from different bits of material.
8. Ribbons and threads of various colours; such odds and ends were used in a variety of ways, to thread through the hair, or to lace through the eyelets of a fastening.

Marco Parenti orders materials for his wife's *giornea, cotta* and *ghirlanda*[1]

In 1447 Marco Parenti, a rich 25-year-old Florentine citizen engaged in his father's silk business, was betrothed to Caterina, the daughter of Alessandra Macinghi negli Strozzi. A dowry of 1000 florins was agreed upon, to be paid in two instalments during the following year. Marco Parenti's own notebook records in detail some of the purchases he made at the time of the marriage, to be given as gifts to his wife. Here follows a list of the cost of materials required for the construction of a *giornea*, a *cotta* and a *ghirlanda*;

GIORNEA

For the *giornea di zetani vellutato di chermisi*:

$24\frac{1}{2}$ *braccia* of the said textile, @ $3\frac{1}{2}$ florins per *braccio*, taken from a length measuring $42\frac{1}{2}$ *braccia*, which came to *fiorini* 85 *soldi* 15 *a oro*. F.85 l.3 s.3.d.3p.[2]

30 braccia of red *valescio* for the lining @ 7 *soldi* per *braccio*; this came to *lire* 10 *soldi* 10 *di piccioli*

13 *braccia* of *guarnello* for lining @ *soldi* 7 *denari* 6 p. per *braccio*; this cost l.4 s.17 d.6.

32 *maglie* @ 8 *denari* each, bought from Deo the goldsmith; F.– l.1 s.8 d.4.

an extra $1\frac{1}{4}$ *braccia* of *zetani vellutato di chermisi* for *guazzeroni* @ $3\frac{1}{2}$ *fiorini* per *braccio*

188 *lattici* (skins of fur) to be used for *fodera d'intagli e orli e filetti*, @ $6\frac{3}{4}$ *fiorini* per hundred; this came to *fiorini* 12 *soldi* 15 *a oro*. F.12 l.3 s.3 d.9.

and for making the said *giornea*, *lire* 7, paid to Andrea di Giovanni, tailor.

COTTA

For a *cotta* of *zetani vellutato di chermisi*:

18 *braccia* of the said textile @ $3\frac{1}{2}$ *fiorini* per *braccio*

20 *braccia* of red *valescio* @ 7 *soldi* per *braccio*, for lining

10 ounces of *bambagia*; F.– l.– s.9 d.2.

120 gilded round *maglie*, for the front of the *cotta* and 100 little

maglie for the sleeves; F.3 s.6 d.9 *a fiorino*

6 *punte* for the laces (*nastri*); 6 *soldi a fiorino*

(the *maglie* and the *punte* altogether totalled F.3 l.1 s.17 d.5.)

pearls for embroidering the sleeves; F.4 l.– s.8 d.6.

26 *lattizi* for the *filetto* round the base of the hem @ $6\frac{3}{4}$ *fiorini* for a hundred; F.1 l.3 s.3 d.9.

paid to Bonifazio, embroiderer, for sewing the pearls on to the sleeves; 2 *soldi di piccioli*

for green and gold fringing to go round the foot of the *cotta*, and *nastri* and *cordelline* of silk; F.2 l.2 s.2 d.6.

for making the garment, I paid Andrea the tailor F.– l.7 s.10 d.–.

GHIRLANDA

For a *grillanda* of peacock feathers (*code di pagone*), decorated with silver and pearls:

500 peacock feathers, best quality, @ l.4 s.8 the hundred; total, 22 *lire*

300 assorted peacock feathers; l.9 s.12 d.6.

gilt *tremolanti* and red and blue enamelled flowers; F.8 l.4 s.9 d.–.

Venetian gold leaf; F.2 l.2 s.17 d.8.

6 ounces of pearls @ 12 *fiorini a oro* the ounce; F.21 l.2 s.11 d.–.

tremolanti and enamelled flowers; F.1 l.– s.8 d.1.

7 large flowers; F.7 l.3 s.3 d.–.

11 roses, made from peacock feathers; for these, and the finishing touches to the *grillanda* made by Niccolò di Bastiano, F.– l.3 s.8 d

1. A. Macinghi negli Strozzi, *Lettere di una donna fiorentina ai figliuoli esuli*, Florence, 1877, pp. 17–20.
2. p. = *piccioli* (see Note on money and measurements). Having first quoted the price in *fiorini* and *soldi a oro*, the sum is then expressed in fractions of the *lira di piccioli*; in this case, 15 *soldi a oro* are worth 3 *lire* 3 *soldi* and 3 *denari* in *piccioli*.

The inventory of Puccio Pucci[1]

The inventory, dated 1449, is typical of most documents of its type, in that it lists a wide range of household items as well as clothing. The entries are recorded room by room, and very often make no distinction between male and female garments; for example, the bedroom of Piero, the second son of Puccio Pucci, includes several *cioppe* belonging to his wife, his own clothes, chests, bed linen and a few gemstones. As usual, each list begins with the most valuable items, in this case, *cioppe*. The following extracts do not appear in the same order as in the inventory, but according to their values, beginning with the most expensive individual item:

fiorini

una cioppa di velluto chermisi paghonazo con maniche aperte, foderata d'ermellini, il busto di pancie (F)	110
uno elmetto con cimiere di liochorno,[2] fornito di perlle	90
uno zetani vellutato chermisi[3] della donna (F)	82
una cioppa rosata della donna con richamo di perlle (F)	80
una cioppa rosata, con maniche aperte, foderata di martore e il busto di faine[4] (F)	80
una cioppa di velluto chermisi a ghozi (F)	60
una giornea di zetani vellutato chermisi (F)	50
una cioppa rosata con maniche aperte, foderata di pancie (F)	40
uno domaschino biancho[5] con richamo di perlle (F)	40
oncie 2 di perlle	35
una cotta di zetani chermisi senza maniche (F)	30
una cioppa rosata con manichette,[6] foderata di pancie (F)	20
uno luccho paghonazo con aliotti[7] di domaschino (M)	18
uno mantello rosato da uomo (M)	15
una saia doppia con maniche di seta[8] (F)	15
una cioppa rosata a ghozi, foderata di dossi	15
una ghamurra rosata con bottoni d'ariento (F)	15
uno mantello e uno chappuccio e una cioppa monachino, nuovo (M)	15
18 chamicie da donna (F)	14
una cintola d'ariento	12
una chotta di velluto verde della donna (F)	12
uno mantello monachino della donna (F)	10
pezze[9] 12 di panno monachino per una cioppa	10
una berretta fornita di perlle (F)	10
uno lucchetto biancho, foderato di pancie	8
una giornea di saia biancha (F)	8
una cotta d'appicciolato, usata (F)	8
uno paio di chorna	8
2 cintole fornite d'ariento	6
uno farsetto di velluto chermisi (M)	6
una chamurra verde di panno con maniche di velluto verde (F)	5
uno giuberello di velluto chermisi (M)	5
una cioppetta di pelo di lione	4
una chioppetta nera rifatta[10]	4
una ghamurra turchina	4
2 mazocchi e 2 berrette con ariento (M)	4
una saia a uccellini[11]	4
uno chappello di raso chermisi (F)	3
2 giornee a divisa (M)	3
una giornea a divisa del conte[12] (M)	3
uno chapello di velluto chermisi da donna (F)	3
una grillanda di penne (F)	2
3 chappelli, uno di velluto nero e 2 di paglia[13]	2
uno lucchetto chatelano[14] bigio (M)	1
3 farsetti vecchi di ghuarnello (M)	1
uno braccio di velluto nero	1
uno farsetto di ghuarnello con maniche di zetani, paghonazo (M)	1
16 cuffie da donna (F)	1
27 benducci da donna (F)	1
uno federo e una giornea di fodero[15] (F)	1
2 farsetti di bochaccino (M)	soldi 10

1. C. Merkel, 'I Beni della famiglia di Puccio Pucci', *Miscellanea Nuziale Rossi-Theiss*, 1897.
2. Such a helmet crowned with a unicorn would probably be worn at a tournament.
3. This entry probably refers to a *cioppa*.

4. *faine* are polecats, less precious than martens, the visible linings of the open sleeves.
5. Another *cioppa*; the name of the garment is left understood.
6. *manichette* are probably short sleeves, turned back at the elbows to reveal the fur lining.

7. *aliotti* may be facings around the side openings of the *lucco*.
8. The *saia* in this case must be a woollen cloth if it contrasts with sleeves of silk.
9. According to Merkel, the abbreviation to 'p' in the original document denotes the term *pezze*, i.e. pieces. Whilst new garments were made up from pieces of other clothing, the number of pieces here do correspond to the quantity of *braccia* needed—around 12 for a *cioppa*.
10. One example of several which prove the extent to which clothes were remade; another entry in the same inventory records a *cioppetta* which had been redyed (*ritinta*), and also listed is a *cioppa disfatta*, presumably unpicked and waiting to be restyled.

11. *a uccellini* = 'with little birds', probably embroidered.
12. In the colours of the Count—i.e. Francesco Sforza, who enjoyed much popularity in Florence at this time.
13. Straw hats appear to have been worn both for riding and as protection against the sun.
14. *chatelano* = catalan; though particularly diffuse in the later part of the Quattrocento, the influence of foreign dress was felt throughout the century.
15. Such inconsistencies of spelling are common; this entry indicates the use of one word to denote both a garment and the kind of cloth normally associated with it.

Conspicuous consumption in dress

The expenditure on clothing, not to mention jewellery, recorded in some trousseaux of the fifteenth century is breathtaking. Invariably, when one or other partner of the betrothed couple was a Sforza, the level of expense was of the highest.

The dowry of Ippolita Sforza,[1] for her marriage with Alfonso of Aragon in 1465, totalled two hundred thousand florins (in Milanese money). The clothes, jewels and other ornaments constituted a third of the total value. Here are some examples of the cost of her clothes:

uno vestito de zetonino raso cremesino cum le manechie ad ale foderate de broccato doro in damaschino verde, et lo busto foderato de sendale verde recamato de perle et de argentaria; it was covered in 8966 pearls estimated at $4492\frac{1}{2}$ ducats; and into the embroidery went 70 ounces of gold and silver thread, estimated with the gold cloth (*drappo doro*), *zetonino*, *raso* and *sendale* at $1106\frac{1}{2}$ ducats; the total value, almost 5600 ducats.

uno vestito de damaschino cremesile cum maneche picole[2] fodrato de sendale verde rechamato de perle, et de argenteria; it had 911 pearls worth 1145 ducats; and the *damaschino*, *sendale* and embroidery[3] came to 85 ducats; the total value, 1230 ducats.

uno vestito de broccato dor cremexile rizo cum le maneche ad ale fodrate tutto d'armelini;[4] estimated at 927 ducats.

vestito uno de broccato doro in damaschino bianco[5] fodrato de sendale de grana cum le maneche ad ale fodrato de broccato dargento in damaschino et cremexile estimato 400 ducati

una mantelina de broccato doro rizo in velluto cremexile fodrato de sendale bianco cum le franze estimato ducati 564

una mantelina de broccato doro rizo in velluto verde fodrata de sendale de grana cum li frapponi de dreto e li franzoni davante[6] estimata ducati 229

una camorra de terzanello cremesile[7] cum uno payro (paio) de maneche de drappo doro in damaschino cremexile valeno ducati 29

tessuto uno de bianco ala damaschina[8] solio cum uno fornimento doro cum zoie[9] vale ducati 104

tessuto uno morello chiaro broccato dargento ala damaschina relevato a raze et colombine[10] cum uno fornimento doro cum zoie vale ducati 155

1. E. Motta, *Nozze principesche nel Quattrocento*, Milan, 1894.
2. *maniche piccole* would be slim-fitting sleeves, reaching to the wrist.
3. This reference to embroidery (*recamo*) means the silver thread worked by a needle, not the applied pearls.
4. This *vestito* was lined throughout with ermine; no expenses were spared by, for example, lining the main body of the gown with a cheaper fur.
5. The white ground of the textile is woven in damask, which is then highlighted by brocaded areas of gold.
6. There is dagged decoration (*frapponi*) on the back of the gown, and fringes in front; as some terms like *mantello* and its diminutives are frequently used in the broadest sense, this *mantelina* could easily refer to a *giornea*, or some kind of sideless

overgarment, the front and back of which are so clearly differentiated as to each warrant its own form of decoration.
7. The difference in quality between the body and the sleeves of the *camorra* is noticeable; only the cloth at the wrists of the sleeves might be seen, for the *camorre* of Ippolita were drowned by the sumptuous *vestiti*.
8. This suggests that there was a recognizable style of textile associated with Damascus, whether Damascus be the place of origin or the trading point whence it was imported.
9. This piece of cloth, and the one listed below, were not items of clothing, for it seems the four edges were finished with gold trimmings and semi-precious stones; they may have been intended as hangings or altar frontals.
10. The radiant dove, one of the Sforza devices.

Letters of Galeazzo Maria Sforza, 1475[1]

In the letters, mainly addressed to Gotardo Panigarole, the generosity of Galeazzo Maria is demonstrated by the presentation of numerous gifts. Not only are these given to the Duke's own circle of friends at court, but to all officials and servants of the household, whether in Milan or in his service abroad. Thus he guaranteed the splendour of his court. These documents are particularly interesting on two accounts; firstly, for the references to the occupations and status of the wearers of the clothes ordered; and secondly, for the specific quantities stipulated for certain types of garments. Here is a list of some of those lengths of cloth:

for men's garments	quantity in braccia	textile	for women's garments	quantity in braccia	textile
zuppone	4	bello veluto	vestimenta	$24\frac{3}{4}$	veluto cremisi alto e basso
	6	brochato d'oro			
	$6\frac{1}{4}$	zettonino raso moretto	camorra	22	zettonino raso cilestro
	$6\frac{1}{4}$	zettonino raso cremexino		16	damaschino cremexino
guardacoro	12	terzanello negro	soca	7	panno turchino
	8	zetonino raso cremexino			
	4	scarlata			
vesta (for wearing in the country)	18	zambelloto cremexino			
	12	tela rossa and panno verde (for lining the same vesta)			
vesta a la castigliana	16	zetonino raso cremexino			
	14	brochato d'argento cremexino			
vesta a la franzesa	14	zetonino raso di morello scuro			
vestito (for a physician)	20	veluto morello			
mantello a la castigliana	16	zetonino raso morello			
mongino	16	zettonino raso cremexino			
ghelero	14	zettonino raso cremexile			
turca	20	brochato d'argento cremexino			
calze	5	scarlata (for making 4 pairs)			

1. G. Porro, 'Lettere di Galeazzo Maria Sforza', *Archivio Storico Lombardo*, ser. I, vol. V, 1878

The possessions of Maestro Bartolo di Tura[1]

Bartolo di Tura was a philosopher and doctor of medicine. Following his death an inventory was made of all the goods belonging to his house in Siena in 1483. Amongst the entries of clothing are some references to very unassuming, practical garments—of interest for their mundane quality.

una gonnella da uomo, di cuoio,[2] grosso

3 invollitoi[3] da fanciulli, vechi, l'uno cilestro, l'altro pavonazzo, e l'altro verde

uno camiciotto da bagno,[4] uso, vechio

uno sparagrembo,[5] uso, di pannolino

un paio di calze pavonaze, da uomo, vechie, fodarate di bianchetta

3 paia di mutande da uomo, nuove

una cuffia lavorata ad reticelle,[6] di seta, di donna

uno paio di guanti di lana bianca, da fanciulle, nuovi

due birette di grana scempie a urechioli,[7] una da uomo, l'altra da fanciulli

uno gurgierino di maglie,[8] bello, fodarato di cremusi

un paio di brache mannesche,[9] di panno rosso

uno lucharello di seta, baldachino nero, vechio, da fanciullo

uno giubbarello di pirpignano rosso con collarino cremusi, uso

un paio di calze di panno verde, solate, use, da fanciulli

uno lucho da donna, con coda, di raso cremusi e tira da piei, fodarato di tela verde

una cioppa (it was Maestro Bartolo's own), *di cremusi vermiglio[10] vellutato facto a la venetiana fodarato di taffetta vermiglio*

1. C. Mazzi, 'La Casa di Maestro Bartalo di Tura', extract from *Bullettino Senese di Storia Patria*, Siena, 1900.
2. This leather *gonnella* must have been particularly practical, probably for use when out riding or hunting.
3. *invollitoi*, cover-ups to be worn by children to protect their better clothes, possibly a garment closely resembling a *giornea*, i.e. open down the sides.
4. A form of chemise worn when taking a bath.
5. An apron.
6. *reticella* is a form of Italian needle lace.
7. *urecchioli* are ear-flaps, to which cords would probably be attached and then tied under the chin.
8. A piece of chain armour, worn to protect the neck and shoulders.
9. Very few references to *brache* appear in the fifteenth century; these are presumably rough red breeches of some kind.
10. *vermiglio* = vermilion, a brilliant red; this description implies the many different shades which may be obtained from one dye, in this case kermes.

Select Bibliography

Select Bibliography of works referred to directly or indirectly in the text.

ACQUA, C. DELL', *Della morte e funerali del duca Gian Galeazzo Visconti, 3 settembre—20 ottobre 1402*, Pavia, 1903.

ADY, C. M., *A History of Milan under the Sforza*, Methuen, 1907; *The Bentivoglio of Bologna: a study in despotism*, Oxford, 1937.

ALBERTI, L. B., *Della Pittura*, ed. L. Mallè, Florence, 1950; *Opere Volgari*, ed., C. Grayson, Bari, 1960. vol. 1, *I Libri della Famiglia*.

ANDERSON, R. M., *Hispanic Costume, 1480–1530*, New York, Hispanic Society of America, 1979.

ANTAL, F., *Florentine Painting and its Social Background*, Routledge Kegan Paul, 1965.

ARESE, G., *L'industria serica piemontese dal sec. XVII alla metà del XIX*, Turin, 1922.

BASEL: CIBA REVIEW, I, 1937, *Medieval Dyeing*; 7, 1938, *Scarlet*; 10, 1938, *Trade Routes and Dye Markets in the Middle Ages*; 62, 1947, *Swiss Fairs and Markets in the Middle Ages*.

BAXANDALL, M., *Giotto and the Orators*, Oxford, 1971; *Painting and Experience in Fifteenth Century Italy*, Oxford, 1972.

BERNARDINO (SAN) DA SIENA, *Le Prediche volgari dette nella Piazza del Campo l'anno 1427*, ed. L. Banchi, 3 vols, Siena, 1880–8.

BIAGI, G., *Due corredi nuziali fiorentini, 1320–1493*, Florence, 1899.

BIRBARI, E., *Dress in Italian Painting, 1460–1500*, Murray, 1975.

BOMBE, W., *Nachlass-Inventare des Angelo da Uzzano und des Lodovico di Gino Capponi*, Leipzig, 1928.

BRENNI, L., *La Tessitura Serica attraverso i secoli*, Como, 1925.

BRUNELLO, F., *L'Arte della Tintura nella storia dell'umanità*, Vicenza, 1968.

BURCKHARDT, J., *The Civilisation of the Renaissance in Italy*, trs. S. G. C. Middlemore, London, 1944.

BURKE, P., *Culture and Society in Renaissance Italy, 1420–1540*, Batsford, 1972.

BUTAZZI, G., *Il Costume in Lombardia*, Milan, Electa, 1977.

CAMPORI, G., *Raccolta di cataloghi ed inventarii inediti, dal sec. XV al sec. XIX*, Modena, 1870.

CAPPI BENTIVEGNA, F., *Abbigliamento e costume nella pittura italiana: Rinascimento*, Rome, Bestetti, 1962.

CARTWRIGHT, J., *Beatrice d'Este, Duchess of Milan, 1475–1497*, Dent, 1899; *Isabella d'Este, Marchioness of Mantua, 1474–1539*, 2 vols, Murray, 1903.

CASTIGLIONE, B., *Il Cortegiano*, ed. B. Maier, Turin, 1969.

CATELLACCI, D., ed., *Ricordanza delle nozze di Francesco de' Medici con la Tessa Guicciardini*, Florence, 1880.

CENNINI, C., *Il libro dell'arte*, ed. F. Brunello, Vicenza, 1971.

CHAMBERS, D. S., *Patrons and Artists in the Italian Renaissance*, Macmillan, 1970.

CHIAPPELLI, L., *La donna pistoiese del tempo antico*, Pistoia, 1914.

CHIAPPINI DI SORIO, I., 'Catalogo delle stoffe antiche della collezione Guggenheim', *Bolletino dei Musei Civici veneziani*, annata XV, n. I, 1970.

CITADELLA, L. N., *Notizie relative a Ferrara*, Ferrara, 1864.

COGNASSO, F., *L'Italia nel Rinascimento*, vol. I, Turin, 1965.

CORAZZA, B. DI MICHELE DEL, 'Diario fiorentino, anni 1405–1438', ed. G. O. Corazzini, *Archivio Storico Italiano*, ser. V, vol. XIV, 1894, pp. 233–98.

CORIO, B., *Storia di Milano*, 3 vols, Milan, 1855–7.

COX, R., *Les soireries d'art depuis les origines jusqu'à nos jours*, Paris, 1914.

DALTON, O. M., *Catalogue of the Engraved Gems of the Post-Classical Periods in the British Museum*, London, 1915.

DEVOTI, D., *L'arte del tessuto in Europa*, Milan, Bramante, 1974.

DINA, A., *Isabella d'Aragona, Duchessa di Milano e di Bari, 1470–1524*, Milan, 1921.

EVANS, J., *A History of Jewellery, 1100–1870*, 2nd ed., Faber, 1970.

FALKE, O. VON, *Kunstgeschichte der Seidenweberei*, Berlin, 1921.

FANELLI, R. B., 'Il Disegno della Melagrana dei tessuti del rinascimento in Italia', *Rassegna della Istruzione Artistica*, anno III, n. 3, 1968.

FLEMMING, E., *Encyclopaedia of Textiles*, Zwemmer, 1958.

FLORENCE, MUSEO MEDICEO, *Il tesoro di Lorenzo il Magnifico, I: Le gemme*, catalogue of exhibition held in the Palazzo Medici Riccardi, Florence, 1972.

FLORENCE, UNIVERSITY (exhibition), *L'Oreficeria nella Firenze del Quattrocento*, Florence, Studio Per Edizioni Scelte, 1977.

GARGIOLLI, G., ed., *L'Arte della Seta in Firenze*, Florence, 1868.

GEIJER, A., *A History of Textile Art*, Sotheby Parke Bernet, 1979.

GHETTI, B., *Di alcune leggi suntuarie recanatesi*, Fano, 1905.

GHINZONI, P., 'Un ambasciatore del Soldano d'Egitto alla Corte milanese nel 1476', *Archivio Storico Lombardo*, ser. I, vol. II, 1875, pp. 155–78.

GIULIANI, M., *La Prammatica Senese per le nozze del' anno MCCCCXII*, Siena, 1879.

GIULINI, A., 'Nozze Borromeo nel Quattrocento', *Archivio Storico Lombardo*, ser. IV, vol. XIII, 1910, pp. 261–84.

GREGORIETTI, G., *Jewelry through the Ages*, Hamlyn, 1970.

GUASTI, C., ed., *Tre lettere di Lucrezia Tornabuoni a Piero de' Medici ed altre lettere*, Florence, 1859; *Le Feste di San Giovanni in Firenze descritte in prosa e in rima*, Florence, 1884.

GUNDERSHEIMER, W. L., *Ferrara: the Style of a Renaissance Despotism*, Princeton, 1973.

HACKENBROCH, Y., *Renaissance Jewellery*, Sotheby Parke Bernet, 1979.

HAY, D., *The Italian Renaissance in its Historical Background*, Cambridge, 1961.

HOWELL, A. G. F., *San Bernardino of Siena*, Methuen, 1913.

LANDUCCI, L., *A Florentine Diary from 1450–1516 . . . continued by an anonymous writer till 1542*, trs. A. de Rosen Jervis, Dent, 1927.

LARNER, J., *Culture and Society in Italy, 1290–1420*, Batsford, 1971.

LAVEN, P., *Renaissance Italy, 1464–1534*, Batsford, 1966.

LEVI PISETZKY, R., *La Storia del Costume in Italia*, vol II, Milan, Fondazione Giovanni Treccani degli Alfieri, 1964; *Il Costume e la Moda nella Società italiana*, Turin, Einaudi, 1978.

LUZIO, A., and RENIER, R., *Delle relazioni di Isabella d'Este Gonzaga con Ludovico e Beatrice Sforza*, Milan, 1890; *Mantova e Urbino, Isabella d'Este e Elisabetta Gonzaga nelle relazioni familiari e nelle vicende politiche*, Turin, 1893; 'Il Lusso di Isabella d'Este, Marchesa di Mantova I, Il Guardaroba di Isabella d'Este', *Nuova Antologia*, ser. IV, vol. LXIII, I Giugno, 1896, pp. 441–69; 'Il Lusso di Isabella d'Este II, Gioielli e gemme', *Nuova Antologia*, ser. IV, vol. LXIV, 16 Luglio, 1896, pp. 294–324.

MACHIAVELLI, N., *Istorie Fiorentine*, in *Opere*, ed. M. Bonfantini, Milan, 1954.

MALAGUZZI VALERI, F., *La Corte di Ludovico il Moro*, vol.I, *La vita privata*, Milan, 1913.

MANFREDINI, M., *Contro i superflui ornamenti delle donne, 12 maggio 1460*, Padua, 1896.

MARCOTTI, G., *Un mercante fiorentino e la sua famiglia*, Florence, 1881.

MAZZI, C., 'La Casa di Maestro Bartalo di Tura', extract from *Bulletino Senese di Storia Patria*, Siena, 1900; *Provvisioni suntuarie fiorentine,*

29 novembre 1464, 29 febbraio 1471, Florence, 1908.

MEEK, C., *The Italian Renaissance, Topics in History Series*, London, 1974.

MERKEL, C., ed., 'I beni della famiglia di Puccio Pucci', *Miscellania Nuziale Rossi-Theiss*, Trento, 1897.

MINUCCI DEL ROSSO, R., 'Invenzione di ferri da tessere drappi di seta e di velluto', *Archivio Storico Italiano*, ser. V, vol. VI, pp. 310–11.

MOLMENTI, P., *La Storia di Venezia nella vita privata*, Bergamo, 1905.

MORASSI, A., *Art Treasures of the Medici: jewellery, silverware, hard-stone*, trs. P. Colacicchi, London, 1964.

MORSELLI, A., 'Il corredo nuziale di Caterina Pico' (1474), extract from *Atti e Memorie della Deputazione di Storia Patria per le Antiche Provincie Modenesi*, ser. VIII, vol. VIII, Modena, 1956.

MOTTA, E., *Nozze principesche nel Quattrocento*, Milan, 1894.

MUNICCHI, A., *Una provvisione suntuaria della reppublica fiorentina*, Florence, 1909.

MÜNTZ, E., *Les collections des Médicis au XVᵉ siècle*, Paris, 1888.

MURALTO, F., *Annalia*, ed. P. A. Donini, Milan, 1861.

NEWTON, S. M., *Renaissance Theatre Costume, and the Sense of the Historic Past*, Rapp and Whiting, 1975.

NICCOLINI DI CAMUGLIANO, G., *The Chronicles of a Florentine Family, 1200–1470*, Cape, 1933.

ORIGO, I., *The Merchant of Prato, Francesco di Marco Datini*, Cape, 1957.

PARDI, G., ed., 'Diario Ferrarese, dall'anno 1409 sino al 1502', by unknown authors, *Rerum Italicarum Scriptores*, vol. XXIV, part VII, Bologna, 1928–33; 'Diario Ferrarese, dall'anno 1476 sino al 1504', by Bernardino Zambotti, *Rerum Italicarum Scriptores*, vol. XXIV, part VII, appendix, Bologna, 1934–7.

PASOLINI, P. D., ed., *Gli experimenti de la Exma S^ra Caterina da Furlj*, Imola, 1894.

PODREIDER, F., *La Storia dei Tessuti d' Arte in Italia (secoli XII–XVIII)*, Bergamo, 1928.

POLIDORI CALAMANDREI, E., *Le vesti delle donne fiorentine nel Quattrocento*, Florence, 1924.

PORRO, G., 'Lettere di Galeazzo Maria Sforza', *Archivio Storico Lombardo*, ser. I, vol. V, 1878, pp. 107–29, 254–74, 637–68.

PORTIOLI, A., 'La nascita di Massimiliano Sforza', *Archivio Storico Lombardo*, ser. I, vol. IX, 1882, pp. 325–34.

PORTOGHESI, L., *Tessuti italiani*, Corsi di storia delle arti applicate, Museo Poldi Pezzoli, Milan, 1978.

POZZO, G., 'Nozze di Beatrice d'Este e di Anna Sforza', *Archivio Storico Lombardo*, ser. I, vol. IX, 1882, pp. 483–534.

PRATO, Istituto Tecnico Industriale Statale Tullio Buzzi, *Il Museo del tessuto a Prato*, catalogue by R. B. Fanelli, Florence, Centro Di, 1975.

REATH, N. A., 'Velvets of the Renaissance from Europe and Asia Minor', *Burlington Magazine*, vol. L, 1927, pp. 298–304.

RICHARDS, G. R. B., *Florentine Merchants in the Age of the Medici*, Cambridge, Massachusetts, 1932.

SANTANGELO, A., *The Development of Italian Textile Design, from the 12th to the 18th century*, trs. P. Craig, Zwemmer, 1964.

SANUTO, M., *I diarii di Marino Sanuto*, vol. I, ed. F. Stefani, Venice, 1879; vol. III, ed. R. Fulin, Venice, 1880.

SERCAMBI, G., *Le Croniche di Giovanni Sercambi*, ed. S. Bongi, 3 vols, Rome, 1892.

SFORZA, B. M., 'Il Corredo Nuziale di Bianca Maria Sforza-Visconti, sposa dell' Imperatore Massimiliano I', *Archivio Storico Lombardo*, ser. I, vol. II, 1875, pp. 51–76.

SIMONETTA, C., 'I diarii', ed. A. R. Natale, *Archivio Storico Lombardo*, ser. VIII, vol. II, 1950. pp. 157–80.

SOLMI, E., 'La Festa del Paradiso di Leonardo da Vinci e Bernardino Bellincione 13 gennaio 1490', *Archivio Storico Lombardo*, ser. IV, vol. I, 1904, pp. 75–89.

STEINGRÄBER, E., *Antique jewellery: its history in Europe from 800 to 1900*, trs. P. Gorge, Thames and Hudson, 1957.

STROZZI, A. MACINGHI NEGLI, *Lettere di una gentildonna fiorentina del secolo XV*, ed. C. Guasti, Florence, 1877.

TAFUR, P., *Travels and adventures, 1435–9*, trs. Malcolm Letts, London, 1926.

TAYLOR, G. and SCARISBRICK, D., *Finger Rings, from Ancient Egypt to the Present Day*, Lund Humphries, 1978; a catalogue of finger rings in the Ashmolean Museum, Oxford.

TERNI DE' GREGORI, W., *Bianca Maria Visconti, duchessa di Milano*, Bergamo, 1940.

VERGA, E., 'Le legge suntuarie milanesi. Gli statuti del 1396 e del 1498', *Archivio Storico Lombardo*, ser. III, vol. IX, 1898. pp. 5–72; *Il Comune di Milano e l'arte della seta dal secolo XV al XVIII*, Milan, 1917.

VESPASIANO DA BISTICCI, *Vite di uomini illustri del secolo XV*, ed. P. d'Ancona and E. Aeschlimann, Milan, 1951.

WEIBEL, A. C., *Two Thousand Years of Textiles*, New York, Pantheon, 1952.

ZAMBRINI, F., ed., *Tratto dell'arte del ballo di Guglielmo Ebreo Pesarese*, Bologna, 1873.

ZANELLI, A., 'Di alcune leggi suntuarie pistoiesi dal XIV al XVI secolo', *Archivio Storico Italiano*, ser. V, vol. XVI, 1895, pp. 206–224.

Acknowledgements

I wish to express my gratitude to all those who have assisted me in the preparation of this book. Firstly, I am indebted to the pioneering research of E. Polidori Calamandrei and Rosita Levi Pisetzky; at the same time, I hope that this study opens some new ideas and points-of-view about the subject of Italian dress in the fifteenth century. In addition, I owe special thanks to Stella Mary Newton and Aileen Ribeiro, for introducing me to the discipline of the History of Dress; to Diana Webb, of the Department of History, University of London King's College, for her stimulating criticism of the historical content, particularly of the introductory chapter; to friends Susie Orso and Richard Schofield; to the staff of the Witt Library, especially Mr Hodge; to my mother and my sister, for being such conscientious typists; to those who helped me in various ways during my travels in Italy; to Michael Stephenson, my editor, for his constant encouragement and advice; and finally to Mary Butler and staff of Bell and Hyman for seeing the book through its final stages of production.

The author and publishers would like to thank the following for providing photographs and giving permission to reproduce them: Staatliche Museen Preussischer Kulturbesitz Gemäldegalerie, Berlin (West); Fratelli Alinari, Florence; Biblioteca Riccardiana, Florence; Gabinetto Fotografico della Soprintendenza ai Beni Artistici e Storici, Florence; Merseyside County Art Galleries, Liverpool; Courtauld Institute of Art, London; Mansell Collection, London; National Gallery, London; Victoria and Albert Museum, London; Scala / Vision International, London; Warburg Institute, London; Pinacoteca di Brera, Milan; Alte Pinakothek, Munich; Metropolitan Museum of Art, New York; Ashmolean Museum, Oxford; Soprintendenza per i Beni Artistici e Storici, Palermo; Giraudon, Musées Nationaux, Paris; Biblioteca Apostolica Vaticana, Rome; Museum Boymans-van-Beuningen, Rotterdam; Osvaldo Böhm, Venice; Soprintendenza per i Beni Artistici e Storici, Venice; National Gallery of Art, Washington; Le Musée des Arts Decoratifs, Paris; Museo Correr, Venice; La Collection du Musée Jacquemart-André, Paris. Illustrations 21, 80 and 112 were reproduced by courtesy of the British Museum; illustration 70 was reproduced by permission of the Museo Provinciale d'Arte, Trento, and illustration 138 was reproduced by permission of the Trustees, The Wallace Collection, London.

Index

The number immediately following an Italian term for a garment indicates the definition in the glossary. Where terms are not referred to in this index, reference should be made directly to the glossary.